T0320436

CREATIVE RESEARCH METHODS FOR CRITICAL EVENT STUDIES

This timely and innovative book offers an introduction to a range of creative methods, providing both empirical and conceptual guidance.

Based upon existing empirical work and richly illustrated throughout, each chapter carefully examines creative methodology and/or methods within an event and festival context. International case studies are incorporated throughout, providing real-world examples of how these methods have been used in practice, as well as highlighting potential ethical issues. Each chapter includes a concise 'how to' set of guidelines to help researchers and students employ creative methods in their own work, as well as a series of 'think points' to help develop ethical practices. Chapters illustrate new pathways or lessons learned from research during the pandemic and other challenging landscapes.

This significant volume offers festival and event researchers and students a different approach to their work that could result in better research, reaching hidden and marginalised groups.

Louise Platt is a Reader in Place Experiences at Manchester Metropolitan University. Her research interests centre on small-scale festivity and mundane leisure practice in relation to identities and place. She is co-editor of the *International Journal of Event and Festival Management*. Her work on processional cultures and urban events has been published in cultural geography and leisure journals. She is a Fellow of the Institute of Place Management. She has co-edited collections including *Gendered Violence at International Festivals* (2020, Routledge), *The Routledge Handbook of Placemaking* (2020, Routledge) and *Research Methods for Critical Event Studies* (2016). She has been invited to speak on panels addressing the value of community events and delivered keynotes on processions and parades in urban spaces.

Rebecca Finkel is a Professor of Critical Event Studies at Queen Margaret University and Senior Fellow of Higher Education Academy. Research frames critical event studies within conceptualisations of social justice, gender in/equality and cultural identity. Co-Editor of Routledge Critical Event Studies Research Book Series as well as *Transforming Leisure in the Pandemic:*

Re-imagining Interaction and Activity during Crisis (2022, Routledge); "Multispecies Leisure: Human–Animal Interactions in Leisure Landscapes" (2021, Routledge); *Gendered Violence at International Festivals* (2020, Routledge); *Accessibility, Inclusion, and Diversity in Critical Event Studies* (2018, Routledge) and *Research Themes in Events* (2014). Published in gender studies, cultural management, urban geography, media, leisure, tourism, and events journals and books, including co-editing special issues on EDI-related topics in highly-rated journals. Rebecca has been invited to deliver keynotes, workshops and seminars throughout the UK, Europe, Trinidad & Tobago, Chengdu (China) and Austin (USA) on festivals and cultural events.

Briony Sharp is a Lecturer in Events Marketing at the University of the West of Scotland and Fellow of the Higher Education Academy. Her research focuses on the social impact and implications of events and leisure practices; including EDI, wellbeing, volunteering and therapeutic leisure. She is co-editor of *Transforming Leisure in the Pandemic: Re-imagining Interaction and Activity during Crisis* (2022, Routledge) and *Accessibility, Inclusion, and Diversity in Critical Events Studies* (2018, Routledge). Briony is the Treasurer of *Leisure Studies Association*, Social Media Editor for the *Journal of Policy Research in Tourism, Leisure and Events* and Executive Board Member of *International Journal of Event and Festival Management*. She is also an Associate Board member of the *Association for British Professional Conference Organisers* (ABPCO).

Routledge Critical Event Studies Research Series

Editors: Rebecca Finkel
Queen Margaret University, UK

David McGillivray
University of the West of Scotland, UK

For more information about this series, please visit: www.routledge.com/Routledge-Critical-Event-Studies-Research-Series/book-series/RCE

CREATIVE RESEARCH METHODS FOR CRITICAL EVENT STUDIES

Edited by Louise Platt, Rebecca Finkel and Briony Sharp

Routledge
Taylor & Francis Group

LONDON AND NEW YORK

Designed cover image: Getty Images

First published 2025
by Routledge
4 Park Square, Milton Park, Abingdon, Oxon OX14 4RN

and by Routledge
605 Third Avenue, New York, NY 10158

Routledge is an imprint of the Taylor & Francis Group, an informa business

British Library Cataloguing-in-Publication Data
A catalogue record for this book is available from the British Library

ISBN: 978-1-032-68641-7 (hbk)
ISBN: 978-1-032-68640-0 (pbk)
ISBN: 978-1-032-68642-4 (ebk)

DOI: 10.4324/9781032686424

Typeset in Times New Roman
by SPi Technologies India Pvt Ltd (Straive)

CONTENTS

FIGURES

TABLES

CONTRIBUTORS

Laura Aguiar, Lecturer in Cinematic Arts, Ulster University, Northern Ireland

Lauren Bouvier, PhD Candidate, Queen Margaret University, Scotland

Alyssa Eve Brown, Senior Lecturer in Tourism and Events, University of Sunderland, England

Leon Davis, Senior Lecturer in Marketing and Events Management, Teesside University, England

Adalberto Fernandes, Research Centre for Tourism, Sustainability and Well-Being (CinTurs), University of Algarve, Portugal

Rebecca Finkel, Professor of Critical Event Studies, Queen Margaret's University, Scotland

Sandra Goh, Senior Lecturer, Auckland University of Technology, Faculty of Culture & Society, School of Hospitality & Tourism, New Zealand

Barbara Grabher, Lecturer in Event Studies, University of Brighton, England

Rita Grácio, Assistant Professor, Centre for Research in Applied Communication, Culture, and New Technologies (CICANT), Universidade Lusófona, Portugal

Christopher J. Hayes, Lecturer in Tourism & Events Management, Teesside University, England

Bronagh McAtasney, Access and Outreach Officer, Northern Ireland Screen

Neil Ormerod, Principal Researcher, Research Centre for Tourism, Sustainability and Well-being (CinTurs), Universidade do Algarve, Portugal

Jenna Pandeli, Associate Professor in Organisation Studies, University of West of England

Louise Platt, Reader in Place Experiences, Manchester Metropolitan University, England

Briony Sharp, Lecturer in Event Marketing, University of the West of Scotland, Scotland

Zorica Siročić, Assistant Professor, Department of Sociology, University of Graz, Austria

Kyla Tully, PhD Candidate, Queen Margaret University and University of Glasgow, Scotland

Trudie Walters, Senior Lecturer, Department of Tourism, Sport and Society, Lincoln University, New Zealand

Briony Whitaker, Senior Lecturer in Events and Festivals Management, University West of England

Fan Wu, Erasmus School of History, Culture, and Communication, Erasmus University, Netherlands

Ian Yeoman, Professor of Disruption, Innovation and New Phenomena in Hospitality and Tourism, NHL Stenden University of Applied Sciences, Netherlands

1

INTRODUCTION

Louise Platt

Metropolitan University, Manchester, UK

Rebecca Finkel

Queen Margaret's University, Edinburgh, UK

Briony Sharp

University of the West of Scotland, Paisley, UK

Events, in their multitude of forms, are considered to be creative endeavours (Silvers, 2012). From design through to implementation of spectacle, they draw on creative skills to deliver experiences that entertain and inspire audiences. Thus, it can be argued that creativity in events requires creativity in researching events. It is from this basis that we, as phenomenological researchers of experiential environments, inquire, are we actually employing similarly creative approaches to researching events? In her comprehensive assessment of creative methods, Kara (2020) comments that creativity in research can help address societal questions that traditional methods cannot, but they are no less robust. Thus far, within event and festival studies, we are yet to see a comprehensive assessment of the use of creative methods. This book addresses that gap while complimenting the work on research methods for critical event studies (Lamond and Platt, 2016; Pernecky, 2016).

As this volume demonstrates, creative research methods are not simply confined to arts-based methods and nor are they always qualitative in approach. Creativity is also not only about data collection or dissemination. Like all good research that is robust and well designed, creativity must emerge from the research question and the context of the work. Creativity is not a bolt-on or an afterthought. Creativity can be both methodology *and* method. In this regard, using creative research methods emerges from the onto-epistemological foundations of the research.

Traditional research methods have the potential to constrain researchers from understanding complex social issues around events and festivals. They also can marginalise some participants from having a voice in research. It is our contention that employing creative methodologies and/or methods in how

DOI: 10.4324/9781032686424-1

we study events and festivals can facilitate more inclusive approaches to research, which do not favour dominant hegemonic narratives and provide diverse perspectives. It is through richer findings that critical event studies can advance as a subject field.

For this edited collection, the chapter authors demonstrate how utilising creative methodologies/methods for their events research developed new pathways (or lessons learned) in understanding critical issues in experiential landscapes. Each chapter examines creative methodology/methods in the critical event context using case study example/s or addresses issues associated with using creative research methods, such as ethics.

Structure of This Book

Broadly speaking, this book focuses on a variety of methodological approaches and applied methods to elucidate what employing creative methods can offer creative events research. The chapters can be seen to concentrate on three main areas of focus: 1) ethics, reflexivity, and positionality; 2) drawing and imagery; and, 3) participatory and co-created research. What follows are different techniques as well as conceptual frameworks drawing on creative ways of designing and (re)doing critical research in events spheres. As demonstrated in the following chapters, going beyond traditional tried-and-true methodological approaches can be risky, and often may require flexibility and pivots; however, the driving force behind each creative methodology/method shows how the results can be richer, more inclusive, and shed more light on understanding the diversified socio-cultural situations being studied. If critical events research is going to develop even further as a discipline, it is through this kind of creative risk-taking to advance comprehension about the complex meanings associated with special events.

The book begins where research begins, with epistemology. Goh and Yeoman's chapter analyses the epistemological dynamics and creative inquiry characteristics in guiding researchers through the subjectiveness of visual and creative research using an analytical framework. By employing an arts-informed approach, they demonstrate the benefits of critical event visual analysis. As in the next stage of research planning, Sirocic[1] focuses on research design aligned with overall research questions and proposes a creative technique for studying several festivals and/or a comprehensive account of different forms in a single festival. The chapter explores the use of multi-sited ethnography as an example of a creative methodology that can respond to the challenge of spatial/temporal de-centeredness and multiple creative forms.

Ethical considerations and approval are compulsory prior to data collection in any research process, and this is especially the case when adopting creative approaches to ensure research is carried out with the highest levels of integrity. Walters examines this in the next chapter, drawing on her own attempts to share the voices of marginalised communities by navigating the tensions between ethics committees' expectations and pragmatic realities in the field. Following this, Whitaker and Pandeli also delve into the ethical challenges of critical events research, focusing on different creative methods for on-site qualitative data collection, including participant consent, at music festivals and which methodological pathways are the most ethical while also being the most effective in collecting useful data.

This brings us into the field with Tully, whose chapter focuses on the utilisation of sketch illustration and still life photography during observations of the management and production of an experimental film festival. Her research details the incorporation of creative methods of field documentation within virtual and in-person ethnographic research. Bouvier focuses on researching arts and cultural festivals by utilising postcards as a tool for accessible data collection. Themes of nostalgia and storytelling are threaded throughout this study of memory making, and a discussion of considerations is proposed for those contemplating using postcards to engage with participants as a creative research method. It is also through creative research responses, specifically applying art-based methods, that Grabher interrogates the wider regenerative ambitions of Bad Ischl-Salzkammergut European Capital of Culture (ECC) 2024. On public transportation, as part of the ECC initiative, she invites participants to respond in drawing to the question, "What does a postcard of the future Salzkammergut look like?" The artistic expression of drawing as a reflective and imaginative practice for research purposes contributes not only to the understanding of challenges and opportunities of this creative approach for critical event studies, but also can appraise the efficacy of the ECC agenda for urban regeneration and future placemaking.

Engaging with event stakeholders during the research process is not a one-size-fits-all endeavour. The following chapters discuss further creative ways to gather innovative findings through favouring relational and diverse perspectives. Davis, Hayes, and Brown investigate strategies for using informal conversations when collecting qualitative research at live events. This chapter elucidates how informal conversations are beneficial as an interactive and creative way to collect data from fans at sport and music events about their lived experiences and perspectives in the moment, offering a rich and nuanced understanding of event participants' experiences and interpretations as well as the event environment. It is through a participatory media research framework that Aguiar and McAtasney engage with marginalised young people at a filmmaking event in an effort to contribute to understandings of complex social issues around events and festivals, particularly issues of accessibility, diversity, and creative and meaningful engagement. In the next chapter, Ormerod argues that social impact monitoring and evaluation are vital for understanding how larger events affect communities. Thus, from a research perspective, it makes sense for social impact monitoring and evaluation to involve local communities more fully in the research process. Based on the Tour de Yorkshire cycle race, this chapter provides guidance to help future researchers achieve the benefits and reduce the challenges of co-creating research with local communities to maximise social impact benefits from big events. The next chapter critically examines Wu's involvement as an action researcher in cross-cultural events, actively engaging in marketing Chinese theatre productions in the UK. Her experiences not only offer innovative insights into the creative application of action research methodology, but also yield practical initiatives within the industry by facilitating collaboration between researchers and practitioners to encourage knowledge sharing and problem-solving.

The book draws to a close with a chapter by Grácio and Fernandes reviewing social sciences' creative methodologies for critical event studies. They set out guidelines in the form of epistemological, ethical, and practical checklists to help critical event researchers develop an awareness of the "critical" dimension when using creative methods in research.

Conclusions

Creative research methods are a growing area of interest and there are recent publications that look at this broadly across the social sciences (Kara, 2020) and within disciplines that could be aligned to event students such as geography (Von Benzon et al., 2021), sport studies (Pang, 2023), and business and management (Ward and Short, 2020). This book complements these by focusing on the cross- and inter-disciplinary nature of critical event studies while making an original contribution to utilising creativity in researching event and festival spaces, and, thus, deepening socio-cultural understanding of contemporary experiential encounters. We hope this volume also encourages event management undergraduate and postgraduate programmes to teach students more creative methods too – to go beyond interviews and surveys when approaching their dissertation projects.

As such, there is still potential for event scholars and students to undertake creative research in this field. For example, visual methods have limited coverage in these chapters, and while we know these methods are being employed in the event studies context, it would be encouraging to see more debate and discussion in event journals and books about these approaches. Another area of development that would facilitate the debates around creative methods in event studies would be for more multi-modal methods of dissemination to be available to researchers. The traditional journal article, while might be open to a few images or a video abstract here and there, is currently not set up to encourage more creative forms of communication. However, as the final chapter by Gracio and Fenandes points out, we need to be cautious in maintaining the critical and not applying the creative for the sake of it. We hope this volume inspires researchers to think creatively *but* carefully about the methods they choose and reflect on what is most suitable for the context of their research.

Notes

1 This chapter uses parts of the book Festivals as Reparative Gender Politics: Millennial Feminism in Southeastern Europe by Zorica Siročić, (Routledge, copyright 2024) to illustrate the methodological approach. Reproduced with permission of The Licensor through PLSclear.

References

Kara, H., (2020). *Creative research methods: A practical guide.* Bristol, UK: Policy Press.

Lamond, I. R., & Platt, L. (2016). *Critical event studies: Approaches to research.* London, UK: Palgrave Macmillan.

Pang, B. (2023). *Creative and inclusive research methods in sport, physical activity and health: Understanding British Chinese children's experiences.* Oxon, Uk: Routledge.

Pernecky, T. (Ed.). (2016). *Approaches and methods in event studies.* Oxon, UK: Routledge.

Silvers, J. R. (2012). *Professional event coordination.* New Jersey, US: John Wiley & Sons.

Von Benzon, N., Wilkinson, S., Wilkinson, C. & Holton, M. (2021). *Creative methods for human geographers.* London, UK: Sage.

Ward, J. & Short, H. (Eds). (2020). *Using arts-based methods: Creative approaches for researching business, organisation and humanities.* London, UK: Palgrave Macmillan.

2

THE EPISTEMOLOGY OF ART

Critical Event Visual Analysis

Sandra Goh

Auckland University of Technology, Auckland, New Zealand

Ian Yeoman

NHL Stenden University of Applied Sciences, Leeuwarden, Netherlands

Introduction

> *Critical Event Studies is emerging as a strong strand within the scholarly study of events, placing it firmly within other areas of multidisciplinary and transdisciplinary research.*
>
> *(Lamond & Platt, 2016, p. 4)*

The adoption of theories and concepts in multidisciplinary studies would entail researchers adapting to research approaches unconventional to their disciplines. This chapter focuses on the combined use of a traditional research approach with creative inquiries and discusses the dilemma of researchers in locating their research paradigm. Novice researchers might be obligated to locate their study under a single paradigm, when, multiple research paradigms actually exist, as this chapter will elaborate.

Just as a religion shapes one's world view and realities, a qualitative researcher's paradigm and philosophy shape the research design (Pernecky, 2016; Denzin & Lincoln, 2011; Leavy, 2014; Silverman, 2013) and is considered to be a higher level of creative thinking in the research design process (Pernecky, 2016). The research paradigm is identified in the methodological approach that aligns with the nature of the study, the types of research questions, and the characteristics of the research participants. Qualitative research is fundamentally aligned with a continuum of constructivism, social constructionism, interpretivism and participatory, that are often problematic to qualitative researchers due to their close attributes, and suggest that more than one paradigm is operational when designing the research problem with creative methods. Using an arts-informed and life history method in a study involving

DOI: 10.4324/9781032686424-2

participants from the arts and events sector about their event travel career trajectories (ETCT), this chapter explores the use of creative inquiries such as mapping, drawings, sketches, sketchnoting, photos, personal items and story-telling technique as an accessible approach in collecting rich and sensitive data. The use of arts in the arts-informed approach is not for art's sake. Instead, the purpose is to involve participants in an active process of meaning-making by relying on the power of art to both inform and engage – epistemologically, it is not only an inclusive, and unintrusive means of collecting data, but it is also an engaging way of sustaining the participants' interest during the course of the research. This chapter would be useful to researchers who are involved in arts, festivals and events academic research and who need to understand the application of more creative techniques that are second nature to their participants. Thus, the purpose of the chapter is to explore the epistemological dynamics and creative inquiry characteristics in guiding researchers through the subjectiveness of visual and creative research using analytical framework.

To provide some context, this chapter will begin with an introduction to a research project before providing an overview of a range of research paradigms. This is followed by a discussion of the dilemma experienced by novice researchers when locating their paradigms in qualitative and mixed research. To illustrate and explore the epistemology discussed in this chapter, a brief discussion of the case has been inserted throughout the text. To aid researchers in event critical studies interested in using visual method, an analytical framework is also provided as an example to add rigour to the analysis.

Case Study

This case is drawn from a PhD research in 2017. According to Getz (2008), "just about every form of organised sport will generate planned events, and they tend to evolve from local to international in attractiveness. This gives rise to event travel careers that evolve and can last a lifetime" (p. 413). These careers follow a pattern that Getz and Andersson (2010) argue can be measured in terms of six dimensions: motivations, travel styles, spatial and temporal patterns, and event and destination choices. The concept of the trajectory suggests changes over time and presents the pattern of travel related to travel trends and demands that applies also to the arts world where artists and producers travel frequently for the purpose of their work (Goh, Smith & Yeoman, 2022).

An arts-informed life history approach was used to gain insights from 19 arts practitioners in Singapore. For most arts practitioners, going on tour with their shows or participating in arts festivals and events is an essential part of promoting and developing their careers. The study reveals their ETCT offering insights into their motivations, constraints, and facilitators to help promote and facilitate future participation in event tourism for both work and leisure.

It is important to mention that the project was inspired by many international artists and producers who have been through the Edinburgh Festival Fringe and were willing to pay their own way to present their work. This study was set as a premise to understand the journey of creative talents with the objective of understanding their motivations and constraints of travelling to participate in international events and festivals. Not every art is considered art by the sponsor, and funding for the arts is limited.

The overarching aim of this research is to investigate how amateur and professional artists and producers develop their event travel careers using the ETCT. The purpose is to ascertain what motivates them to travel to participate in events, how they make decisions about their travel destination, and what type of events they participate in at different stages of their event careers. The research questions are:

1 How do amateur and professional artists and producers develop an ETCT?
2 What are the factors that constrain or facilitate their career on the ETCT?
3 To what extent do amateur and professional artists and producers conceptualise themselves as serious event tourists?
4 What role do open-access events play in the ETCT of the amateur and professional artists and producers?

When mentioned, the cohorts in this chapter refer to participants who represent three different generations of artists and producers in Singapore. The study was conducted between 2016 and 2017 and the participants for the study were purposefully selected to observe different perspectives of their event careers and event travel careers under different cultural and historical time periods.

Negotiating Research Paradigms: Ontologies, Epistemologies, and Method and Methodologies

It is important to clarify the basic beliefs of the researchers when designing a project. Our perspectives are often taken for granted (Pernecky, 2016) and this becomes apparent when researchers decide on the research method before first locating their research philosophy. Guba and Lincoln (1994) identify three levels of basic beliefs: ontology, epistemology, and methodology. Ontology is "the study of being" (Crotty, 1998, p. 10). Ontological assumptions are concerned with what constitutes reality (Scotland, 2012). "Epistemology is concerned with the nature and forms of knowledge" (Cohen, Manion & Morrison, 2007, p. 7). In other words, epistemology is concerned with how knowledge can be created, acquired, and communicated, and what it means to know (Scotland, 2012). Epistemology is also concerned about the nature of the relationship between the would-be knower and what can be known (Guba & Lincoln, 1994).

As such epistemology determines the methodology of the research project. It should be noted that a clear distinction exists between method and methodology (Stanley & Wise, 1990). Methods include specific techniques or research practices (surveys, interviews, or artistic practices such as storytelling, popular theatre, photo-story production, songwriting, etc.), and methodology refers to a broader theoretically informed framework (e.g. participatory research).

Over the years Lincoln Guba and Denzin have updated the handbook of qualitative research to include emerging research paradigms (2011). Each research paradigm has its own set of beliefs that differ in its ontology and epistemology. Geertz's (1988) prediction about the "blurring of genres" came through. While novice researchers would look for one such paradigm to fit within their research design (Asghar, 2013), the case demonstrates that more than one paradigm represents the researcher's position. Table 2.1 presents five types of research paradigms. Of the five, the case presented in this chapter was able to identify with three paradigms: Constructivism, Participatory, and Critical Theory.

The terms constructivist and social constructionist are problematic and need to be clarified (Ching, 2017). Although Lincoln, Lynham and Guba (2011) consider them together as constructivist, researchers such as Crotty (1998), Young and Collin (2004), and Pernecky (2012, 2016), argue that constructivism adopts a more individualistic outlook while social constructionism offers a more holistic approach to include the perspective of the social world or collective generation. The critical theory paradigm extends the knowledge by considering the transformation (Guba & Lincoln, 2005) that has taken place and that which is required to take place.

Within the event travel career literature, it is not explicit what the philosophical ideas are behind the research design, although, according to Slife and Williams (1995), they are largely embedded in research and are not explicit to readers. Early researchers of event travel career concept have displayed a post-positivist approach, making use of hypotheses and quantitative surveys, and have acknowledged that a different approach would further the knowledge of the concept. Cohen, Duberley, and Mallon (2004) further affirm that when examined across different philosophical perspectives, new discoveries can be made. The case design offers a constructivist and social constructionist approach, further incorporating an alternative inquiry – the creative inquiry (Cole & Knowles, 2008; Montuori, 2012), to study event travel careers.

Ontologically, both positivists and post-positivists believe in a single reality, although the latter acknowledge that what is unknown is less than absolute. Social constructionism has a different set of beliefs. It adopts a relativist ontology that multiple realities exist, whether locally or specifically constructed, or co-constructed (Guba & Lincoln, 2005). This study supports the ontological consideration of social constructionism as it adds depth and breadth to the study, to also discover any association with early foundations

TABLE 2.1 Research paradigms

Paradigms	Positivism	Postpositivism	Critical Theory et al.	Constructivism	Participatory
Ontology	Naive realism a "real" reality but apprehendible	Critical realism – virtual reality shaped by social, political, cultural, economic, ethnic, and genre values; crystalized over time.	Historical realism – virtual reality shaped by social, political, cultural, economic, ethnic, and gender values; crystallized over time	Relativism – Local and specific Co-constructed realities	Participative Reality - Subjective-objective Reality, co-created By mind and given cosmos
Epistemology	Dualist/objectivist; findings true Not concern with who or what researchers study	Modified dualist/ objectivist; critical tradition/community; findings/ probably true	Transactional/ subjectivist; value-mediated findings	Transactional/ Subjectivist; Co-created findings	Critical subjectivity in participatory transaction with cosmos; extended epistemology of experiential, propositional, and practical knowing; co-created findings
Methodology	Experimental/ manipulative; verification of hypotheses; chiefly quantitative methods	Modified experimental/ manipulative; critical multiplism, falsification of hypotheses; may include qualitative methods	Dialogic/dialectical Open to adopt any methodology contributing to a better world or social system (Asghar, 2013)	Hermeneutical/ dialectical	Political Participation in Collaborative action inquiry; primacy of the practical; use of language grounded in shared experiential context

Source: (Adapted from Lincoln, Lynham & Guba, 2011, p. 100).

and exposure to specific form of leisure activities (or form of arts) that might lead to the epistemological consideration of answering the research question. It is where I would argue that the authenticity of lives lived emerges to make sense of their world in relation to others. Such authenticity was displayed through the stories narrated by the individuals that date back to the time before their event career actually started. For example, the participants shared about their upbringing and their initial exposure to the arts. This study is built on the basis that social constructionists construct knowledge with different individuals and are also interested in the background of the individuals and how they make sense of their past to explain their present ETCT. An individual's past could be located in a different context, and, ontologically and epistemologically, it is sensible to separate the two to provide a meaningful study of individual's event career development in the context of their historical timeline. This is contradictory to Gergen (1994) and Andrews' (2012) position, renouncing ontological issues to only deal with knowledge creation epistemologically. As an epistemology, social constructionism asserts that knowledge is historically and culturally specific. According to Stead (2004), meanings differ across cultures and contexts and no word or thought is an expression of a reality. Culture is not perceived as static as it is co-constructed in a changing environment (e.g. technologies, travel, and migration) and as people meet another from other cultures. There are therefore multiple "truths" (Stead, 2004; Guba, 1996) and what I considered as multiple realities in the individual stories narrated in the context of its time. These stories are again negotiated and renarrated from the perspective of the researcher both as an insider and an outsider. Social constructionism views people as having multiple personalities and these personalities are displayed under different contexts and times (Stead, 2004). This means that selves take on meaning in relation to other people in different contexts (Stead, 2004; Young & Collin, 2004) and is therefore subjective. However, this is not to disregard objectivity; rather, I believed that people have identities that evolve as they move from one social-cultural setting to another over time.

Under the critical theory paradigm, realism is based historically and is shaped by social, political, cultural, economic, ethnic, and gender values over time. Epistemologically, research is therefore driven by the social structures as discussed under social constructionism. The methodology is also participatory which sits well with the participatory and collaborative paradigm (see Figure 2.1). We know very little about the paradigm of the critical theory. While noncritical paradigms present what is observable in a situation, critical paradigm goes beyond the observation and seeks to find out what's transformational for a better world. Critical paradigm is more versatile, philosophical and progressive and therefore there is no known concept of critical methodology. It is less concerned with the independent nature of the reality of life.

Researchers are called to a more liberal vision of epistemological and methodological freedom, in a post-paradigmatic future. The visual research approach enables the researcher to do more than adopt one such research paradigm. The case researcher could consider the research subject constructively with the participants (constructivism), with the participatory principles of co-creating the data with the individuals and their cultural cohorts (participatory), while critically considering the historical realism that impacts on the participants and their cohorts (Critical Theory et al) as can be seen in the case example. For the purpose of this chapter, the research paradigm for the case has been updated to include the participatory and critical theory as it was previously considered in Goh, Smith and Yeoman (2019) and Ching (2017) but was not explicitly articulated.

The Art of Visual Research

Participatory techniques in visual research are well-liked these days, partly because of the idea that research should also benefit those who are subjected to it and more specifically that researchers should engage themselves in helping to solve problems of communities without thinking primarily about their own professional gains (the "ethical" motive) (Pauwels, 2015, p. 96).

Sensitive issues are best visualised by the participants rather than to be spoken about. It is also accessible where participants are unable to: draw, speak, or describe their emotions under different or constraint circumstances. The creative inquiries here are not created for art's sake, instead, they are created to provide participants with a form to work on.

Underlying the ontological, epistemological and methodological perspectives are the research questions that formed the choice of the research method. The first two research questions, "How do amateur and professional artists develop an ETCT?" and "What are the factors that constrain or facilitate their career on the ETCT?", relate to the differing trajectories of artists and producers at different stages of their career over time. The third and fourth research questions are more conceptual but require in-depth interviews with the participants to reconstruct their lived experiences. The research questions are: "To what extent do amateur and professional artists and producers conceptualise themselves as serious event tourists?" and "What role do open access events play in the ETCT of the amateur and professional artists and producers?"

Methodologically, this study is rooted in both the traditional qualitative research method and a non-conventional research method that seeks to understand the past in different cultural, historical and also political contexts. The interpretive approach of social constructionism employs methods that create dialogue between the researched and the researcher in order to collaboratively construct a meaningful reality (Angen, 2000). A life history research approach will be used alongside an arts-informed research approach. The arts-informed approach adds another dimension to life history, allowing the creative exhibition of lives using the creative inquiries. Such creative inquiries have included respondent-produced narratives, photographs, memory maps, and artefacts (Knowles & Thomas, 2001), visual timeline (Harper, 2002) and auto-driven image or respondent-generated visual images/data used to generate verbal feedback (Pauwels, 2015).

Life history is an ideal research method to draw meaning from the past to give meaning to the present (Goodson & Sikes, 2001). In life history, researchers study and analyse how people talk about their lives, their experiences, events in life and the social context they inhabit (Germeten, 2013; Riessman, 2003; Goodson & Sikes, 2001). Life history research is "slow work" (Germeten, 2013, p. 620) and often requires several rounds of interviews. In order to explore the ETCT of the amateur and professional artists and producers as serious event tourists, it was necessary to trace the development of the participants over time. The arts-informed life history inquiry approach has the added feature of creative inquiries besides the use of life history and narratives. According to Cole and Knowles (2001), such a creative inquiry process could be an alternative form of visual communication tools that helps in the construction of fuller and richer ideas. Poland and Pederson (1998) suggest that we do more with the images before we put them into words, as nonverbal expression adds other dimensions into the research – also known as the "imagistic subtext". In this study, participants were invited to recall their past by forming a memory map of their ETCT. They were left to their creativity in how they interpreted the memory map (whether as text, visual, or a combination of both).

In order to gain a social world perspective of an event travel career, it was pertinent to examine the individual's account of their event travel career before comparing it with their cohort's event travel careers. Thus, for the purpose of studying the ETCT of artists and producers, meaning is reconstructed in relation to an individual's social and cultural background before comparing it with their cohort's backgrounds across the same historical and cultural periods. Social constructionist approaches do not consider that people have a discoverable nature (Burr, 1995) but instead theorise multiple realities, and that individual stories are narrated in the context of different periods of time. These stories are again negotiated and renarrated from the perspective of the researcher both as an insider and an outsider. Ontologically, the individual realities are viewed as adding depth and breadth to the study, to help with the discovery of any association with their earlier foundations and exposure to specific forms of leisure activities (or art forms) that might lead to the epistemological consideration of answering the research question.

The critical theory paradigm incorporates a critical dimension that is valuable in considering change and development on the ETCT. It "ask[s] a new set of questions — often evaluative, political, and pragmatic — regarding the choices one makes" (Gergen, 2001, p. 2). The interpretive approach of social constructionism employs methods that create dialogue between the researched and the researcher in order to collaboratively construct a meaningful reality (Angen, 2000). Although narratives provide a framework for studying people's ideas about their experiences and the development of self (Gergen & Gergen, 2006; McAdams, 2001), van Schalkwyk (2010) argues that there is a need to help participants with their autobiographical memory. With the provision of such support in mind, an arts-informed research approach was used alongside the life history research approach. The use of language is dominant in this latter approach, as storytelling is fundamental in reconstructing the stories of the participants.

It is important to consider the design of a research by considering who the participants are and how long the enquiries would take. On that basis, the various methods were explored to align with the participants' interests and strengths, as well as to consider how the research process would sustain the attention span of the participants. In this study, data were collected during two life history interviews, scheduled a week or so apart. Prior to the first interview, the researcher (Goh) organised a more informal meeting with each participant to introduce the study and to enable them to prepare for the creative inquiry aspect of the research. For the first interview, this was to create a life history memory map and select an artefact (which could include photographs) to represent the early stages of their event travel career. To prepare for the second interview, participants could revisit and review their memory map and select an artefact to represent the more recent period of their career. The life history conversation began with the question, "Tell me about your life ..."; by "life", the researcher explained that she meant the event travel career. Nineteen people took part in the study; they represented a sample of artists and producers (including those performing and producing) currently residing in Singapore. They were drawn from the performing (rather than visual) arts, including music, dance, and theatre. Many were currently professionals, some were amateurs, and many had moved between amateur and professional status during their careers. Epistemologically, the arts-informed life history approach is an inclusive, natural, and engaging way of prompting and constructing data (Goh, Smith & Yeoman, 2019; Ching, 2017).

While good examples and discussions of particular types of visual research do exist and remain useful, few authors have ventured to provide an analytical and integrated approach to visual research as a whole. And so the field continues to give a highly dispersed impression (Pauwels & Mannay, 2020). The next section attempts to introduce the analytical model that blends visual research.

The Art of Analysing Visual and Text Data

The relationship between the social constructionist (the researcher), the participants in the research, and the participants in the social world is paramount to the formation of meaning in the real world. This belief orients the epistemology of this study and, in turn, the methodological decisions (Phillips & Hardy, 2002) and the analytical approach. An approach that involves an all-encompassing analytical framework is therefore essential to capture the self, the cohort, and the researcher's perspective, in addition to the changing environment (Goh, Smith & Yeoman, 2019; Ching, 2017).

This section introduces the Zoom Model, an analytical model that employs the metaphor of a camera to unveil the multiple layers of meaning inherent in a life history (Goh, Smith, & Yeoman, 2019; Pamphilon, 1999). Operating like the lens of a camera, the model encompasses four levels of zoom, and refocusing the lens encourages the examination of life histories from four different perspectives: Meso-Zoom, Mirco-Zoom, Macro-Zoom, and Interactional-Zoom.

The analytical framework was adapted from Pamphilon's (1999) Zoom Model for life history analysis incorporating the creative inquiry/arts-informed approach grounded in a social constructionist research paradigm along with participatory and critical theory. As shown in Figure 2.1, the "Meso-Zoom" focuses on the individual participant and how they create their narratives; the "Micro-Zoom" focuses on the oral (including pauses and emotions), visual aspects of the inquiries were added to address the creative inquiries alongside the Meso-Zoom; "Macro-Zoom" is the critical zoom that focuses on the individual and society and considers the individuals with the others within their "cohorts" (other participants in the field being interviewed); and the "Interactional-Zoom" focuses on the researcher and the researched,

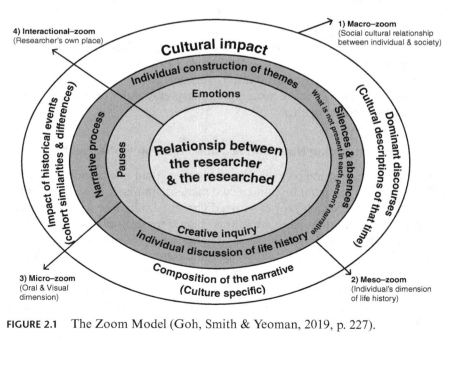

FIGURE 2.1 The Zoom Model (Goh, Smith & Yeoman, 2019, p. 227).

privileging the role of the researcher as both the insider and the outsider (Goh, Smith & Yeoman, 2019; Ching, 2017).

For Pamphilon (1999), "at the macro level, the focus is on dominant discourses, narrative form, and cohort effect" (p. 397); this can "reveal the variable impact of historical events on the lives of individuals by illuminating cohort similarities and differences" (p. 125). However, it was observed in this study that this zoom cannot be executed without first using the meso-zoom on at least three or four participants. The cohort's similarities and differences could then be observed across different life histories. The possibility to do so enabled the researcher to move back and forth with the macro- and meso-zooms (individual), observing factors such as the age of the individual and the cultural and social atmosphere during their era.

Epistemologically, the issue of multiple realities could be addressed with the use of the analytical Zoom Model. In order to capture the different cultural and historical contexts of lives lived, which is the central tenet of social constructionism, the analytical Zoom Model was an ideal companion as an analytical tool throughout the research process. The macro-zoom enabled the researcher to consider the lived experiences under different cultural and historical contexts and to seek similarities and differences with the participant's cohort. The key strength of social constructionism is the reflexivity it offers the researcher (Johnson & Duberley, 2000). The interactional-zoom provided a space in which the researcher and the researched can be epistemologically engaged, and their relationship is key for sense-making and the co-construction of meaning. Cohen, Duberley, and Mallon (2004) caution us "to reflect critically on our own intellectual assumptions in our social construction of any version of reality" (p. 420). The use of the Zoom Model has helped with averting or at least minimising such assumptions. Further, the researcher's lived experiences as a researcher-producer (insider) and researcher-academic (outsider) co-existed to make meaningful interpretation by fusing the subjectivities of these lives together.

Reflection, Concluding Note, and Recommendation for Researchers

Researchers are encouraged to explore using more than one paradigm in critical event studies for qualitative and mixed method approach. It is also possible to view previous research project with a different paradigm to gain a different perspective on the study. The case in this chapter for example, could consider the application of the critical theory in practice to progress desired transformation, adding value to critical event studies. For example, the economic, cultural and physical constraints experienced by the participants (artists and producers), could be made known to the policymakers in the arts to formulate a more desiring artistic platform and environment for Singaporean artists and producers to develop and grow more competitively.

As shown in Table 2.1, these paradigms provide a set of guidance for researchers and it should be updated given the openness and progressive nature of the critical paradigm. Akin to the versatility of the critical paradigm, the Zoom Model offers researchers interested in using visual or creative methods an analytical structure for future studies. With multiple lenses, the Zoom Model offers researchers a holistic perspective that are all encompassing of the research to oneself, others, and the greater society at large.

References

Andrews, T. (2012). What is social constructionism? *Grounded Theory Review: An International Journal, 11*(1). Retrieved from http://groundedtheoryreview.com/2012/06/01/what-is-social-constructionism/

Angen, M. J. (2000). Evaluating interpretive inquiry: Reviewing the validity debate and opening the dialogue. *Qualitative Health Research, 10*(3), 378–395.

Asghar, J. (2013). Critical paradigm: A preamble for novice researchers. *Life Science Journal, 10*(4), 3121–3127.

Burr, V. (1995). *An introduction to social constructionism*. London: Routledge.

Ching, S. G. M. (2017). Event Travel Careers of Singaporean Artists and Producers: An Arts-Informed Life History Approach. *Doctor of Philosophy Thesis, Victoria University of Wellington*.

Cohen, L., Duberley, J., & Mallon, M. (2004). Social constructionism in the study of career: Accessing the parts that other approaches cannot reach. *Journal of Vocational Behavior, 64*(3), 407–422.

Cohen, L., Manion, L., & Morrison, K. (2007). *Research methods in education* (6th Edition). London: Routledge.

Cole, A. L., & Knowles, J. G. (2001). *Lives in context: The art of life history research*. Walnut Creek, CA: AltaMira Press.

Cole, A. L., & Knowles, J. G. (2008). Arts-informed research. In A. L. Knowles & J. G. Cole (Eds.), *Handbook of the arts in qualitative research: Perspectives, methodologies, examples, and issues* (pp. 55–70). Thousand Oaks, CA: Sage Publications.

Crotty, M. J. (1998). *The foundations of social research: Meaning and perspective in the research process*. Thousand Oaks, CA: SAGE.

Denzin, N. K., & Lincoln, Y. S. (2011). *The Sage handbook of qualitative research*. United States of America: Sage Publications.

Geertz, C. (1988). *Works and lives: The anthropologist as author*. Stanford, California: Stanford University Press.

Gergen, K. J. (1994). Mind, text, and society: Self-memory in social context. In U. Neisser & R. Fivush (Eds.), *The remembering self: Construction and accuracy in the self-narrative* (78–104). Cambridge: Cambridge University Press.

Gergen, K. J. (2001). *Social construction in context*. Thousand Oaks, CA: Sage.

Gergen, M. M., & Gergen, K. J. (2006). Narratives in action. *Narrative Inquiry, 16*(1), 112–121.

Germeten, S. (2013). Personal narratives in life history research. *Scandinavian Journal of Educational Research, 57*(6), 612–624. https://doi.org/10.1080/00313831.2013.838998

Getz, D. (2008). Event tourism: Definition, evolution, and research. *Tourism Management, 29*(3), 403–428. https://doi.org/10.1016/j.tourman.2007.07.017

Getz, D., & Andersson, T. D. (2010). The event-tourist career trajectory: A study of high-involvement amateur distance runners. *Scandinavian Journal of Hospitality and Tourism*, *10*(4), 468–491. https://doi.org/10.1080/15022250.2010.524981

Goh, S., Smith, K. A., & Yeoman, I. (2019). Zooming in: An arts-informed life history approach to the analysis of event travel career narratives. *Event Management*, *23*(2), 223–238.

Goh, S., Smith, K. A., & Yeoman, I. S. (2022). We are serious event travelers: Event travel careers and the social worlds of arts practitioners to international arts festivals and events. *Event Management*, *26*(6), 1275–1296.

Goodson, I. F., & Sikes, P. J. (2001). *Life history research in educational settings: Learning from lives.* Buckingham, England; Phildelphia, PA: Open University Press.

Guba, E. G. (1996). What happened to me on the road to Damascus. From positivism to interpretivism and beyond: Tales of transformation. In L. H. & K. Ballard (Ed.), *From positivism and interpretivism and beyond: Tales of transformation in educational and social research* (pp. 43–49). New York, NY: Teachers College.

Guba, E. G., & Lincoln, Y. S. (1994). Competing paradigms in qualitative research. In N. K. Denzin & Y. S. Lincoln (Eds.), *Handbook of qualitative research* (pp. 163–194). Thousand Oaks, CA: Sage.

Guba, E.G., & Lincoln, Y.S. (2005). Paradigmatic controversies, contradictions, and emerging confluences. In N. K. Denzin & Y. S. Lincoln (Eds.), *The SAGE handbook of qualitative research* (3rd ed., pp. 191–215). Thousand Oaks, CA: Sage.

Harper, D. (2002). Talking about pictures: A case for photo elicitation. *Visual Studies*, *17*(1), 13–26. https://doi.org/10.1080/1472586022013734

Johnson, P., & Duberley, J. (2000). *Understanding management research: An introduction to epistemology.* Thousand Oaks, CA: Sage Publications.

Knowles, J. G., & Thomas, S. (2001). Inisghts and inspiration from an artist's work, envisioning and portraying lives in context. In G. J. Cole, & Ardra L. Knowles (Ed.), *Lives in context: The art of life history research* (pp. 203–207). Lanham, Maryland: AltaMira Press.

Lamond, I. R., & Platt, L. (2016). *Critical event studies: Approaches to research.* London, UK: Palgrave Macmillan.

Leavy, P. (Ed.). (2014). *The Oxford handbook of qualitative research.* USA: Oxford University Press.

Lincoln, Y. S., Lynham, S. A., & Guba, E. G. (2011). Paradigmatic controversies, contradictions, and emerging confluences, revisited. *The Sage Handbook of Qualitative Research*, *4*(2), 97–128.

McAdams, D. P. (2001). The psychology of life stories. *Review of General Psychology*, *5*(2), 100–122.

Montuori, A. (2012). Creative inquiry: Confronting the challenges of scholarship in the 21st century. *Futures*, *44*(1), 64–70. https://doi.org/10.1016/j.futures.2011.08.008

Pamphilon, B. (1999). The zoom model: A dynamic framework for the analysis of life histories. *Qualitative Inquiry*, *5*(3), 393–410. https://doi.org/10.1177/1077800 49900500306

Pauwels, L. (2015). 'Participatory' visual research revisited: A critical-constructive assessment of epistemological, methodological and social activist tenets. *Ethnography*, *16*(1), 95–117.

Pauwels, L., & Mannay, D. (2020). Visual dialogues across different schools of thought. In E. Margolis & L. Pauwels (Eds.), *The Sage Handbook of Visual Research Methods* (2nd ed., 1–11). London: SAGE Publications.

Pernecky, T. (2012). Constructionism critical pointers for tourism studies. *Annals of Tourism Research*, *39*(2), 1116–1137. https://doi.org/10.1016/j.annals.2011.12.010

Pernecky, T. (2016). *Epistemology and metaphysics for qualitative research*. London: Sage Publications.

Phillips, N., & Hardy, C. (2002). *Discourse analysis: investigating processes of social construction*. Thousand Oaks, CA; London England: Sage Publications.

Poland, B., & Pederson, A. (1998). Reading between the lines: Interpreting silences in qualitative research. *Qualitative Inquiry*, *4*(2), 293–312.

Riessman, C. K. (2003). Performing identities in illness narrative: Masculinity and multiple sclerosis. *Qualitative Research*, *3*(1), 5–33.

Scotland, J. (2012). Exploring the philosophical underpinnings of research: Relating ontology and epistemology to the methodology and methods of the scientific, interpretive, and critical research paradigms, *5*(9), 9–16. https://doi.org/10.5539/elt.v5n9p9

Silverman, D. (2013). What counts as qualitative research? Some cautionary comments. *Qualitative Sociology Review*, *9*(2), 48–55.

Slife, B. D., & Williams, R. N. (1995). *What's behind the research?: Discovering hidden assumptions in the behavioral sciences*. London, England: SAGE Publications Ltd.

Stanley, Liz, & Wise, Sue. 1990. *Feminist Praxis: Research, theory and epistemology in qualitative research*. London: Routledge.

Stead, G. S. (2004). Culture and career psychology: A social constructionist perspective. *Journal of Vocational Behavior*, *64*(3), 389–406. https://doi.org/10.1016/j.jvb.2003.12.006

Van Schalkwyk, G. J. (2010). collage life story elicitation technique: A representational technique for scaffolding autobiographical memories. *Qualitative Report*, *15*(3), 675–695.

Young, R. A., & Collin, A. (2004). Introduction: Constructivism and social constructionism in the career field. *Journal of Vocational Behavior*, *64*(3), 373–388. https://doi.org/10.1016/j.jvb.2003.12.005

3

MULTI-SITED RESEARCH AS A CREATIVE METHODOLOGY FOR CRITICAL EVENT STUDIES

Zorica Siročić

University of Graz, Graz, Austria

Introduction: Challenges of Studying Events/Festivals

Because of their widespread presence, their importance to their communities, and their economic value, to name just a few factors, there is a vital need to study festivals and alike social events. After developing a specific research question, it is necessary to develop a research design and make methodological choices appropriate to the goals of the study. In doing so, it is worth keeping in mind that festivals are unique social phenomena that often require a holistic approach due to their complexity and diverse facets – these are the factors that will have an impact on the methodological choices. To illustrate, a common approach to the study of festivals would be the use of ethnographic methods such as observations and interviews. (Traditional) ethnography is based on the idea of acquiring intimate knowledge of everyday "face-to-face communities and groups" (Marcus, 1995, p. 99) and "the idea of such a thorough, formative, exclusive engagement with a single field" and its participants (Hannerz, 2003, p. 202).

However, there are several features specific to festivals that make us reconsider whether traditional ethnography is an appropriate methodology and method to study them. Specifically, a festival is per definition a temporary site that simultaneously encompasses a multitude of nested sites, has a fluctuating audience, and is often spatially and temporally dispersed. These are just some of the characteristics that require an adapted and creative approach to fieldwork. Though creativity is, as Helen Kara (2015, p. 10) writes "notoriously difficult to define" and its definitions depend on socio-cultural, linguistic, and geographical contexts, to name a few factors, this chapter understands creativity in research as an innovative, adaptive, flexible, and open approach to the social context and phenomenon in question, including the use of one's physical

DOI: 10.4324/9781032686424-3

presence in the field. Kara (2015), for example, divides creative research methods into four key areas: arts-based research, research using technology, mixed methods research, and transformative research (such as participatory, feminist, or decolonizing). Kara (2015) further links creativity in research with the uncertainty that research entails and with the potential to redefine or bring together existing elements in new ways. These aspects of creativity in research are particularly relevant to critical event studies, as one often needs to be prepared to meander and explore, expecting the unexpected. In other words, events are spontaneous phenomena that depend on numerous factors that the researcher cannot take all into account in advance, but must be prepared to adapt to the logic and flow of the event.

Specifically, a festival is a phenomenon that relies on creativity in its organisational conception over the content, which encompasses a range of artistic and creative forms. Unless primarily dedicated to a single art form, festivals usually include workshops, exhibitions, fairs, concerts, and many other forms. Consequently, this *multiplicity of forms* requires a researcher to be creative in the choice of methods and methodology. Specifically, at a festival a researcher is confronted with nested dislocations within a site – which in practice would require shorter visits to different sites, that is festival forms. Consequently, the multiplicity of festival's content entails the use of different methods of data collection and analysis. These range from field techniques such as participant observation and interviews to, for example, discourse analysis or art interpretation. It is useful for a researcher to be familiar with different data collection techniques in order to decide which is most appropriate for a given situation.

Some additional characteristics of festivals that further account for a creative approach include, for example, the *diversity of organisational practices* in events. Festivals are often organised as small, do-it-yourself events run by a team of ad hoc volunteers, or as large events managed by a professional team and selectors who plan and work on the festival throughout the year. These differences have implications for budget, programming choices, and the access a researcher may have to the event. In other words, a researcher often explores micro, meso, and macro levels of social analysis or needs to make a choice between these levels.

Another characteristic of the festival that should be kept in mind when considering methodological choices is that they are, by definition, *exceptional* (cf. Falassi, 1987) *"chronotopes"* (Bakhtin, 1994) or occasions that function as ruptures in the everyday life and/or work routine of a given community. As such, festivals can sometimes even be spatially isolated, yet they are still embedded in the socio-political, economic, and cultural context, either through identification or "disidentification" (Muñoz, 1999) with the broader community. This specificity requires the researcher to strike a balance between the specific insights related to the event in question, on the one hand, and a more general acquaintance with the broader socio-political, cultural, and economic environment, on the other.

In order to address the contextual significance of the event and demonstrate contextual competence, one may need to leave the particular event setting and collect data in the surrounding context. This is necessary even if one is not primarily studying the relationship between these contexts, but in order to make sense of the event in general. Because of the exceptional nature of the festival, one must be careful not to overgeneralise findings to the field, as these may differ significantly from or even contradict the findings that apply to the festival and should reflect on the one's positioning when accessing/entering the field.

Festivals gather *diverse and fluctuating audiences* that require creative approaches to ethnographic data collection techniques such as observation and interviewing, as they don't allow for the traditional ethnographic practice of intimate familiarity with the members of a community. Although the audience is often the primary research interest for an event studies scholar, one should not lose sight of the organisers and participants who bring together different professions and lifestyles. The relationships between these groups may also be of interest. These different roles of interviewees entail from a researcher familiarity with the organisational practices and the organising team, as well as with the history of the event.

The *temporal character* of the festival is another feature with implications for methodological choices. Specifically, a given event may occur only once, or it may have regular annual editions. Similarly, a researcher may wish to take a snapshot of an event in question, noting its specifics in detail, or a researcher may want/need to follow an event over the course of several years, using a longitudinal perspective to observe its constants and changes. Both perspectives are valuable, and the choice between them depends on the research question and the time and material resources available. In any case, the temporal (i.e. temporary) nature of festivals will challenge the assumptions of the traditional ethnographic approach, in which a researcher stays in a field for an extended period of time.

Finally, *the location* of the festival has significant implications for research design. Festivals can be locally bound or geographically dispersed. In the latter case, we can speak of editions of the same festival or of a specific type of festival (e.g., Ladyfest). Regardless of this difference, in the case of different locations/sites, as well as in the case that a researcher is interested in one or a few particular aspects of festivals (e.g., exclusion, inclusion) – this often requires the comparison of either several editions of a single festival or of different festivals. In other words, one will have to engage in spatially decentred research, which means following events in several different places and inevitably in different time periods. The *spatial and temporal dispersion* is further complicated by possible differences in languages, cultures, and political and economic regimes, which require context-specific knowledge and sensitivity to the existence of the aforementioned differences. A similar requirement applies to the study of an event over the course of several years, when this period presupposes significant transformations of socio-political and economic regimes.

How, then, does one conceptualise a creative yet coherent and systematic research design that takes into account the challenges posed to methodological choices by festival-specific characteristics such as multiplicity of forms, organisational diversity, simultaneous exceptionality and embeddedness, diverse and fluctuating audiences, and temporal and spatial decentrality? This chapter proposes multi-sited research as a methodology capable of offering creative – in the sense of flexible and adaptable – solutions to a research question or research objectives. Drawing on previously mentioned Kara's (2015) systematisation, multi-sited research would be an example of creative mixed methods. The chapter first outlines the basic principles of multi-sited research and then illustrates its application in the book *Festivals as Reparative Gender Politics: Millennial Feminism in Southeastern Europe* (Siročić, 2023), and finally it ends with the methodological reflection, providing a list of concrete guidelines and tips for practical use.

Multi-Sited Research

Definition

Whereas in traditional ethnography a researcher spends an extended period of time immersed in the community of interest, in multi-sited research a scholar follows the object of interest and collects data in several spatially or socially distinct locations over shorter periods of time. Or, in the words of one of its chief proponents and initiators, George Marcus (1995, p. 96, 1999), this "mobile ethnography" traces cultural formation across and within multiple sites of activity. Although one might debate what defines a "site" (whether that might also mean, e.g., a perspective), "multi-sited" is commonly understood to imply geographical, spatial decentredness (Falzon, 2016a, p. 2). In other words, multi-sited ethnography shifts the focus from the situated object of traditional ethnography to the systems of relations that define it (Marcus, 2016, p. 19). Instead of the "thick descriptions" (Geertz, 1973) of a more or less static social space characteristic of ethnography, multi-sited ethnography places at its core strategies of following connections, associations, relationships (Marcus, 1995, p. 97), and exploring assemblages and networks. Multi-sited ethnography is an "exercise in mapping terrain; its goal is not holistic representation" (Marcus, 1995, p. 99). In other words, when using this methodology, one must come to terms with maintaining a fragmented perspective while balancing thick and thin descriptions.

Context

Multi-sited ethnography emerged in the early 1990s as an epistemological, methodological, and practical adaptation of ethnographic research to conceptual and theoretical developments in the social sciences and humanities.

Particularly influential seem to have been strong social constructivist approaches and poststructuralist and postmodern theories that conceptualised social complexity, materiality, and territoriality in terms of assemblages (Deleuze and Guattari, 1987) and actor-networks (Law, 1992; Latour, 1996). Mark-Anthony Falzon (2016a, p. 4) specifies the conditions that explain the need for this shift from traditional ethnography to multi-sited research: this is to begin with the idea of space as socially produced. Equally influential was the perceived inadequacy of the local (perspective) and the awareness of the need to conceptualise societies as situated within larger wholes (Mark-Anthony Falzon, 2016a, p. 5). Also, the ever-growing scholarly interest in international and transnational flows and migrations (of people, ideas, objects, etc.) could no longer be ignored. Finally, there are the historical-pragmatic reasons that have made shorter field studies an accessible research alternative to longer periods of time (Mark-Anthony Falzon, 2016a, p. 6), which often cannot be afforded due to private or professional constraints.

Objects of Study

Multi-sited ethnographers define their objects of study through several different modes or techniques, which can be understood as "practices of construction through (pre-planned or opportunistic) movement and tracking within different settings of a complex cultural phenomenon [....]" (Marcus, 1995, p. 106). Marcus (1995) lists what these modes and techniques might include:

a Following the people: migrations studies, diaspora studies
b Following the thing: material object of the study (commodities, gifts, money, art work, intellectual property)
c Following the metaphor: realm of discourse and modes of thought; circulation of signs, symbols, metaphors (language, print, visual media)
d Following the plot, story, or allegory (narratives, social memory)
e Following the life or biography (life histories)
f Following the conflict

Since the initial formulation of these techniques by Marcus in the mid-1990s, there has been a proliferation of studies empirically addressing the proposed research programme. Since each of the proposed techniques, as well as their possible combinations (e.g., one could combine following the people and following the thing, etc.) imply different circumstances, it is difficult to provide a concrete list of recommendations for each one of them. Therefore, to get an impression of the good practices, it is advisable to read some of the empirical studies, for example in the edited volumes by Coleman and Von Hellermann (2011) and Falzon (2016b).

Research Logic and Methodology

While traditional ethnography is strongly associated with the inductive principles that characterise for instance grounded theory (Glaser, 1998; Charmaz, 2014), multi-sited research also accommodates the deductive and abductive research logic that characterises comparative and theoretically driven interpretive designs. As Marcus (1995, p. 102) puts it

> [t]he object of study is ultimately mobile and multiply situated, so any ethnography of such an object will have a comparative dimension that is integral to it, in the form of juxtapositions of phenomena that conventionally have appeared to be (or conceptually have been kept) 'worlds apart'.

In other words, the comparative translation and tracing between sites is the basis of the multi-sited methodology (Marcus, 1995, p. 111). Consequently, the sampling strategy and ultimately the analysis of the material can follow the inductive principles of theoretical sampling and grounded theory (cf. Glaser, 1998; Charmaz, 2014) or situational analysis[1] (cf. Clarke, Friese, and Washburn, 2017; Clarke, 2003; Clarke, Friese, and Washburn, 2015), which postulate the collection of more data until the point of saturation. However, the analysis may follow a more deductive and abductive logic, as in the comparative designs, where the sampling strategy and the interpretation of the material draw on pre-existing theoretical knowledge and concepts. Which logic is followed depends on the nature of the research question.

Methods of Data Collection and Analysis

Multi-sited fieldwork research engages with other than exclusively ethnographic perspectives, methods, and informants, or as Marcus (2016, p. 23) puts it, this methodology can be understood as "para-ethnography". In the words of Hannerz (2003, p. 212), "skills of synthesis" are valued in contemporary ethnographic research, which refers, for example, to

> interacting with informants in a series of dispersed sites, but also doing fieldwork by phone and email, collecting data eclectically in many different ways from a variety of sources, paying close attention to popular culture, and reading newspapers and official documents.

In other words, contemporary multi-sited research recognises the (epistemological) value of "following" the field before, after, or in between visits, for example by reading reports, using archives, and following relevant social media accounts. This condition is not only relevant in cases where the object of our study has, for example, different annual editions or is spatially dispersed. Fewer, shorter research visits may have pragmatic reasons, as in some cases private or professional conditions do not allow for an extensive fieldwork visit. The latter situation accounts for one of the most common objections to multi-sited ethnography, which is that a researcher does not spend enough time getting to know the community and field in question in order to draw well-informed conclusions. To address this objection, it is advisable to supplement shorter research stays with (extensive) background research.

In other words, multi-sited research is an example of "mixed-methods" programme, that is qualitative and qualitative, or several qualitative methods can be combined, and allows for "triangulation" (Jick, 1979; Flick, 2004; Mertens and Hesse-Biber, 2012) or the use of several data collection and analysis methods. For example, to address the previously mentioned objections in relation to the short stays, one can combine multi-sited fieldwork with archival research or with "digital ethnography" (Murthy, 2008; Kaur-Gill and Dutta, 2017) as another methodological programme that responds to the situation in which large parts of social life and interactions are displaced into a virtual realm. As mentioned above, the para-ethnographic methodological framework allows for the use of different methods of sources, data collection, and data analysis that go beyond the usual ethnographic methods (such as interviews and observations). These other methods of data collection can include archival research or policy analysis to familiarise with the field or context of the phenomenon in question. Likewise, events as intellectual and creative endeavours often require the combination of ethnographic methods with methods such as discourse analysis or other qualitative and interpretive designs appropriate for the analysis of art production, for example. Although most work is done with qualitative data, multi-sited research allows for the collection of quantitative data, such as demographic data, that can be mixed and triangulated with other qualitative data sources. This "para-ethnographic" condition of the research design, as well as the described compatibility with non-ethnographic research methods and methodologies, make the use of the term *"multi-sited research"* rather than the usual "multi-sited ethnography" appropriate for this chapter.

In summary, multi-sited research is a creative methodological programme that allows for the combination of different techniques, data collection methods, and modes of analysis. As such, multi-sited research is well suited to mapping the terrain and highlighting relationships, as in situational analysis, or juxtaposing aspects of interest, as in comparative designs. The innovativeness, flexibility, and adaptability that characterise multi-sited research are particularly useful in the study of creative phenomena – such as festivals – because they often involve a range of creative and artistic forms that require the researcher to adapt their tools to the particularities of the situation. *Festivals as Reparative Gender Politics*, as the study of gender-centred (women's, feminist, and LGBTQ+) festivals detailed below, is an example of such an approach. The research flow described (Figure 3.1) should be understood as a

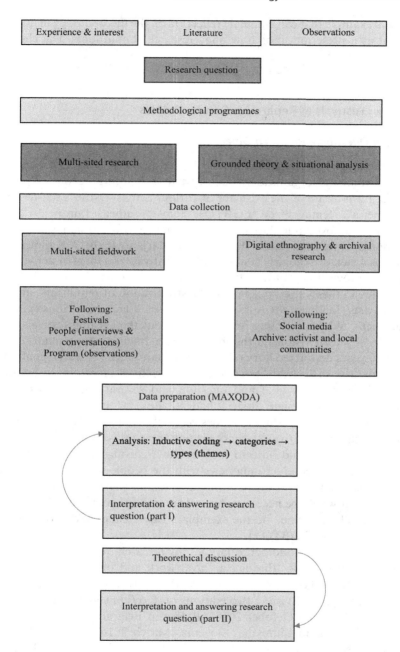

FIGURE 3.1   Research design summary.

practical example that can stimulate reflection on the methodology in question, and not as a prescription of how one's research should look. The choice of research design will depend on the research question, the characteristics of the field, the availability of data and sources, etc.

Example: Festivals as Reparative Gender Politics

Research Question – Research Object

As a scholar of social movements and having previous work experience in a non-governmental organisation dedicated to promoting gender equality in Croatia, I was aware of the existence of various activist festivals self-described as "women's", "feminist", or "LGBTQ+" across Southeast Europe[2]. Although the festivals enjoyed popularity among feminist and queer activists, with the exception of three case studies (Hvala, 2010; Marjanović, 2017; Kajinić, 2010), there was a lack of scholarly research on the festivals as a form of activism and even less recognition that a festival would have a political value. One could hear and read theses that spoke of the "festivalization of feminism", implying that activists' fondness for festivals presupposes a lack of serious (political) engagement. While collecting information about the existing festivals, I was fascinated by their rise from the initial 2–3 in 2000 to approximately 15–20 within 20 years on the territory of Southeast Europe. My research goal was to explain the rise of festivals' popularity in the activist repertoire in Southeast Europe. This research goal and question had several implications for the research plan and design: first, I had to look at the beginnings of the "festivalization" trend, which includes not only festivals that exist, but also those that have ceased to exist. Since visiting these festivals was not an option, this meant that I would have to look at the archival material documenting these festivals and conduct interviews with the people who attended, organised, and initiated them. Furthermore, the research question around the trend implied that it would be necessary to visit several different festivals connected to an overarching theme – in the exemplary case, gender and sexual equality (women's, feminist, LGBTQ+).

In multi-sited methodological jargon, my research question implied that I would "follow festivals" through archival work and physical visits to those events that were theoretically relevant and empirically accessible. Over the course of two years, I visited two editions of *VoxFeminae* in Zagreb, Croatia (November 2015 and October 2016), *BeFem* in Belgrade, Serbia (December 2015), *Red Dawns* in Ljubljana, Slovenia (March 2016), *City of Women* in Ljubljana, Slovenia (October 2016), *Firstborn girl!* in Skopje, Macedonia (March 2016), and *PitchWise* in Sarajevo, Bosnia and Herzegovina (September 2016). To avoid the risk of not getting to know the research situation in detail, I triangulated the observational data with interviews and textual sources, but I also familiarised myself with the rest of the local scene before or after visiting a festival. I did this by reading up on the mainstream, countercultural, and subcultural sites of creative, artistic, and political production, by having informal meetings with actors who have direct experience of the local scene, and by visiting current exhibitions, protests, and meeting places. In between visits, I would follow the social media accounts of activist collectives and official festivals, complementing physical fieldwork with digital ethnographic tools. For the general methodological guidelines (e.g., sampling strategy, conducting interviews, accessing the field, documenting the research, preparing the material, and analysis), I relied in the beginning on the basic principles of grounded theory (see Glaser, 1998; Charmaz, 2014) and situational analysis (see Clarke, 2003; Clarke, Friese, and Washburn, 2015) as examples of the more systematically elaborated programmes for conducting qualitative research.

Research Material – Collecting the Data

The data collection process began by first identifying the ongoing festivals in the region and contacting their organisers via email. I would introduce myself and the research interest and usually schedule an interview with the person. Some *interviews* were scheduled around the time of the festival, while others were scheduled before or in between festivals so that organisers could focus on the event that was taking place. In selecting interviewees, I relied on the official information on the festival websites and on a snowballing strategy – that is, interviewees would give me the names of other people involved in the organisation of that particular event and/or similar ones. I conducted a total of 23 anonymous (interviewees were given pseudonyms in the book), semi-structured interviews, ranging from 25 to 90 minutes, with the initiators, programmers, and organisers of current and past events. These interviews focused on three broad and open-ended questions that addressed interviewees' motivations and interests in activism, the organisation of festivals, and perceptions of the broader activist scene. The majority of the interviews were conducted in person, with only three conducted online over the course of a year and a half, between 2015 and 2016.

Another source of oral data is *informal conversations* I had on the spot with about 20 festival participants. I did not record these conversations so as not to interfere with the benefits of spontaneous socialisation that characterise festivals, although I did take notes afterwards. These conversations drew my attention to various sites of production by groups and individuals outside the immediate festival setting that nevertheless connected these events to the local art and activist scene. The notes and memos served as a base from which to expand the empirical investigation, following the strategy of theoretical sampling. The informal conversations were also important for uncovering the silent voices and issues.

Other data sources include *participation and direct observation* of festivals. After compiling a list of ongoing festivals, I attended and observed seven festivals that took place in 2015–2016 (see list on the previous page). I tried to follow as many different programme forms as possible and to engage in conversations with organisers, performers, and visitors of these events over the course of two to five days. The festivals I visited were mixed art-activist festivals, characterised by their diversity of forms. Consequently, I would visit a range of art and creative forms – including concerts, film screenings, performances, art and photography exhibitions, comedy, to name a few. In addition, I would attend discussion forums and panels discussing some aspects of feminist and LGBTQ+ politics and life. Finally, I made sure to spend enough time hanging out in a casual atmosphere between programme slots, talking to people and soaking up the atmosphere. The festivals are not only sites for socialisation and negotiation of activist practices, but they also disseminate ideational and artistic production, so my task was to collect different examples of such production and analyse them later.

Finally, *extant texts* are another source of data. According to Kathy Charmaz (2014, p. 35), extant texts include various documents that exist independently of the researcher. In this case, extant texts include the available programmes for each festival included in the study, but also the promotional materials (such as badges, posters, and flyers) that could be found online, on site, or given to me by the organisers. In addition, some panels and discussions were recorded, transcribed, and/or extensive notes taken. The documentary data also included the textual production within the festival communities and their online representation through official websites and social media channels (at the time mostly Facebook), which I collected through digital ethnography. This meant following the exemplary collectives and their postings in order to know when certain events took place, how the collective communicated the content, and to familiarise myself with the rest of the activities beyond festivals that these groups were engaged in. The online postings were also a convenient place to get better quality images documenting the festivals, as they were often taken by professional photographers and cameras, because the ones I took with my own phone were not of the quality for commercial publication.

Entry to the Field and Reflections on the Research Process

In making initial contacts, I was able to take advantage of my previous work experience in one of the gender equality NGOs, as some of the people I contacted knew me from seeing me or had worked with me in some way. I suspected that the fact that I was once part of the same networks and that I had some familiarity with the activist experience and with some of the people in the regional activist scene contributed to the sense of trust and openness during interviewing. However, for some, my background may have had the opposite effect, as some may have perceived me as belonging to one group or another, or felt that I might share their stories with other colleagues. Although the region I was interested in included countries where different languages are spoken, I was able to use my native language, Croatian, when interviewing the majority of activists. I used English when interviewing people from Slovenia and Kosovo, and North Macedonian activists adapted to me by speaking Serbo-Croatian.

Before the event I would scan the programme to see what I would not want to miss, during the event I would try to make contact with the audience and the organisers, and after the event I would take extensive notes in two forms. One form, the *fieldwork diary*, served the purpose of recording unstructured personal impressions, more or less stream-of-consciousness observations, including not only reflections on the events and people observed, but also on the impact of the experience on myself. Festivals have been educational and inspirational places that have led me to consult further literature sources, look for similar examples, and reflect on how exposure to the context is not only important in terms of research findings, but also how it has affected me on a personal level.

The other structured forms included the *protocols of the events and the interviews*, in which I noted information according to the given structure of time and place; the description of what was observed (written in a neutral tone/ report); information about the context (usually based on the information provided in the programme booklets); and finally, interpretation and methodological reflection. This last part was particularly important, as it was here that I identified and noted the progress of the research, things that were new to me and that required further familiarisation in a theoretical sense. These notes helped me identify places and people to look for in terms of theoretical sampling. Finally, the rough interpretative sketches of the events later became a backbone for analysis, interpretation, and theory building. The similar protocol was used in the case of interviews, where after an interview I would write down information about the time and place, the context in which the interview took place, and my observations, tips on where to look for additional information, and initial interpretation.

The multi-sited fieldwork, which included the festival visits listed above, took place during my doctoral studies, which were funded by various grants. Although this situation meant financial precariousness, not having a full-time position at an institution gave me the opportunity to follow the festivals as they were happening and to spend a considerable amount of time doing background fieldwork and travelling around the region. While the festivals typically lasted anywhere from two days to a week, I spent few weeks before and after in the local context, familiarising myself with the local community and conducting interviews. For scholars in different work and life situations, it is advisable to plan ahead and check what is possible given time, material, and work constraints.

Data Analysis

Material Preparation – Sorting Out

After almost two years of data collection, the empirical material had to be sorted and prepared for analysis. Since I used different types of data, I sorted them into different folders from the beginning, which proved to be extremely useful in this preparation phase. While most of the observation diaries, event logs, and interview logs were typed in Word, I scanned those that weren't, as well as some of the promotional material I received at the site. Transcribing interviews and discussions was one of the most time-consuming activities in this phase, but while I was preparing the material, I was able to get a first idea of what would later become the categories for analysis. After transcribing and scanning the material, I sorted the data into the following folders 1) fieldwork (participant observation notes, diaries, interview transcripts, interview protocols, conversations, programme/events); 2) background information (festivals, festival promotional materials; various sources of information about their activist and local communities).

MAXQDA – Coding and First Findings

In the next step I transferred the prepared and sorted material to the software for qualitative analysis – MAXQDA. This software is made keeping in mind the methodological and epistemological postulates of grounded theory, and for that matter it fitted into my initial research design, so I started inductively – doing open coding of the research material, and later on sorting codes into categories. Thus, in terms of data analysis methods, I chose inductive thematic analysis, building categories and typologies. Finally, I identified generational change, organisational practices, and ideological positioning as the overarching themes around which I wrote my dissertation. Specifically, I argued that festivals became a popular choice in activist repertoires because they allowed for generational change, creativity in organisational practices, and ideological positioning that was alternative to their predecessors. The answer to the research question was based on inductive reasoning and built on the most salient themes in the research material.

While the research could have been finished at this point, and for many this will be the end point, I introduced another phase with the preparation of the book manuscript. Having received a postdoctoral fellowship to turn the dissertation into a book and to prepare a postdoctoral project, I had the opportunity to engage more closely with the theoretical sources. Because I had to do extensive empirical work within the time and financial constraints of doctoral programme, I relegated the theoretical literature to the background. Although I drew on the literature of social movement studies, I used it as a conceptual toolbox. Consequently, my doctoral thesis primarily made an empirical contribution to the studies of feminist and queer festivals and activism in Southeast Europe, and to the mapping of transnational trends in contemporary gender equality politics outside the usual Anglo-American context.

While preparing the book proposal, I engaged closely with feminist, queer, and political theory – sources that I had collected over the years as literature that spoke to me and that would be relevant reading material. From this point, I engaged in deductive and abductive reasoning, weaving together empirical material and theory. This engagement with theory provided me with a more nuanced and precise terminology to apply to the material and relate it to existing research and theoretical considerations. Specifically, I divided the overarching themes into belonging, play, dissent and reflection, and fun; and finally, I situated the study within the existing theoretical literature in feminist, queer, and political theory. I did this by arguing that festivals (for enabling belonging, play, dissent and reflection, and fun) can be interpreted as a specific form of political action – what I called "reparative" politics, initially inspired by Eve Kosofsky Sedgwick's seminal essay (Sedgwick and Frank, 2003) "Paranoid reading and reparative reading; or, you're so paranoid, you probably think this introduction is about you". In this way, the book moved from being primarily empirical to relating and situating these empirical findings within existing theoretical debates.

Concluding Remarks, Reflection, Guidelines, Tips for Practical Use

In conclusion, multi-sited research is a prime example of creative methodology, as it allows one to combine different techniques, methods of data collection, and modes of analysis depending on the research object. Often, a researcher (especially at the beginning of the career), when considering the methodological choices that would be appropriate for the research in question, is confronted with guidelines that are formulated in such a way as to ensure a kind of methodological purity. In such cases, one gets the impression that such methodological programmes often don't allow or take into account the messiness and exploration – leaving one in doubt about how to approach one's own research, which will most likely deviate from the textbook examples in one way or another. Multi-sited research, on the other hand, provides enough space for adaptability and flexibility of research design, which is well suited to the messy reality of fieldwork. The latter will most likely require a researcher to modify their initial approach once confronted with the variety and specificity of different data sources – which in turn would entail different methods of analysis. In this sense, multi-sited research can be seen not only as an example of creative methodology, but also as a methodological choice suitable for the analysis of different creative forms – precisely because of the possibility of combining different data sources and methods of analysis.

Nevertheless, multi-sited research provides enough structure to the methodological programme to ensure the quality of qualitative research. Ines Steinke (2004) offers several such quality criteria that are specific to qualitative research. The first concerns *intersubjective comprehensibility*, which can be achieved through documentation of the research process, interpretation in groups, and the use of codified procedures. The second is *the indication of the research process*, where one should distinguish the appropriateness of the research question, the choice of methods, the transcription rules, the sampling strategy, the individual methodological choices in the context of the entire research process, and the evaluation criteria in relation to the research object. The third is the *empirical foundation* of the research, which can be tested through the use of codified methods, written support for the theories developed, analytical induction, prediction, and communicative validation. The fourth is the awareness of *limitations*, which can be demonstrated through the use of case contrasting – looking for and comparing maximally and minimally different cases in relation to the theory, and through the explicit search and analysis of deviant cases. The fifth is *coherence* in terms of the theory developed and in terms of the treatment of contradictions. The sixth is the *relevance* of the research question and the contribution of the theory developed. The last criterion is *reflective subjectivity*, which is achieved through self-observation, reflection on personal preconditions, the existence of a relationship of trust, and if there are any reflections during the entry into the field.

In the light of these criteria, one of the most important tips for researchers is to document the entire research process – from the moment of formulating the research question, through the application of data collection, to the interpretation of the results. To ensure the consistency of the documentation process in the face of the chaos of fieldwork, it is useful to create in advance templates for recording observations and interviews, including separate descriptive and interpretative parts, along with reflection on the choice of methods and subjective positioning. It is advisable to fill in these templates for each data collection occasion with the exact time and place immediately after its completion or shortly thereafter, while impressions and memories are still fresh. These notes not only ensure intersubjective comprehensibility, indication of the research process, and empirical foundation, but also form the basis for the analytical, interpretive, and theory-building phases. Furthermore, working in a qualitative tradition requires reflection on one's subjective positionality as a researcher and on the limitations of the findings, which should also be kept in mind and noted during the research process. In addition, the reflective notes help to keep track of one's personal and professional development, which is a rewarding experience.

Finally, on the practical side, it is advisable to familiarise oneself in advance with the main features of the field in order to be prepared in terms of linguistic or cultural competence. This can be done through short visits to the field during the exploratory phase of the research; through conversations with people from the given context or through expert interviews; through extensive online work. This will make it possible to estimate the approximate length of each research stay. When planning stays, one must consider how and when to combine fieldwork with other methods, such as archival research or interviews. This also has implications for planning accommodations and intervals in which to combine field visits, as well as for obtaining funding and/or permission to conduct fieldwork.

Notes

1 Adele Clarke (2003, 2005) places the notion of the "social world" or "social arena" in the centre of her conceptual and methodological expansion of grounded theory that she labelled "situational analysis". In doing so, she shifts the analytical focus from the human action (traditional grounded theory) towards the situation of the inquiry (situational analysis). Consequently, in the situational analysis the situation of interest is empirically constructed through making and subsequently analysing situational maps, maps of social worlds, and positional maps (Clarke 2003, p. 554; Clarke, Friese, and Washburn 2015, p. 172).

2 In the book and in this chapter, I use the term "Southeast Europe" to designate the post-socialist and post-conflict parts of this region, including the territories of Bosnia and Herzegovina, Croatia, Kosovo, Northern Macedonia, Serbia, and Slovenia.

References

Bakhtin, M. M. (1994) *The dialogic imagination: Four essays*. Edited by C. Emerson and M. Holquist. Austin: University of Texas Press (University of Texas press Slavic series, 1).

Charmaz, K. (2014) *Constructing grounded theory*. 2nd edition. London: SAGE Publications.

Clarke, A. E. (2003) 'Situational analyses: Grounded theory mapping after the postmodern turn', *Symbolic Interaction*, 26(4), pp. 553–576. Available at: https://doi.org/10.1525/si.2003.26.4.553

Clarke, A. E. (2005). *Situational analysis: Grounded theory after the postmodern turn*. Sage Publications.

Clarke, A. E., Friese, C. and Washburn, R. (eds) (2015) *Situational analysis in practice: Mapping research with grounded theory*. Walnut Creek, California: Left Coast Press.

Clarke, A. E., Friese, C. E. and Washburn, R. S. (2017) *Situational analysis: Grounded theory after the interpretive turn*. 2nd edition. Thousand Oaks: SAGE Publications, Inc.

Coleman, S. and Von Hellermann, P. (eds) (2011) *Multi-sited ethnography: Problems and possibilities in the translocation of research methods*. New York: Routledge. (Routledge advances in research methods, 3).

Deleuze, G. and Guattari, F. (1987) *A thousand plateaus: Capitalism and schizophrenia*. Minneapolis: University of Minnesota Press.

Falassi, A. (1987) "Festival: Definition and morphology", in Falassi, A. (ed.) *Time out of time: Essays on the festival*. Albuquerque: University of Mexico Press.

Falzon, M.-A. (2016a) 'Introduction: Multi-sited ethnography: Theory, praxis and locality in contemporary research', in M.-A. Falzon (ed.) *Multi-sited ethnography: Theory, praxis and locality in contemporary research*. Milton Park, Abingdon, Oxon: Routledge, pp. 1–23.

Falzon, M.-A. (ed.) (2016b) *Multi-sited ethnography: Theory, praxis and locality in contemporary research*. Milton Park, Abingdon, Oxon: Routledge.

Flick, U. (2004) 'Triangulation in Qualitative Research', in U. Flick, E. von Kardorff, and I. Steinke (eds) *A companion to qualitative research*. London; Thousand Oaks, Calif: Sage Publications, pp. 178–183.

Geertz, C. (1973) *The interpretation of cultures: Selected essays*. New York: Basic Books.

Glaser, B. G. (1998) *Doing grounded theory: Issues and discussions*. First printing. Mill Valley, Calif: Sociology Press.

Hannerz, U. (2003) 'Being there… and there… and there!: Reflections on multi-site ethnography', *Ethnography*, 4(2), pp. 201–216. Available at: https://doi.org/10.1177/14661381030042003

Hvala, T. (2010) 'The Red Dawns Festival as a feminist-queer counterpublic', *Monitor ISH*, 12 (1): 7–107.

Jick, T. D. (1979) 'Mixing qualitative and quantitative methods: Triangulation in action', *Administrative Science Quarterly*, 24(4), p. 602. Available at: https://doi.org/10.2307/2392366

Kajinić, S. (2010) '"Battle for Sarajevo"' as "Metropolis"': Closure of the First Queer Sarajevo Festival according to Liberal Press', *The Anthropology of East Europe Review*, 28(1), pp. 62–82.

Kara, H. (2015) *Creative research methods in the social sciences: A practical guide*. Bristol: Policy Press.

Kaur-Gill, S. and Dutta, M. J. (2017) 'Digital ethnography', in J. Matthes, C. S. Davis, and R. F. Potter (eds) *The international encyclopedia of communication research methods*. 1st edition. Wiley, pp. 1–10. Available at: https://doi.org/10.1002/9781118901731.iecrm0271

Latour, B. (1996) 'On actor-network theory: A few clarifications', *Soziale Welt*, 47(4), pp. 369–381.

Law, J. (1992) 'Notes on the theory of the actor-network: Ordering, strategy, and heterogeneity', *Systems Practice*, 5(4), pp. 379–393. Available at: https://doi.org/10.1007/BF01059830

Marcus, G. E. (1995) 'Ethnography in/of the world system: The emergence of multi-sited ethnography', *Annual Review of Anthropology*, 24(1), pp. 95–117. Available at: https://doi.org/10.1146/annurev.an.24.100195.000523

Marcus, G. E. (1999) 'What is at stake–and is not–in the idea and practice of multi-sited ethnography', *Canberra Anthropology*, 22(2), pp. 6–14. Available at: https://doi.org/10.1080/03149099909508344

Marcus, G. E. (2016) 'Multi-sited Ethnography: Notes and Queries', in M.-A. Falzon (ed.) *Multi-sited ethnography: Theory, praxis and locality in contemporary research*. Milton Park, Abingdon, Oxon: Routledge, pp. 181–196.

Marjanović, I. (2017) *Staging the Politics of Interconnectedness between Queer, Antifascism and No Borders Politics. The Case of QueerBeograd Cabaret*. PhD Dissertation. Academy of Fine Arts Vienna, Institute for Art Theory and Cultural Studies.

Mertens, D. M. and Hesse-Biber, S. (2012) 'Triangulation and mixed methods research: Provocative positions', *Journal of Mixed Methods Research*, 6(2), pp. 75–79. Available at: https://doi.org/10.1177/1558689812437100

Muñoz, J. E. (1999) *Disidentifications: Queers of color and the performance of politics*. Minneapolis: University of Minnesota Press (Cultural studies of the Americas, v. 2).

Murthy, D. (2008) 'Digital ethnography: An examination of the use of new technologies for social research', *Sociology*, 42(5), pp. 837–855. Available at: https://doi.org/10.1177/0038038508094565

Sedgwick, E. K. and Frank, A. (2003) *Touching feeling: Affect, pedagogy, performativity*. Durham: Duke University Press (Series Q).

Siročić, Z. (2023) *Festivals as reparative politics: Millennial feminism in Southeastern Europe*. S.l.: Routledge.

Steinke, I. (2004) 'Quality criteria in qualitative research,' in U. Flick, E. von Kardorff, & I. Steinke (eds), *A companion to qualitative research* (pp. 184–190). Sage Publications.

4

THROWING OUT THE RULE BOOK

A Creative Approach to Researching Events with Integrity

Trudie Walters

Lincoln University, Lincoln, New Zealand

Introduction

The concept of creative research methods does not simply refer to qualitative, arts-based methods, but extends to thinking creatively about methodology and the ethics of research practice (Kara, 2020). Indeed, Mumford et al. (2010) argue that adopting a creative approach to research can make research more ethical. Research should always be carried out ethically and with integrity, and academics are almost universally required to complete a university ethics approval process prior to collecting data in the field. Research with children or vulnerable population groups, research involving sensitive topics, or research that necessitates collection and storage of personal information, are often subject to greater scrutiny by university ethics committees. This may deter some researchers from carrying out studies that could have potentially significant benefits through addressing questions and issues of importance to under-researched populations, further marginalising their voices. In addition, there are often tensions between the ideal and the real, where the expectations of the ethics committee do not necessarily align with the practical reality of event studies research.

This chapter presents three case studies based on my personal experiences of using creative methods to respond to challenges while in the field. In order to meet the needs of event attendees and remove barriers to their participation in the research, I had to think on my feet and creatively adapt previously approved research methods. I hope to demonstrate that by adopting creative yet pragmatic methods it is possible to research ethically and without compromising one's integrity. I provide a series of think points after each case study for the reader to consider while conceptualising their research and developing their ethics application.

DOI: 10.4324/9781032686424-4

A Brief History of Research Ethics

Prior to the 1960s, research ethics were not a concern for social science researchers; they perceived themselves as objective, value-free collectors of data in much the same vein as hard scientists (Sieber, 2004; Traianou, 2014). They recognised no relationship with their human research "subjects" and indeed, believed that the existence of such a relationship would contaminate the data (Sieber, 2004). However, from the late 1960s this began to change. In both the UK and the US, Institution Review Boards (IRBs) were established to counteract some highly questionable medical research practices and provide regulations for the protection of human participants (Cheek, 2005; Juritzen, Grimen and Heggen, 2011; Traianou, 2014). At a similar time, social scientists working in medical research began investigating issues such as drug abuse and racism which were highly context-specific, dynamic social phenomena. They realised that they brought attitudinal "baggage" to their research and that research participants would only provide candid responses if they felt comfortable. The researchers' ability to generate useful, valid data was contingent on ensuring that their research participants felt respected and fairly treated (Sieber, 2004).

Research ethics has evolved further since that time (Juritzen, Grimen and Heggen, 2011). In universities around the world, research ethics is highly formalised and, while no longer confined to medical research, university ethics policies nevertheless often remain strongly influenced by these traditions (Christians, 2005; Lincoln, 2005). Research, especially funded research, cannot usually be carried out until ethics approval from the IRB, Human Research Ethics Committee, ethics committee, or other similarly named regulatory body has been gained (Balon et al., 2019; Cheek, 2005; Christians, 2005). Some argue that qualitative research is disadvantaged by this historical hangover and ethics committee review process. With a traditional bent towards "scientific" positivist quantitative research methods that produce generalisable results, ethics committees may reject qualitative research on the basis that it is "unscientific" and therefore not valid, with the findings being of no use to society (Cheek, 2005; Drolet et al., 2023; Lacey, 1998; Lincoln, 2005; Juritzen, Grimen and Heggen, 2011).

Critiques of Research Ethics: Power and Processes

Ethics committees require researchers across all disciplines to take more into account than simply making sure research participants are respected and treated fairly (Beauchemin et al., 2022; Cheek, 2005; Juritzen, Grimen and Heggen, 2011; Sieber, 2004). In what is an increasingly bureaucratic environment arguably aimed more at protecting the institution from reputational and legal risk than the principle of causing no harm, researchers must address concerns around informed consent, confidentiality and privacy, how participants are recruited, cultural considerations, and what methods are used (Balon et al., 2019; Beauchemin et al., 2022; Cheek, 2005; Christians, 2005; Hickey et al., 2022; Lincoln, 2005; Juritzen, Grimen and Heggen, 2011). A number of scholars make the point that through this scope creep, the power of ethics committees has moved beyond their remit to protect the research participant, to determine the very nature of the knowledge that can be produced: an issue of epistemic injustice (Cheek, 2005; Drolet et al., 2023; Lincoln, 2005; Juritzen, Grimen and Heggen, 2011; Traianou, 2014). For example, the ideal of informed consent is predicated upon the competence of research participants to provide that consent: children, speakers of other languages, and those with literacy, cognitive and intellectual challenges are thus often excluded from participation – and research that has the potential to benefit them may not be carried out (Juritzen, Grimen and Heggen, 2011). Thinking more creatively about the methods used to determine "competence" may provide an opportunity to overcome such barriers to participation for marginalised groups (Mumford et al., 2010).

Perhaps unsurprisingly then, there is a corresponding growing body of literature that is critical of ethics review boards and processes alike (Hickey et al., 2022). There is a sense that for some researchers the process of gaining ethics approval (or formal exemption) is too burdensome, time-consuming, and even intimidating (Balon et al., 2019; Hickey et al., 2022). Others believe that standards promoted by ethics committees are "disconnected from the reality of the field" (Drolet et al., 2023, p. 281). However, Hickey et al. (2022, p. 550, emphasis in original) note, "the ethics review process, enacted by an ethics review board that functions as the point of activation for dialogue around the ethical dimensions of research practice, holds significant potential to support researchers *and* inform research cultures." Where there is a hierarchy of ethics review committees (for example, one person may be responsible for reviewing ethics applications for less "risky" research projects within a university department, but is required to escalate higher risk projects to a university-level committee) it may be possible that such personalised approaches can be adopted. Yet even where one person is charged with this responsibility, if they adopt a pedantic "gatekeeper" attitude or there is interpersonal conflict between themselves and the researcher applying for approval, the process will remain bureaucratic, adversarial, and intimidating (Drolet et al., 2023; Hickey et al., 2022).

In addition to issues of informed consent, confidentiality and privacy, participant recruitment and the research methods used, must be added conflicts of interest, falsification of data, plagiarism, ensuring accurate representation of participant voice, ownership of research findings, and how to engage with participants who do not have English as their first language (Drolet et al., 2023; Fitzpatrick et al., 2016). There is also sometimes a disconnect between what is approved by the IRB, and what happens in practice. For example, researchers may commit to protecting research participants' confidentiality via password-protected computer storage or locked filing cabinets, but in reality they may lack the resources or infrastructure to fulfil this (Drolet et al., 2023).

Sieber (2004) observed that the ethical issues faced by researchers are not solved by adhering to the rules of ethics boards: it is possible to research ethically and with integrity, without adhering to ethics committee rules. Please note I am not arguing here that there is no place for ethics review in human/social research, or that researchers should ignore rules. Rather, I am seeking to highlight some of the challenges faced by (particularly) qualitative researchers resulting from formal university research ethics approval processes, that are themselves a result of the history of the origins of the IRB itself. There is increasing recognition of the need for ethics review processes to take into account the ontological and epistemological underpinnings of qualitative research, acknowledging that qualitative methods are different – but no less valid (Drolet et al., 2023). In a similar vein, Beauchemin et al. (2022) have called for more and deeper researcher consideration of the ethical issues faced when conducting research, and more transparent discussions of how these were conceptualised and addressed. In writing this chapter I hope to demonstrate why this is necessary for critical event studies researchers whose field, by its very nature, creates some unique challenges and tensions. Our ability to adopt creative methods is pivotal to this argument.

Challenges and Tensions in Conducting [Ethical] Events Research

Critical event studies researchers are often embedded within a business- or tourism-focused department or faculty, and those reviewing ethics applications may be unfamiliar with the nature of events research. Reviewers may therefore be uncomfortable when presented with creative research methods that are outside the "tried and true." But what is it about events research in particular that makes it different, and what does this mean for research ethics? Events are dynamic, complex social phenomena that positivist approaches cannot capture adequately (Jaimangal-Jones, 2014). The interplay of time, location, and the human dimension results in a certain degree of unpredictability, and each iteration or experience of the same event is unique (Jepson and Clarke, 2016; Pavoni and Citroni, 2016; Getz and Page, 2020). This suggests the need for a hermeneutic qualitative approach that can be adapted to the context and capture the individuality of the event experience, but that is sometimes misinterpreted as being methodologically unsound (Alvesson and Sköldberg, 2000; Creswell, 2013; Jaimangal-Jones, 2014; Jennings, 2012).

Arguably most important for the purposes of this chapter, events are creative endeavours, planned and designed as experiences to be consumed. Therefore, whether free or paid/ticketed, whether for education or entertainment, events function as "time out of time" for attendees, a liminal zone that they seek to immerse themselves in (Getz and Page, 2020; Jaimangal-Jones, 2014).

For event staff, volunteers, participants, performers/exhibitors, producers and organisers, an event is a time of work. From an ethical standpoint, this means that the research must be carried out in such a way that it does not detract from the enjoyment of the experience for attendees, nor distract volunteers or paid staff from doing their work. From an ethics standpoint, how does this align with an ethics committee's traditional requirement for each research participant to read a project information sheet and sign a consent form? With regards to recruitment, how does the researcher select which people to approach in a crowd, and does this introduce bias? What about the power dynamics of researcher/participant? Depending on the event, there may be a diverse range of attendees with varying levels of competency in the language of the researcher – how does the researcher include their perspectives in the research? This also raises questions when the research is carried out in one language and then translated into another language for publication: how is this managed ethically? How can creative methods help us to find answers to these ethical questions?

Events by their very nature are time-bound: there is a fixed start and end time, and they may be one-off or periodic. For example, a music event featuring a specific line-up of musicians may only be held once, whereas the Olympic Games occurs every four years; and recurring events such as this are often held in a different destination when they do occur again. Furthermore, unlike these large events which have marketing lead-in times of many months and across many channels (such as local, regional and national print newspapers and magazines, television, social media, and digital billboards), many smaller events may only advertise locally and via social media in preceding weeks. Ethics committees often work to a set schedule; they may meet only once a month. Thus, where a smaller event only comes to the attention of a researcher one or two weeks in advance, the window of opportunity for ethics approval may be tight, especially if the ethics committee requires one or more rounds of revisions. Where the event is held annually, this creates even more time pressure, as the researcher will need to wait another year to carry out their research if they cannot gain their approval in time. How long will it take to contact event organisers and gain their permission to carry out research at the event? What might the event organisers need to know to make an informed decision about whether to allow the research to be carried out? In an event lasting only a few hours, how can the researcher ensure sufficient empirical material is collected for robust findings to be generated? Can we think creatively to provide more IRB flexibility, to help us deal with these temporal challenges?

It is not only time that is delimited: events are also usually confined to a specific space or place. In addition to the location being subject to change for recurring events, for other events the location may not be revealed until close to the time. For example, for safety reasons the organisers of the Marathon of Afghanistan (the country's first public, outdoor, co-ed sport event) kept both the date and the location of the event a closely guarded secret until just days before (Orr and Baeth, 2019). If the event is not publicised in advance, or is being held in a location that is unfamiliar to the researcher, it may be difficult to determine with any certainty where and how the research may be carried out safely for all parties. Ethics committees may need to know how participants' privacy will be respected, or how the physical safety of both researcher and participant will be assured – how does the researcher deal with this? Where should the researcher position themselves within the event if they are using participant observation? Is their observation overt or covert?

These are doubtless more factors that make events research distinctive, and that must be taken into account for research to be conducted ethically. However, despite these unique qualities a search of the event studies literature reveals few examples explicitly discussing ethical considerations. Notable exceptions include Jaimangal-Jones (2014) who presents a valuable reflection on the ethical issues around the use of ethnography and participant observation in festival and event research. Dashper's (2016) discussion of the complexity of ethics when using autoethnography in critical event studies is brief but well-considered and a must-read for those using this method – and indeed, for those peer reviewing such work. Jepson and Clarke (2016) provide a good high-level overview of ethical considerations in events and festival research, but it is arguably more idealistic than realistic. For example, they mention the importance of informed consent but do not give an example of how this may be achieved practically in the field. While Biaett (2019) investigated the ethics of estimating the number of attendees at events, it was from the standpoint of corporate social responsibility rather than research ethics.

What follows, then, is an autoethnographic account of a series of illustrative cases that detail the practical application of creative methods to ethical decision-making in the field, in an attempt to address this gap. I hope this will encourage more critical event studies researchers to be both creative and transparent about how they addressed and overcame ethical considerations when writing their methodology section in publications.

Case Studies: Throwing Out the Rule Book

The three case studies that follow are organised in chronological order. However, as I was writing them, I noticed that doing so meant the evolution of my thinking about ethical considerations, and the complexity of the challenges I was grappling with, also became evident.

Researching in a Marginalised Community

The problem: Unsurprisingly, most researchers have a personal interest in what they are researching. Some even have a personal connection with the community or the individuals they are seeking to research with. In these circumstances, how can they use creative methods to deal ethically with the issues of power and trust, especially when they transition into the role of researcher in a community they are familiar with? In a marginalised community, these issues are particularly salient. Due to prior negative experiences with people and organisations in authority, often spanning many years, the community may naturally be mistrustful of "outsiders" – or even "insiders" who have become "outsiders" simply by stepping into the role of researcher. I reflect on some of these questions using a case study from my experience as an early career researcher, where I was quickly humbled by the realisation that I was not an insider at all. I also highlight how the very process of completing the university ethics application (the nature of the questions asked and the answers expected) created barriers to participation.

The case study: I had worked in a bank in this community for 5 years before and during my time as a PhD student. The suburb (in Ōtepoti/Dunedin, Aotearoa New Zealand) has long been stigmatised. Its population is older, with more refugee and ethnic minority peoples than the wider city, and has a higher deprivation across all measures (income, employment, level of education, access to communication technology, car and home ownership) (StatsNZ, 2018). I believed that my time working in the community gave me a familiarity that I could capitalise on to investigate the impact of a local street festival designed to celebrate the people and place and strengthen the sense of community:

> I observed and was immersed in both the lives of my customers and the wider South Dunedin community… As a result, I developed a strong affection for many of the former and a protective attitude towards the latter. I therefore cannot help but carry these emic perspectives and experiences into this research; they have been instrumental in the conceptualisation of this project, have shaped how I think about marginalised communities, and have (I believe) helped me to be a more empathetic, compassionate researcher.
>
> *(Walters, 2019, p. 38)*

In addition to collecting demographic information from participants, my (approved) ethics application noted the following:

> Project information provision and participant consent: all participants will be provided, in advance, with an Information Sheet (refer to attached) to advise them of the nature of the research study, what their participation will entail, that their conversations will be recorded for later analysis by the researcher, and that they will be asked to discuss their perceptions of the South Dunedin Street Festival and its contribution to community celebration, pride, cohesiveness and wellbeing. A signed Consent Form (refer to attached) will be obtained from each individual.

Conforming to university expectation and tradition, the information sheet and consent form were long (three pages in total) and written in formal rather than conversational English. At the time, I perceived no scope for creativity. I printed off 25 copies, attached them to a clipboard, clipped my university ID to a university-branded lanyard and ensured my digital voice recorder was charged. I wore casual clothes but in hindsight I am sure I still looked "official" and out of place. I arrived just before the event was scheduled to start and, after walking the length of the street to scope out the layout, stalls and music stages, stationed myself near what I hoped was a suitable shop doorway. In the book chapter about this project, I felt it was important to discuss the fatal weaknesses in my approved ethics application which revealed themselves almost immediately:

> First, the power inherent in my new academic role presented a barrier to people's willingness to participate. As the Festival began, I approached a woman walking past. She glanced at me (and my official-looking clipboard and name badge) and declined to engage in conversation, saying "I don't want to talk to a university person" and walking quickly away. Second, it became evident that not all event attendees were able to read the consent form, and third, those with children were not willing or able to spend time talking to me. My preconceived notions of my familiarity with the community were clearly flawed and a new approach was needed.
>
> *(Walters, 2019, p. 40)*

My ability to employ creative methods resulted in an ethical solution that enabled me to continue with data collection at the approved event. The book chapter details the rapid change of plan developed on the spot:

> …Event attendees were approached (without the clipboard), given a brief verbal overview of the project, and asked whether they would be interested in a quick chat about the Street Festival. If so, I verbally conveyed the contents of the consent form and asked them to sign it, and the "in-the-moment" conversation ensued. These conversations were semi-structured and lasted 3–8 minutes. Immediately after the conversation, I quickly took detailed field notes about the thoughts and experiences that they shared with me, and included as many quotes as I could capture.
>
> *(Walters, 2019, p. 40)*

This creative method allowed me to engage with people casually, but at the same time make sure they understood what the project was about and therefore give informed consent. I was guided by the desire to do no harm and pose no risk to participants in a pragmatic way that still enabled me to uphold the principles of the ethics application. Furthermore, while I asked whether they lived in South Dunedin or somewhere else, I did not ask anyone's name and simply estimated their age. In these ways, the power imbalance and resulting intimidation were reduced such that they felt comfortable telling me about their experience of the event, and both their anonymity and dignity were preserved.

Had I not been able to engage in such a creative way with the challenge I faced and simply walked away disheartened from the research, I would not have had the opportunity to demonstrate the many positive outcomes of this festival as seen through the eyes of local residents, and contribute to an affirming counternarrative of a stigmatised community. This experience also highlighted to me the importance of minimising the disruption to event attendees: their purpose for being there was not to take part in my research, it was to take part in the event. While I had spoken with the event organisers prior and gained permission to carry out my research, I had not discussed the more detailed logistics with them. In hindsight, I wonder had I done this, whether they may have immediately realised the flaws in my plans.

Think points:

- Be aware of your assumptions and cognisant of the power dynamic when you move into the role of researcher in a community that is familiar to you.
- Consider how you may be perceived by participants – what you are wearing, how you speak, where you stand/sit – and how this may create a barrier to participation.
- Ask yourself whether what you are asking of them is going to interrupt their enjoyment of the event. For example, will it take longer than a few minutes, is it during a break in the event programming (and if so, are they making a beeline for the bathroom or refreshments), do they need to read and sign a document before they chat to you?
- What creative methods could you use to facilitate your data collection?

Researching with Speakers of Other Languages

The problem: In my experience, ethics committees seldom if ever require researchers to consider how to include speakers of other languages. There is no recognition of the ethical implications of conducting research in English, and even if the research is conducted in the source language there are no questions asked about the ethics of translation. The translator is often rendered invisible in methodology sections of publications, and the issue of the timing of translation during the analysis phase is also seldom made explicit. I acknowledge that finding a bilingual co-researcher is difficult. I acknowledge that thinking about translation is difficult. But I also believe that we must be more explicit about these ethical challenges in our publications, detail any creative attempts to overcome them, and discuss the implications of not overcoming them. Otherwise, we perpetuate inherent bias in our research and convey a subtle message that this is acceptable. We also need to put pressure on funders to adequately fund cross-language research, recognising the higher cost incurred by the need for a bilingual research team to ensure authentic representation.

So how does this relate to critical events researchers and creative methods? For multicultural events in particular, there may be a large number of attendees for whom English is not their first language and who are therefore not comfortable participating in research conducted in English – there may also be cultural factors at play and/or issues of trust and power to consider. This is a situation seldom addressed in ethics applications, where the focus is on informed consent and participant safety rather than the ethical implications of representation and translation. In this instance then, rather than throwing out the rule book, I suggest an addition to it. I believe there are two ethical challenges for the critical event studies researcher that require creative methods to overcome them: first, to consider how to engage with speakers of other languages and ensure their voices are represented; and second, if they are able to participate in their own language, how to ensure the methodological practice of translation is ethical.

Dealing with the first challenge can be difficult for many reasons. It may not be possible to find a bilingual co-researcher or research assistant. Funding constraints may mean that it is not possible to employ anyone. However, conducting research in English immediately introduces inherent bias (Temple, 2005) and it is important that researchers recognise this and attempt to overcome it. One way is to build a relationship with the event organiser or the communities represented at the event, as this may lead to a creative solution that meets the needs of all parties. The second challenge is arguably a little more straightforward to address. However, despite the ethical implications of translation on data analysis and reporting, it is seldom discussed in the methodology section of publications.

The case study: We wanted to investigate the contribution made by cultural events to the subjective wellbeing of ethnic minority migrant communities in Aotearoa New Zealand (Walters and Venkatachalam, 2022). We focused on Diwali/Deepavali, the Hindu Festival of Light, in two locations. My bilingual co-author was a Singaporean Indian with lived experience of Deepavali in her home country and a native Tamil speaker. Her involvement not only enabled a far broader and deeper understanding to be gained, but facilitated the participation of attendees with English as a second language and arguably enabled even those with a better command of English to convey their experiences more clearly. This project not only demonstrated the importance of communicating with participants in their own language, but as we worked through the methodology of data collection and analysis it also highlighted the ethical consideration that neither ethics committees nor funders took into account:

Very few of those approached (approximately 6 in total over both events) did not wish to participate, of which around half cited a lack of confidence in speaking English. Although the second author is a native Tamil speaker, which enabled two participants to feel comfortable sharing their experiences, the voices of speakers of other languages may be underrepresented. This is a limitation of the study, and one that is unfortunately common within critical event studies; therefore, we use this article to call not only for funders to recognise the need to provide interpreters, but also for universities to support those from ethnic minority backgrounds to join the academic community.

(Walters and Venkatachalam, 2022, p. 146)

What we did not make explicit in the methodology section, however, was how we dealt with the translation of the interviews conducted in Tamil during the analysis. Much to my shame, this was despite me having previously published a paper that developed a cross-language thematic analysis translation timing tool, discussing the importance of the timing of translation from an ethical standpoint, and calling for more transparency from researchers (Esfehani and Walters, 2018). The application of creativity in the research methods here is crucial if we are to ensure authentic, respectful representation of speakers of other languages.

Thematic analysis is a common tool in qualitative research, valued for its flexibility and ability to provide nuanced findings when investigating complex social phenomena (Braun and Clarke, 2006). It is an iterative process, meaning it is important to be explicit about decisions made when needing to translate interviews carried out in one language into the language of publication – at what point in the process was translation carried out, and why, and by whom? What implications were considered, and how were these balanced against pragmatic time/resource considerations? This is particularly important in qualitative research, where language itself and the interpretation of meaning are central to the research process (Lopez et al., 2008; van Nes et al., 2010). While our publication discussed translation in thematic analysis, I believe the same principles and questions around the ethics of translation apply to other methods of data analysis.

Think points:

- If you are not a bilingual researcher, engage early in the process with event organisers and/or members of the community – be creative as you seek to identify the most appropriate way to include speakers of other languages in your research.
- Consider cultural aspects that may preclude participation. Some people may only engage as a group, or if you have taken the time to build a relationship of trust with them in advance.
- Take time to think about the ethical implications of when and how to translate their words, and be explicit about these decisions in your methodology.

Researching with People with Disabilities

The problem: This final case study was undoubtedly the most challenging, ethically speaking. I grappled with the ethics of this project for some time and was very nervous both when I approached the event organisers with my idea and then when the first journal article was published. Not because I was considering being unethical, but because of the multiple layers and complexity surrounding research with disabled people. The sharp-eyed reader may already have noticed the first challenge: terminology! Without going into a deep discussion of the history of perspectives on disability, suffice it to say that terminology is very important. Those who subscribe to the social model of disability will use the term "disabled people" to indicate that the disability exists not because of the person, but because of physical and attitudinal barriers created by society. Proponents of the people-first movement, however, prefer the term "people with disabilities" to put the person before their disability (Mullen and Wills, 2016). I believe that, ethically, (able-bodied) researchers need to acknowledge the debates around terminology, and should provide a rationale for their choice. This leads me to the second ethical question: should able-bodied researchers be conducting research with disabled people?

The case study: As part of my wider project to examine the contribution of events to marginalised communities, I had hoped to find an event with/by/for disabled people. I initially envisaged this being a Riding for the Disabled event or similar, but I was delighted to see an arts festival advertised in another city. This was at short notice, meaning the pressure was on to contact the event organisers to get permission and then get an amendment to my overarching project ethics application approved. It was at this point that I also started to dive into the disability studies literature to understand how I might best approach this particular situation. In regard to the contested space around the language of disability, I chose to use "disabled people" which is the current official consensus in Aotearoa New Zealand (Office for Disability Issues, 2020).

Whilst that was the first ethical consideration addressed, the more background literature I read while I was conceptualising this project, the more unsure of myself and my idea I became. I reflected deeply on what I was reading, and incorporated some of this into the journal article as I sought to be transparent and situate myself within the research:

> … researchers must also be cognisant of issues with agency and power in the research relationship that are often exacerbated by the disabled/non-disabled binary, and the complex arguments about whether non-disabled researchers should be researching disability. At the same time, there have been calls for critical event studies scholars to engage with disabled people and enable their stories to be heard. I am a non-disabled person with no lived experience of the subject I am researching here. Nor do I have lived experience as

a family member, support worker or carer of a disabled person. As such, I grappled with the ethical considerations of researching an event with/by/for disabled people as an outsider. With these concerns in mind, I discussed my research idea and the motivations behind it with the Chair of the InterACTing Trust and the InterACT Disability Arts Festival organiser. Both were enthusiastic and supportive, providing input and insight into the research design.

(Walters, 2023, pp. 210–211)

While I did not have the luxury of time in which to build a relationship, I nevertheless had multiple conversations and emails with the organisers leading up to the event as we co-designed the methodology. They were immensely generous with their time and expertise, and I could not have done this research without them. They helped me understand the physical layout of the event, which was held across two large, interconnected warehouse spaces and a third, smaller outbuilding. They talked me through the myriad activities that would be held over the three-day programme (theatre and music performances, short film screenings, sculpture and photography exhibitions, and numerous hands-on activities such as jewellery and card making). They guided me through a number of creative methods to recruit participants. First, they invited me to help with the bump-in so that I could develop rapport with the volunteers and speak with them. Second, they suggested that during the event proper I also (a) approach people for a quick chat while they were engaged in various activities, and (b) set up a couch with a sign saying "InterACT with me" (a play on the title of the event) for people to self-select. They were also happy for me to do the more "standard" participant observation, and included mention of me and my research in their communications with participants as a means of informed consent. Rather than using the (completely inappropriate and uncreative) university project information sheet and consent form, they suggested I use an Easy Read format developed in Aotearoa New Zealand especially for those with learning disabilities – which they subsequently approved.

On the day of the event, however, things inevitably changed and once again I found myself having to use creative methods and think creatively to ensure my research remained ethical. I had my Easy Read forms printed off, but no one was interested in reading them. People simply came to join me on the couch, bringing whatever they had made to show me. Some came multiple times over the course of the three days. When I approached people at the different activity stands, they waved away the paperwork. I sat down with one of the organisers at the end of the first day for our more formal interview, and raised this with him but he was unconcerned at this deviation from the official ethics approval. As an ex-academic himself, his view was that university ethics was something to be ticked off and that in this case the reality of the situation meant that I should just be creative and go with the flow. Given his deep familiarity with both the event and the disabled community attending, I accepted his relaxed approach to throwing out the rule book.

Think points:

- Understand and articulate the sensitivities of the language, issue or community you are working with, and be explicit about any decisions you have had to make.
- Acknowledge the issues of power and agency, and how you addressed them in your research – for example, what creative methods did you use to recruit participants and gain informed consent? Were they effective, and how can other researchers learn from your experience?
- Think creatively about how to with the event organiser and/or the community to develop the methodology, and the ethics application, so that it is ethically appropriate and meets their needs.
- Within reason, be guided by the event organisers if things should change during the course of the event – be prepared to be creative while of course adhering to the principles of ethical research.

Conclusion

In this chapter I set out to demonstrate how creative methods can be used to address and overcome some of the unique ethical challenges posed by of critical event studies research. The autoethnographic case studies showcase how I have dealt with specific considerations in creative ways, sometimes during the data collection phase, in a manner that was ethical but not necessary strictly "by the book" and as approved by the ethics committee. I hope this chapter has (or will) help you, the reader, to think creatively about ethical issues that are beyond informed consent or what the ethics form may ask of you: what creative methods could you use to make research participation accessible and comfortable for the community, and ensure their voices are accurately and authentically represented in your findings? As my own journey has revealed, I believe the answer lies in throwing away the rule book and adopting creative methods to guide your ethical decision-making. This seems to be particularly important when researching with/for marginalised groups, where employing "traditional" methods may not be the most appropriate way of meeting their needs.

References

Alvesson, M. and Sköldberg, K. (2000) *Reflexive methodology: New vistas for qualitative research.* London and Thousand Oaks, CA: SAGE Publications.

Balon, R., Guerrero, A. P. S., Coverdale, J. H., Brenner, A. M., Louie, A. K., Beresin, E. V. and Weiss Roberts, L. (2019) 'Institutional Review Board approval as an educational tool', *Academic Psychiatry*, 43, pp. 285–289.

Beauchemin, E., Côté, L. P., Drolet, M-J. and Williams-Jones, B. (2022) 'Conceptualising ethical issues in the conduct of research: Results from a critical and systematic literature review', *Journal of Academic Ethics*, 20, pp. 335–358.

Biaett, V. (2019) 'An ethical conundrum: The estimation of event attendance', *International Journal of Tourism Cities*, 5(2), pp. 188–199. https://doi.org/10.1108/IJTC-12-2017-0080

Braun, V. and Clarke, V. (2006) 'Using thematic analysis in psychology', *Qualitative Research in Psychology*, 3(2), pp. 77–101.

Cheek, J. (2005) 'The practice and politics of funded qualitative research', in N. K. Denzin and Y. S. Lincoln (eds.) *The SAGE handbook of qualitative research*. Third edition. London and Thousand Oaks, CA: SAGE Publications, pp. 387–409.

Christians, C. G. (2005) 'Ethics and politics in qualitative research', in N. K. Denzin and Y. S. Lincoln (eds.) *The SAGE handbook of qualitative research*. Third edition. London and Thousand Oaks, CA: SAGE Publications, pp. 139–164.

Creswell, J. W. (2013) *Qualitative inquiry and research design: Choosing among five approaches*. London and Thousand Oaks, CA: SAGE Publications.

Dashper, K. (2016) 'Researching from the inside: Autoethnography and critical event studies', in I. R. Lamond and L. Platt (eds.) *Critical event studies: Approaches to research*. London: Palgrave Macmillan, pp. 213–229.

Drolet, M. J., Rose-Derouin, E., Leblanc, J. C., Ruest, M. and Williams-Jones, B. (2023) 'Ethical issues in research: Perceptions of researchers, research ethics board members and research ethics experts', *Journal of Academic Ethics*, 21, pp. 269–292 https://doi.org/10.1007/s10805-022-09455-3

Esfehani, M. and Walters, T. (2018) 'Lost in translation? Cross-language thematic analysis in tourism and hospitality research', *International Journal of Contemporary Hospitality Management*, 30(11), pp. 3158–3174.

Fitzpatrick, E. F. M., Martiniuk, A. L. C., D'Antoine, H., Oscar, J., Carter, M. and Elliott, E. J. (2016) 'Seeking consent for research with indigenous communities: A systematic review', *BMC Medical Ethics*, 17, Article 65. https://doi.org/10.1186/s12910-016-0139-8

Getz, D. and Page, S. (2020) *Event studies: Theory, research and policy for planned events*. Fourth edition. Abingdon: Routledge.

Hickey, A., Davis, S., Farmer, W., Dawidowicz, J., Moloney, C., Lamont-Mills, A., Carniel, J., Pillay, Y., Akenson, D., Brömdal, A., Gehrmann, R., Mills, D., Kolbe-Alexander, T., Machin, T., Reich, S., Southey, K., Crowley-Cyr, L., Watanabe, T., Davenport, J., Hirani, R., King, H., Perera, R., Williams, L., Timmins, K., Thompson, M., Eacersall, D. and Maxwell, J. (2022) 'Beyond criticism of ethics review boards: Strategies for engaging research communities and enhancing ethical review processes', *Journal of Academic Ethics*, 20, pp. 549–567.

Jaimangal-Jones, D. (2014) 'Utilising ethnography and participant observation in festival and event research', *International Journal of Event and Festival Management*, 5(1), pp. 39–55. https://doi.org/10.1108/IJEFM-09-2012-0030

Jennings, G. R. (2012) 'Qualitative research methods', in L. Dwyer, A. Gill and N. Seetaram (eds.) *Handbook of research methods in tourism: Quantitative and qualitative approaches*. Cheltenham, UK and Northampton, MA: Edward Elgar Publishing, pp. 309–323.

Jepson, A. and Clarke, A. (2016) 'Creating critical festival discourse through flexible mixed methodological research design', in I. R. Lamond and L. Platt (eds.) *Critical event studies: Approaches to research*. London: Palgrave Macmillan, pp. 59–83.

Juritzen, T. I., Grimen, H. and Heggen, K. (2011) 'Protecting vulnerable research participants: A Foucault-inspired analysis of ethics committees', *Nursing Ethics*, 18(5), pp. 640–650.

Kara, H. (2020) *Creative research methods: A practical guide*. Bristol: Bristol University Press.

Lacey, E. A. (1998) 'Social and medical research ethics: Is there a difference?' *Social Sciences in Health*, 4(4), pp. 211–217.

Lincoln, Y. S. (2005) 'Institutional Review Boards and methodological conservatism: The challenge to and from phenomenological paradigms', in N. K. Denzin and Y. S. Lincoln (eds.) *The SAGE handbook of qualitative research*. Third edition. London and Thousand Oaks, CA: SAGE Publications, pp. 165–181.

Lopez, G. I., Figueroa, M., Connor, S. E. and Maliski, S. L. (2008) 'Translation barriers in conducting qualitative research with Spanish speakers', *Qualitative Health Research*, 18(12), pp. 1729–1737.

Mullen, M. and Wills, R. (2016) 'Re-storying disability through the Arts: Providing a counterpoint to mainstream narratives', *New Zealand Journal of Research in Performing Arts and Education: Nga mahi a Rehia no Aotearoa*, 6, pp. 5–16.

Mumford, M. D., Waples, E. P., Antes, A. L., Brown, R. P., Connelly, S., Murphy, S. T. and Devenport, L. D. (2010) 'Creativity and ethics: The relationship of creative and ethical problem-solving', *Creativity Research Journal*, 22(1), pp. 74–89.

Office for Disability Issues (2020) *Disability etiquette*. Available at: https://www.odi.govt.nz/home/about-disability/disability-etiquette/ (Accessed 6 November 2023)

Orr, M. and Baeth, A. (2019) 'Creating safe space in a hostile place: Exploring the Marathon of Afghanistan through the lens of safe space', in T. Walters and A. S. Jepson (eds.) *Marginalisation and events*. Abingdon: Routledge, pp. 193–207.

Pavoni, A. and Citroni, S. (2016) 'An ethnographic approach to the taking place of the event', in I. R. Lamond and L. Platt (eds.) *Critical event studies: Approaches to research*. London: Palgrave Macmillan, pp. 231–251.

Sieber, J. E. (2004) 'Empirical research on research ethics', *Ethics and Behaviour*, 14(4), pp. 397–412.

StatsNZ. (2018) *2018 Census place summaries*. Available at: https://www.stats.govt.nz/tools/2018-census-place-summaries/ (Accessed 6 November 2023).

Temple, B. (2005) 'Nice and tidy: Translation and representation', *Sociological Research Online*, 10(2). Available at: www.socresonline.org.uk/10/2/temple.html (Accessed 6 November 2023)

Traianou, A. (2014) 'The centrality of ethics in qualitative research', in P. Leavy (ed.) *The Oxford handbook of qualitative research*. Cary: Oxford University Press, pp. 62–77.

van Nes, F., Abma, T., Jonsson, H. and Deeg, D. (2010) 'Language differences in qualitative research: is meaning lost in translation?', *European Journal of Ageing*, 7, pp. 313–316.

Walters, T. (2019) '"Proud to be South D": Perceptions of a street festival in a marginalised community in New Zealand,' in T. Walters and A. Jepson (eds.) *Marginalisation and events*. Abingdon: Routledge, pp. 36–43.

Walters, T. (2023) 'The InterACT Disability Arts Festival: Creating revolutionary futures?', *International Journal of Event and Festival Management*, 14(2), pp. 205–220.

Walters, T. and Venkatachalam, T. S. (2022) 'The difference Diwali makes: Understanding the contribution of a cultural event to subjective well-being for ethnic minority communities', *Event Management*, 26, pp. 141–155.

5

CREATIVELY NAVIGATING ETHICAL APPROVAL IN ETHNOGRAPHIC FESTIVAL RESEARCH

Briony Whitaker

University West of England, Bristol

Jenna Pandeli

University of West of England, Bristol

Introduction

This chapter discusses how the challenges of obtaining ethical approval from university ethics committees can be overcome by thinking creatively during the research planning and application process. Qualitative research projects are often considered more high risk and unpredictable (Øye et al., 2016), and therefore can face greater scrutiny from ethics committees due to concerns around the chosen methods or a lack of understanding of the research site (Øye et al., 2016). The focus of this chapter is how we can utilise the concept of habitus (Bourdieu, 1990) and ethnography as creative ways of justifying "high-risk" research when applying for ethical approval, specifically in the context of festival research.

Ethical approval applications often follow a generic structure, the design of which is often more accommodating to quantitative research (Bell & Wynn, 2023). This chapter explores creative thinking to justify qualitative research to ethics committees in sites that are fairly new to research – in this particular instance, music festivals. We call for a reimagining of the ethical approval process to properly reflect the diverse research within the social sciences as well as the unpredictability of qualitative research, namely ethnography.

This chapter focuses on research conducted by the first author that explores sustainability and festival attendees. The research looks to create a sustainability value segmentation framework to help festival organisers understand attendees' values specifically whilst inside the festival setting in order to design targeted interventions for behaviour change related to sustainability. This research required access to music festivals to collect data on-site, and to understand the

DOI: 10.4324/9781032686424-5

disconnect between assumed values and beliefs and what those values look like when actually inside a festival.

We will first justify the need for ethnographic research to contribute a qualitative perspective to the existing, largely quantitative, literature in the festival sector. We will then discuss the challenges associated with ethical approval and ethnographic and other qualitative research, exploring current debates in the field to present a picture of the current bureaucratic processes and explain how they are flawed. Using vignettes, the first author's experiences will then be presented to provide insight into her experiences of navigating the ethical approval process for festival ethnography; this will be broken into two parts to unpack the creative ways the author overcame barriers to her research. Firstly, we show how conceptualising the research as ethnography acted as an anchor in securing ethical approval, and secondly, we explore the first author's habitus and explain how an understanding of habitus is a crucial element of research and something that needs to be considered more formally as part of the ethical approval process. Finally, we call for changes in the ethical approval processes and propose recommendations for how researchers considering ethnographic research at festivals can creatively develop much-needed (ethically approved) qualitative research projects.

Ethnography and Festivals

Whether for entertainment, economic growth, and regeneration (Frost, 2015), social inclusion, or even political messaging (Laing & Mair, 2015), music festivals have become a growing area in academic research across multiple disciplines (Frost, 2015). However, there is an identified lack of qualitative research in the Events Management subject field, and ethnography in particular "remains an underused method" (Dashper, 2016, p. 217) despite "its appropriateness and value for researchers into the event experience" (Holloway, Brown & Shipway, 2010, p. 75). Quantitative methods, such as surveys and questionnaires, have been widely used to "measure" experiences and intentions to return to festivals (Holloway, Brown & Shipway, 2010) but leave literature with a gap to fill for a more in-depth qualitative exploration of the music festival sector.

The music festival environment is renowned for its impulsivity and ability to transport attendees (physically and metaphorically) away from the mundanity of daily life "through improvised action and kinetic excitement" (Frost, 2015, p. 572), and so it is important to understand the "phenomenon from the perspective of the participants" (Skilling & Stylianides, 2020, p. 543). Where quantitative research often relies on survey responses outside of the festival setting (Holloway, Brown & Shipway, 2010), ethnography gives the researcher access to immerse themselves into the festival and engage with attendees as an "observant participant" (Rossetti, 2024, p. 3) rather than as an external entity to the event. The methodological opportunities presented for ethnographic researchers inside the festival setting, for example, the opportunity for interviews and observations, provide "a wealth of rich data that can be triangulated" (Holloway, Brown & Shipway, 2010, p. 76). There is an importance in the interaction and understanding between the researcher and those being researched – ethnography facilitates this and means that the researcher can engage with attendees and ask questions about exhibited behaviours, motivations etc, but also allows the researcher to reflect upon their own experiences as a participant in the festival setting.

There are evidenced challenges with an ethnographic approach to festival research, one of which is access to the festival itself. The "gatekeepers" to the festivals may take issue with any unfavourable findings (Holloway, Brown & Shipway, 2010, p. 80) which could enforce a bias on any published data. "Gatekeeping" can also be in reference to ethics committees that are unfamiliar with festival environments as settings for research. There is also the difficulty that arises with the "sensory excess" (Frost, 2015, p. 573) that often underpins the design of the festival itself, which can lead to doubts that any account by a researcher will be fundamentally individual and will also be "found wanting" (Frost, 2015, p. 573). It is the job of the qualitative ethnographic researcher, therefore, to identify creative ways to address these challenges or acknowledge the potential limitations of the findings alongside making valuable and much-needed qualitative contributions to the field.

Despite a clear need for more qualitative research needed in the field, and strong justifications for its use, ethnography and highly qualitative research are typically met with challenges when applying for ethical approval. The following section will explore the process of ethical approval for ethnographic research and the common frustrations for researchers.

Ethics and Ethnography

This section aims to critique the ethical approval process for social science research in order to think creatively in reimagining how we might want this process to look in the future. To do this we will first introduce the complexities of the ethical approval process and discuss previous literature that focuses on ethics and ethnography.

Ethical guidelines are considered necessary as a way of regulating what the researcher can, cannot, or should not do in certain areas of research. In some healthcare and social welfare research areas, for example, "ethical approval" is absolutely essential as a way of safeguarding patient and client interests and privacy (see Coffey, 1999). But does this mean that all research needs to be, or should be, so tightly regulated? (Ferdinand et al., 2007).

According to Bell and Wynn (2023) ethics review processes can be conceptualised as an area of "violent simplification", they overly simplify something incredibly complex that cannot be easily addressed in a nice, neat form. Graeber

(2012, p. 109) argues that "paperwork… is designed to be maximally simple and self-contained", even when the content and the area of interest are complex, complicated, and evolving, thus, very often, there is no room for our ethics applications to discuss the real ethics of our methods and research projects, there is no room for this on the overly simplistic (yet often confusing!) ethics forms. For example, Opsal et al. (2016) found that review boards' current use of population "vulnerability" and topic "sensitivity" to assess project risk does not adequately determine the benefits, risks, or ethicality of research and instead researchers should be encouraged to attend to relationships in their projects. Whilst we do occasionally see attempts made by university ethics processes to update and adapt to the changing environment, the capacity of research ethics bureaucracies to accommodate plural methodologies and epistemologies remains the focus of much debate (Bell & Wynn, 2023).

Many researchers have become exhausted and frustrated by an administrative system that is considered to focus on form over substance (Bell & Wynn, 2023). Universities might assume that this aversion to the internal ethics processes would mean that researchers are "anti-ethics", desperate to be free of the university shackles and take high-level risks in their research – which seems absurd – why would we want to purposefully put ourselves and our participants at risk? Surely, what universities should instead take away from this aversion is that the ethics process, particularly for qualitative, social science research, is not fit for purpose. In fact, researchers want to make research ethics about "more than research applications" (Bell & Wynn, 2023, p. 538). In an academic world, "formalised" ethical approval at institutions seems to take precedence over the "everyday ethics" that ethnography demands (Russell & Barley, 2022, p. 3). But to what extent can a "one-off administrative task" (Russell & Barley, 2022, p. 3) truly comprehend the many complexities that come with data collection? It is certainly often the case that "codes of ethics practice lack sensitivity to particular methods…and thereby more-or-less inadvertently constrain the conduct of empirical research" (Tummons, 2022, p. 12) which perhaps results in the view that the ethical approval process is simply "an annoying list of things you are not allowed to do" (Bos, 2020, p. 31).

If we specifically consider ethnography, it is argued that university ethics committees have a tendency to be overly cautious and often struggle with the unknown and constantly developing nature of ethnography (Atkinson, 2009). Sluka (2018) identifies that anthropologists and ethnographers have had particular difficulty with ethics committees because the committees are often based on biomedical or laboratory models of research ethics which are not well suited for application to qualitative or fieldwork-based research approaches. Thus, it is not that ethnographic research does not get approved by ethics committees, but that ethnographers have to jump through many hoops to reduce the fear and anxiety that institutions attach to this method. Sluka (2018) is particularly critical of the underlying ethos or attitude of such boards which he finds to lack trust and confidence in researchers. He argues that ethics boards suggest that researchers cannot be fully trusted, and their work requires deep ethical and safety scrutiny and management oversight, including that they cannot be trusted to make their own informed, independent decisions regarding accepting and managing risk in their fieldwork.

Therefore, in order to smoothly progress through the ethics committee and achieve ethical approval on our research projects we need to tick all the right boxes, play the game and, at times, think creatively to overcome the hurdles of ethical approval in riskier research settings.

Ethnography as an Anchor in Obtaining Ethical Approval

Despite the fact that getting ethical approval for ethnography is notoriously stressful and difficult as outlined by the literature in the previous section, for the first author, it was in fact the concept of ethnography that saved her research. Trying to obtain ethical approval for a project with multiple qualitative methods within festival sites was proving to be tricky with a lot of push back and complications from the ethics department. However, when the project was framed under the concept of ethnography this made it much easier for the ethics committee to understand and helped to alleviate some of the issues as outlined in the following vignette:

When applying for ethical approval through my institution, I was told that there would be issues with conducting interviews and observations on site. There were concerns that participants who had been consuming alcohol and taking drugs would be unable to give consent. The proposed approach returned to me was to ask participants to be interviewed, give them 24 hours to consider their consent, and then return to find them in the same spot the next day to conduct the interview. Seriously!? Having been a festival attendee myself many times, I knew that it was very unlikely for me to find the same participants in the same spot after 24 hours, and that spending time searching for them would waste valuable time on-site. It would also mean that the first day of the festival would be essentially useless, as it would be spent simply collecting potential participants rather than collecting valuable data. The size and scale of festival sites can be enormous (Glastonbury Festival, for example, has been estimated to be the size of 500 football pitches), different acts play across multiple stages and people are constantly on the move. Ultimately, when time is so limited and with so much to explore, it would be more likely that participants would decline to be a part of the data collection due to it requiring a specified time and meeting spot in an environment which is so spontaneous and fluid, rather than them declining to consent due to ethical issues. To me this proposition seemed ridiculous and completely unrealistic and impractical.

This proposal was incredibly stressful to me, when I received this response from the ethics committee, I panicked that this might be the end of my PhD – with festival season fast approaching and with a research plan proposed by the ethics committee that was simply not feasible, I was beginning to lose hope in collecting qualitative data at festivals.

Rather than spiral, I arranged a meeting with my supervisors to problem solve and come up with a solution to this issue. I had only just returned from maternity leave and was a still finding my feet with returning to my research. But as luck would have it, I had recently brought on an additional supervisor onto my panel who had expertise in research methods and was also a member of the university ethics committee. When I explained the dilemma to my research panel she said plainly "Briony, you are doing ethnography, why aren't you calling it that?". Despite the fact that I was using multi- methods – observations, interviews, diaries etc. it hadn't yet occurred to me that this was ethnography! By drawing on this label, it allowed me to anchor my methodology, hold it all together and use this to explain my approach more clearly to the research ethics panel. This paid off as after a bit of editing, my ethics application was accepted! I found this so confusing, as my previous application was essentially asking to do the same thing! So why was this new application accepted just because I called it "ethnography"? I found it even more confusing after I started reading about all the difficulties that ethnography can often bring when applying for ethics. For my situation, ethnography was what had saved my application.

The creative thinking in this instance – in reframing research from separate interviews and observations to all being under the ethnography umbrella – ensured that the ethics committee felt the research had been justified. Whilst ethnography is a complex ethical methodology, it does allow the committee a clearer picture of what the research will be doing on-site. Using ethnography was a creative way to justify the research where it was not required for the ethics committee to have an understanding of the festival site.

However, what is important to note here is that without the author's experiences and intrinsic understanding of festival sites, she might not have known that the committees' solutions were unworkable, and the research would have taken a very different, poorer approach (or may not have happened). Thus, in the following section, we detail the significant role that the researcher plays in navigating the field sites and potentially minimising ethical concerns.

Habitus, Research Ethics, and Safety

Whilst we fully understand the need for formalised ethical reviews of research, and the importance of ethical conduct in research, the tick box exercise of most university ethics applications often misses fundamental fragments of what might actually make research high risk or potentially pose ethical dilemmas. We argue that the knowledge, experience, and skills of the researcher play an important role in mitigating risk in research and the role of the researcher is completely underestimated in the process. A first-time researcher with no knowledge or previous experience in the research setting is likely to be vulnerable to ethical issues arising on-site. In contrast, an experienced researcher, with knowledge and previous experience and familiarity with the research site is likely to be more prepared for ethical dilemmas if they arise. It is far more complex though than simply "experienced or unexperienced", there are multiple, sometimes conflicting factors at play that enhance or reduce the risk of research. We argue that these ethical issues are impacted by the habitus of the researcher:

> *The notion of habitus has several virtues. … agents have a history and are the product of an individual history and an education associated with a milieu, and … also a product of a collective history …*
>
> *(Bourdieu & Chartier, 2015, p. 52)*

Habitus is an internal archive of personal experiences rooted in the distinct aspects of individuals' social journeys. Individuals' dispositions are a reflection of their lived trajectories and justify their approaches to practice (Costa et al., 2019; Bourdieu, 1990). Thus, the researcher brings their lived experiences to the field which will impact their comfort level, knowledge, behaviours, and attitudes. Festival research as noted previously is fraught with ethical issues, particularly when we consider that they are sites for alcohol consumption and drug taking (Palamar & Sönmez, 2022). In this context, a seasoned festival goer who has lots of previous experience of the drugs, alcohol, music, and people at festivals will likely seamlessly blend in and be at ease in the setting; data collection can begin almost instantaneously without trying to "figure out" what's going on. We always bring our culturally inscribed "habitus" (Wacquant, 2016), our social interests and passions with us into the field, which shape our fieldwork interactions in advantageous or disadvantageous ways in regard of the informational yield of our studies (Schmid & Eisewicht, 2022, p. 18). According to Schmid and Eisewicht (2022) "when evenly matched with the field, the researcher's socialisation and symbolic body can become a beneficial resource for their fieldwork". And this is what we see here; the researcher having a great affinity to the field site, fitting in, and using this socialisation to her advantage.

Schmid and Eisewicht (2022, p. 17) go on to argue that:

> *For ethnography, the ethnographers themselves must be assessed for their fitness with the method and the field of research. This is the reason why ethnography is so socially discriminating in regard of the researcher, and this is also*

why ethnography must be taken personally. A long- term immersion in deviant or criminogenic settings may not be suited to an anxious personality. For the immersive study of elites in investment banking or the high fashion industry, a researcher with a lower working- class habitus is probably not your best choice.

Whilst some of the ideas presented here are debatable and potentially controversial, there is an interesting argument being made. And whilst we might contend that there is in fact merit and value in undertaking research outside of your comfort zone and being an "outsider", we agree that research is potentially safer and easier to navigate for those whose habitus "fits" with the research site. Ethnographic researchers are not required to pass as a native, but sociocultural affinities can help to generate feelings of sympathy and affection between the researcher and the researched via a kindred habitus or lifestyle, common interests, or shared life experiences (Schmid & Eisewicht, 2022; Schmid, 2021) allowing them to move seamlessly through the field. Thus, the researcher's habitus function is a key tool of the research.

In the following Vignette, we see how Briony's habitus facilitated data collection, and a smooth, relatively stress-free research experience.

I've been going to festivals since I was a teenager as an attendee in my teens, as an attendee and employee in my twenties and finally as a researcher in my thirties, so I've seen them from multiple perspectives. The first festival I went to as a teenager was Glastonbury, and the setting alone was overwhelming from the start- rain, mud, tents, large crowds, alcohol, drugs, and long drop toilets for a solid five days. It was absolutely massive. The scale of it - there are 170,000 attendees, so I already knew that the ethics committees proposals or waiting 24 hrs and then going to re-find the potential participants would immediately fail.

The first time I was ever offered drugs was at the first festival I attended. Someone approached me and my friends and asked us if we wanted any mushrooms. It wasn't a big deal, it was very friendly and none of us felt uncomfortable, we just started chatting, declined and explained that it wasn't our "cup of tea" and that was that. The more time I spent at festivals, the more I saw people using drugs and to be honest, I feel like it's become a "part of the scenery". It didn't particularly bother me in the first place, but it was something I did notice at first – but now I don't give it a second thought if I see someone doing them openly. Drugs at festivals are a fairly open secret.

So, when I was interviewing a group of men aged around 25–30 one year, and one of them came out of a tent with white powder around his nose, it wasn't anything that I found threatening or unusual and felt more than capable of handling the situation to ensure the research went smoothly, safely and without harm. Once all his friends and I noticed the white powder, we all had a bit of a laugh and I explained it was probably best to leave the research there, we chatted a bit and I thanked them for their time and moved on. They weren't embarrassed, we all laughed it off and it was fine.

Festivals are my happy place; the music, the people, the atmosphere, the freedom, I still cannot believe my luck that this is what I get to focus on for my work! I feel at home here, I feel at ease. However, I know colleagues who couldn't think of anything worse – sitting in fields and being surrounded by people high or drunk, I can imagine how uncomfortable they would be here.

Through Briony's lived experience she has built up a fundamental understanding of the festival environment, allowing her to be able to see potential ethical issues as they arise and have a good understanding of how to overcome them. In contrast, people without this experience may need a lot more help and support in navigating ethics through this environment. It is because of Briony's knowledge of festivals that she immediately knew the ethics committees proposal of giving participants 24 hours to think about consent and then finding them again was never going to work. This is just one example of how habitus is likely to have an impact on the safety and risk of research for both the researcher and participants. Therefore, we argue that we need to consider this more formally in the ethics process and think creatively in reconsidering what that process could look like.

Reimagining the Ethics Process

In this chapter we have presented an insight into the complexities of obtaining ethical approval to conduct qualitative social science research and the creative choices made by the researcher to overcome these hurdles. We present the concept of habitus to draw attention to the researcher's own lived experiences to highlight how this can impact how a researcher may be better equipped to tackle issues of ethics and safety in the field. Based on these discussions, here we propose a reimagining of the ethics process, presenting creative solutions to the current practices that, as we have suggested are not fit for purpose for qualitative, social science research.

It has been stated that researchers want to make research ethics about "more than research applications" (Bell & Wynn, 2023, p. 538) and as we have outlined, at present this is what is missing in the ethics application. We need universities to acknowledge the misalignment between ethics applications and real-world research ethics. Whilst the current set-up may serve to facilitate researchers' compliance with "auditable" regulatory requirements, and to reassure risk-averse universities that they can demonstrate rigorous oversight, it does nothing to skill researchers in assessing the ethical implications of their own research. Mastering the skills to address and mitigate the moral dilemmas that can emerge during a research project involves more than having a pre-determined set of options for research practice (Palmer and Forrester-Jones, 2018).

Ethical conduct is understood as an ongoing, critical and dialogical engagement with the moral and political questions of conducting research (Cannella & Lincoln, 2011). Ethics in research is processual (Harvey, 1990). It requires "self-regulation" (Hallowell et al., 2005), mediated through "self-reflexivity" (Alvesson & Deetz, 2000) about the possible effects or implications of the researcher's presence within, and representation of, the communities they research (Harvey, 1990) on the one hand, and the potential implications and consequences of reporting certain findings on the other. This does not mean that ethnographers ought to be allowed to do whatever they like, to make up research rules as they go along, but rather to assess the actual situation in which they conduct research (Wray-Bliss, 2005; Ferdinand et al., 2007). This is not reflected in the current university ethics processes. Thus, we propose several ideas that will put a thoughtful and nuanced understanding of ethics back into the research ethics processes.

The experiences of the first author presented above provide some insight into the confusing and ineffective nature of the ethics process. In the initial rejected application, the ethics committee recommended providing festival goers with participant information sheets and consent forms and then returning to them in 24 hours to check they were able to consent. As a result of the researcher's habitus, her experience and knowledge of festivals and festival goers, she knew that this was not a realistic research plan. Ethics committee's work to remove *all* risk from research rather than realising that we need to work with and manage the risk that is inherently there in all field settings. We need to prioritise equipping researchers with skills and knowledge to manage these risks. If we work to only remove all risks, we are severely limiting the settings we can research and the people we can research. For example, as already mentioned festivals settings are full of risk in terms of research ethics, ethics committees will most likely ask researchers not to interview intoxicated people, but if we are being completely honest, for many festivals this rules out a vast number of people from participating in research and our sample will therefore unlikely reflect the festival population. Instead, would it not be more sensible to ensure researchers are able to make informed and thoughtful decisions in the field about whether or not someone is able to participate in research? Rather than asking them to complete a form and then returning 24 hours later, wouldn't it be more sensible to have an open and honest conversation with participants about consent, ensure they have your contact details and all the information and allow them to consider withdrawal afterwards if they wish?

We must instead consider whether the researcher is "fit for the field" and has everything they need to navigate through their fieldwork to manage risk and ethics. This is where we see the importance of habitus. We do not argue that people have to have the "right" habitus to conduct research, but they need to reflect on their habitus and how it fits with the field and what this might mean for ethics. Similarly, this is something ethics committees could consider – a "one size fits all" form does not acknowledge the level of experience and knowledge researchers have in certain areas, whether that be experience of conducting research, experience of conducting high-risk research or experience with the participants or research setting. Thus understanding habitus plays a vital role in managing access, safety, and risk in research.

So, what do we propose? Firstly, we call for wide-scale formalised and personalised yearly training for research-active staff in higher education to equip them with skills and knowledge of research ethics. At present, research ethics training is not standard practice across PhD programmes, putting PhD students in a particularly vulnerable position, especially if they are not working with proactive and supportive supervisors. Understanding ethics is as essential to research as philosophy, literature and methodology and is also the area which has the potential to cause serious harm to the participants, researcher and university institution if not handled appropriately. Thus, we call for greater care and effort going towards training and development in research ethics which should allow for a much more "light touch" ethics application that should be less bureaucratic. Instead of submitting a 10-page form most of which is not even directly relevant to the research project, researchers could simply submit a research proposal and draw attention to some of the ethical challenges of the research and how they might be managed. With full training, researchers will be equipped with knowledge of university codes of practices, ethics conduct, and principles in order to ensure they conform to university policies and procedures in their research. But they will also be equipped with reflexive skills in considering issues that might arise and will be more well-rounded in their approach to consider their own role in the research, their identities and what this might mean for ethical conduct in the field.

We propose researcher ethics training include several key areas that might include but are not restricted to:

- University codes and principles of practice
- Confidentiality, anonymity, and consent
- Obtaining access
- Safety and mental wellbeing of the researcher
- Safety and mental wellbeing of the participants
- Navigating risks and problem solving in the field
- Recording data
- Storing data
- Vulnerability
- Relationships
- Reflexivity

Alongside ethics training and development, we also propose department ethics mentors who researchers can go to for informal conversations relating to ethical dilemmas and talking over solutions or plans. Mentors should be colleagues with experience in the field that they can draw on to advise others. We argue that these creative suggestions for reimagining the ethical approval process will move us towards putting a real ethics of care back into research and ensure that researchers are able to overcome ethical challenges in the field without completing violently simplified ethics applications.

Final Thoughts for Embarking on a Qualitative Journey in Festival Research

This chapter has hopefully highlighted how creative thinking can assist with the complexities of ethical approval as it did in this case. Although there are challenges in getting qualitative research approved, there is a strong case that more research is needed in the emerging field of music festivals, so we should not be deterred despite the additional explanations that may be required over quantitative research. The following tips have been developed by the authors and will hopefully assist those keen to undertake research in this area.

1 Utilise your Habitus: If you have been to festivals before, consider your personal experiences and identify where you can contribute to gaps in existing literature. Having an understanding of the research setting can help not only with ethical approval (or any potential suggestions provided by an ethics committee), but also the practicalities of planning data collection.
2 Allocate a familiarisation period: If you have not been to a festival before, consider a familiarisation period. As Barley and Bath (2014, p. 182) note "including such a preparation stage can enhance the quality of data that is collected at a later stage". Attending a convenient, local festival prior to ethical approval or data collection may be beneficial as it will give the researcher an insight into the festival setting and what will/won't work in terms of collecting data. Experiences gained through familiarisation can start to contribute to developing habitus. The cost of this could also potentially be included on funding applications, as there is academic justification for the benefits of familiarisation before ethnographic research.
3 Reflect on the benefits of both an insider and outsider perspective: There are some scenarios in which you may never be able to achieve a full insider perspective/habitus – for example, if you are a female researching male experiences at music festivals you will be able to draw upon your experiences as an attendee at a festival, but the aspect of gender will rely on other participants. But this should not diminish the passion for the research! There is a clear need for more qualitative/ethnographic research in the (literal) festival field and having both insider and outsider perspectives are important contributions. Think about how your "outsider" perspective and reflections can be used alongside data collection from other participants.

4 Think creatively in the ethical approval process to justify your choices: If you are struggling with qualitative ethical approval, think creatively about how you can reframe your justifications. Here, it was the application of "ethnography", but there may be another methodological approach that helps justify your qualitative research.

References

Alvesson, M. and Deetz, S. (2000) *Doing critical management research*, London: Sage.

Atkinson, Paul (2009) *Ethics and ethnography*, *Twenty-First Century Society*, 4:1, 17–30

Barley, R. and Bath, C. (2014) The importance of familiarisation when doing research with young children. *Ethnography and Education* 9(2), pp. 182–195.

Bell, K. and Wynn, L. L., (2023) Research ethics committees, ethnographers, and imaginations of risk. *Ethnography*, 24(4), pp. 537–558.

Bos, J., (2020) *Research ethics for students in the social sciences* (p. 287). Switzerland: Springer Nature.

Bourdieu, P 1990[1980], *The logic of practice*. Cambridge: Polity Press.

Bourdieu, P. and Chartier, R., (2015) *The sociologist and the historian*. Cambridge: Polity Press.

Cannella, G. S. and Lincoln, Y. S., (2011). Ethics, research regulations, and critical social science. *The Sage handbook of qualitative research*, 4, pp. 81–90.

Coffey, A. (1999) *The ethnographic self*. London: Sage.

Costa, C., Burke, C. &Murphy, M (2019) Capturing habitus: Theory, method and reflexivity, *International Journal of Research & Method in Education*, 42:1,19–32, https://doi.org/10.1080/1743727X.2017.1420771

Dashper, K. (2016) Researching from the inside: Autoethnography and critical event studies. In: Lamond, I. R. & Platt, L., (eds) *Critical event studies, approaches to research* (pp. 213–229). London: Palgrave Macmillan.

Ferdinand, J., Pearson, G., Rowe, M. and Worthington, F., (2007) A different kind of ethics. *Ethnography*, 8(4), pp. 519–543.

Frost, N. (2015) Anthropology and festivals: Festival ecologies. *Journal of Anthropology* [online]. 81(4), pp. 568–583.

Graeber D (2012) Dead zones of the imagination: On violence, bureaucracy, and interpretive labor. *Hau: Journal of Ethnographic Theory* 2(2): 105–112.

Hallowell, N., J. Lawton and S. Gregory (2005) *Reflections on research: The realities of doing research in the social sciences*. Milton Keynes: Open University Press.

Harvey, L. (1990) *Critical social research*. London: Unwin Hyman.

Holloway, I., Brown, L. and Shipway, R. (2010) Meaning not measurement using ethnography to bring a deeper understanding to the participant experience of festivals and events. *International Journal of Event and Festival Management* [online]. 1(1), pp. 74–85.

Laing, J. and Mair, J. (2015) Music festivals and social inclusion – the festival organizers' perspective. *Leisure Sciences* [online]. 37(3), pp. 252–268.

Opsal, T., Wolgemuth, J., Cross, J., Kaanta, T., Dickmann, E., Colomer, S. and Erdil-Moody, Z. (2016) "There are no known benefits…" Considering the risk/benefit ratio of qualitative research. *Qualitative Health Research*, 26(8), pp. 1137–1150.

Øye, C., Sørensen, N. Ø. and Glasdam, S. (2016) Qualitative research ethics on the spot: Not only on the desktop. *Nursing Ethics*, 23(4), pp. 455–464.

Palamar, J. J. and Sönmez, İ., (2022) A qualitative investigation exploring why dance festivals are risky environments for drug use and potential adverse outcomes. *Harm Reduction Journal*, 19(1), p. 12.

Palmer, N. and Forrester-Jones, R., (2018) Research Ethics Training: Using a virtue ethics approach to training to support development of researcher integrity. In N. Emmerich (ed) *Virtue ethics in the conduct and governance of social science research* (pp. 65–82). US: Emerald Publishing Limited.

Rossetti, G. (2024) Conceptualising participant observations in festival tourism. *Current Issues in Tourism* [online], 27(12), pp. 1884–1897.

Russell, L. and Barley, R., (2022) Is this ethical? Using this question as a starting point. In L. Russell, R. Barley & J. Tummons (eds.) *Ethics, ethnography and education* (pp. 1–10). UK: Emerald Publishing Limited.

Schmid, C. J., (2021) Ethnographic gameness: Theorizing extra-methodological fieldwork practices in a study of outlaw motorcycle clubs. *Journal of Contemporary Ethnography*, 50(1), pp. 33–56.

Schmid, C. J. and Eisewicht, P., (2022) Check yourself before you wreck yourself! Are you cut out for ethnographic fieldwork? In J. Pandeli, N. Sutherland, and H. Gaggioitt (eds.) *Organizational ethnography: An experiential and practical guide* (pp. 15–33). London: Routledge.

Skilling, K. and Stylianides, G. J. (2020) Using vignettes in educational research: A framework for vignette construction. *International Journal of Research & Method in Education* [online]. 45(5), pp. 541–556.

Sluka, Jeffrey Alan (2018) Too dangerous for fieldwork? The challenge of institutional risk management in primary research on conflict, violence, and 'terrorism'. *Contemporary Social Science*, 15(2) 241–257.

Tummons, J., (2022) The many worlds of ethics: Proposing a latourian investigation of the work of research ethics in ethnographies of education. In L. Russell, R. Barley, & J. Tummons (eds.) *Ethics, ethnography and education* (pp. 11–28). UK: Emerald Publishing Limited.

Wacquant, L. (2016) A concise genealogy and anatomy of habitus. *The Sociological Review*, 64(1), pp. 64–72. https://doi.org/10.1111/1467-954X.12356

Wray-Bliss, E. (2005) Abstract ethics, embodied ethics: The strange marriage of Marx and foucault and positivism in labour process theory. In H. Willmott and C. Grey (eds) *Critical management studies: A reader*, pp. 383–414. Oxford: Oxford University Press.

6

EMBRACE THE STRANGE

Creativity within Festival Research

Kyla Tully

*Queen Margaret University and University of Glasgow,
Edinburgh, Scotland*

Introduction

In 2019 Alchemy Film and Moving Image Festival, an experimental film festival in Scotland, adopted the tagline "Embrace the Strange" to its festival marketing and branding materials. A tongue-in-cheek acknowledgement of the avant-garde nature of the films and exhibitions as well as the influx of experimental film enthusiasts to the rurally situated festival, the incorporation of this motto resonated with attendees to such a degree that it became a permanent fixture of the festival. While the popularity of this branding approach is undeniably tied to the contexts of the Alchemy Film and Moving Image Festival in particular, it can also be extrapolated to the shared experiences of engagement with festivals in general. As noted by festival researchers, the intense and immersive nature of festivals is itself a strange phenomenon to experience, let alone document: festival research itself involves significant immersion in "physically demanding and high-stimulus environments" (Ruane, 2017, p. 10) wherein regardless of their role, researchers as well as festival workers are also participants in the festival (Najera-Ramirez, 1999; Duffy et al., 2011; Ruane, 2017).

In navigating the strangeness of festival research in terms of the intense and immersive nature of the festival experience, the incorporation of creative methods within fieldwork alongside or in place of conventional approaches may help to not only better reflect the experiences of the research but also better suit the needs and abilities of the research within the field. For instance, the inclusion of arts-based research methods such as drawing allows for the communication of multifaceted information about feelings and experiences (Broussine, 2011; Leavy, 2020), while the creative incorporation of established

DOI: 10.4324/9781032686424-6

visual documentation methods such as photography can help to encapsulate singular moments and elements of interest to the researcher (Pauwels and Mannay, 2020). However, while there is a growing amount of literature surrounding the application of creative methods in general (see Kara, 2020) as well as in specific fields such as organisational research (see Broussine, 2011; Ward and Shortt, 2020) and the arts (see Skains, 2018), there are few texts regarding creative research specifically within festivals and events research. Given this limited research guidance, the decision to make adjustments to traditional fieldwork within festival and events research to include creative methods requires a notable degree of creative thinking, methodological flexibility, and ultimately confidence on the part of the researcher. As such, using examples from my research fieldwork involving two productions of the Alchemy Film and Moving Image Festival, this chapter is structured to provide a reflection of my experiences integrating creative research practice within my ethnographic research. Through the outlining of the different stages of my research development and execution, I will contextualise my decision-making processes as my research plan expanded from a structured text-based project to an immersive experience incorporating visual data generation. Following a summary of foundational information about the overall project and my original plan for conducting fieldwork and data analysis, I detail the different ways my research methods and focus continually deviated from my initial plan to incorporate creative methods, the ethical and practical considerations I encountered, and the evolution of how I understand creativity to relate to festival research practice. The ultimate aim of relating my experiences of using creative methods in festival research is to demonstrate their role within such fieldwork and how sometimes it is necessary to embrace the strange – that is to say, give in to the immersive unknown of the creative process within the broader chaos of festival work.

Research Context

The examples I use to illustrate the development of creative practice within my festival fieldwork are from my doctoral research project, which took place as an Applied Research Collaborative Studentship with Edinburgh's Queen Margaret University and the University of Glasgow from September 2020 to March 2024. With an aim to generate an understanding of the demands, expectations, and processes of professionalisation within a rural arts organisation, I was provided with a research residency at Alchemy Film and Arts (Alchemy), an experimental film organisation situated in the town of Hawick in the Scottish Borders. Founded in 2010 as the Alchemy Film and Moving Image Festival, over the next decade the capacity of the festival steadily expanded, transitioning into a year-round organisation in 2014 with artist retreats and exhibition projects outside the festival's five-day timeframe and further expanding in 2018 to incorporate community engagement programming and artist residencies within Alchemy's ongoing programming. Since the departure of the festival founder and Creative Director in 2018, Alchemy has been managed by a dual-leadership team who have overseen the organisation through significant development as well as the coronavirus pandemic.

The initial aim of my research was to utilise participant observation to identify the management practices at Alchemy as they were designed and implemented during a period of organisational formalisation and expansion. A key aspect of my initial line of inquiry was the notation of practices and structures distinct to the organisation's rural contexts, which I planned to distil into a management framework that could be replicated within other similarly situated cultural organisations. However, after three months of virtual observation of strategic planning and programming meetings I decided that this goal did not align with the operational patterns I was observing within Alchemy; I felt the personalities and values of the individual staff members and their interpersonal relationships were enmeshed within the organisation's management structures and practices to a degree that crafting a replicable framework devoid of these individualised and influential aspects would be disingenuous. Therefore, I shifted both my research focus and overall methodological framework from a case study that looked to isolate replicable processes and structures (Suryani, 2008) to an ethnography that framed Alchemy as a unique cultural phenomenon (O'Reilly, 2012; Barbour, 2014). The aim of my research then became to generate an illustrative account of Alchemy as a collective of people as well as a place of work, which I hoped would provide a descriptive encapsulation of the unique contexts rural arts organisations operate within that could be useful for policy makers, funders, and other similarly situated cultural organisations.

My original timeline involved a year of preparation before beginning fieldwork in the autumn of 2021, a plan that was interrupted by the fluctuation of lockdown restrictions related to the COVID-19 pandemic. In response to the limitations of Scotland's 2020 lockdown, Alchemy had begun implementing several structural changes within the organisation, and with lockdown restrictions progressively easing since June 2020 (Scottish Parliament, 2022) the end of the pandemic appeared imminent. As such, after obtaining ethical approval for my study from the Queen Margaret University Research Ethics Panel, I began virtual fieldwork via video-calling platforms in November 2020; it seemed more efficient use of my fieldwork to document the changes as they were occurring rather than retroactively attempting to recall the context of the pandemic and its role in organisational decision-making. The shared assumption that the pandemic was drawing to a close was undeniably incorrect, evidenced by the introduction of a second lockdown in Scotland in January 2021 (Scottish Parliament, 2022). In response to the fluctuating lockdown restrictions over the next two years, my fieldwork took place within a wide variety of virtual and in-person contexts until I ended my official field visits in August 2022.

While my fieldwork consisted of over 530 hours of participant observation spanning 22 months, my anecdotal points of reference for this chapter stem from two bouts of fieldwork during the Alchemy Film and Moving Image Festival in 2021 and 2022: the first over a five-day period wherein I conducted 72 hours of in-person participant observation, and the second over a ten-day period wherein I conducted 112 hours of in-person participant observation. I clarify these time-scales not to encourage such intensive research practices, but to provide context for the environment within which my field observations took place, as the creative methods I used for documentation and sense-making were curated in real-time in response to the continual environmental, mental, and emotional fluctuations of the research field, research participants, and myself as the researcher.

The Initial Approach

Building on my interpretivist understanding of both reality and knowledge as socially crafted through the mediation of personal interpretations (Barbour, 2014), my initial research proposal looked to combine participant observation, interviews, discourse analysis, and practice-based research within a case study framework. I planned to alternate between periods of data collection and data analysis, two separate processes that I would supplement with an intensive period of practice-based research to generate an embodied understanding (Candy, 2006) of what it was like to work within the Alchemy Film and Moving Image Festival. My approach shifted within the first five months to focus on participant observation, interviews, and thematic analysis, or the identification of themes and patterns of collected data (Coffey, 2018), within an ethnographic framework. The adaptation to my research approach was in response to both my previously described observations of the organisation and the realities of conducting fieldwork: the inclusion of discourse analysis meant I was examining the role of language within the organisation, which necessitated intensive tran-scriptions of verbal interactions (Barbour, 2014). However, I soon realised I found the social and physical contexts surrounding the observed conversa-tions to be of equal or greater interest than the conversations themselves, which divided my attention within the observational process. The subsequent refram-ing of my research as a cultural study provided space to follow these interests and establish methods of documenting my observations that came to me natu-rally, as opposed to forcing a framework that I was not invested in. I was able to develop and put a new plan to action with my first round of in-person fieldwork in April 2021, observing the Alchemy Film and Moving Image Festival as it was streamed online by a small team in the Alchemy office. I had a clear vision for what my fieldwork would entail: spending my days in the office taking observa-tional notes and documentational photos, then returning to my accommoda-tion in the evenings to transcribe my fieldnotes and thematically categorise my observations in a spreadsheet that I would later revisit during my analysis stage.

The Virtual Festival: Creative Deviations and Complications

I arrived at the Alchemy office the day before the launch of their eleventh film festival, the second virtual festival the organisation was conducting since the first pandemic lockdown in 2020. After officially meeting the staff in-person, getting a tour of the building, and reviewing the schedules for the festival, I joined the team of four for dinner at a nearby restaurant before returning to my accommodation to prepare for the week. Following my return to the Alchemy office the next morning, I realised that following the previous night's meal the staff had returned to the office to continue work for another four hours, which was notable from a series of inside jokes that this timeframe seemed to have generated. Panicked by having potentially missed foundational data so soon within my in-person research, I abandoned my structured field-work plan and decided that I would stay in the office as long as any member of the team was still present. This decision was the beginning of a series of deviations from my planned approach.

Illustrations of a Virtual Festival

The first deviation from my initial fieldwork plans involved the incorporation of drawing as a creative substitute for documentational photography. For the duration of the festival, the majority of the work involved the four members of staff situated at adjacent workspaces within the Alchemy office, with two members running the livestream at one table and two others engaging with event moderation and coordination tasks from their computers at a second table where I usually sat. Within my first hours of in-person fieldwork during the 2021 virtual film festival, I realised that although my research participants had become accustomed to my observational presence in virtual meetings, the dynamics of our relationship were drastically altered by my physical presence in the room. Without the restrictive framing of a video-call screen limiting the visibility of my note-taking and visual focus, my observational role seemed more explicit and unnerving, in particular due to the participants' new ability to see the direction of my focus when I was documenting their movements and interactions. I found the awareness of my presence in the room was most explicitly demonstrated when I attempted to take a photo of the team gathering for the first morning meeting of the festival, my raised phone causing everyone to freeze until it was lowered. Aware of the discomfort I was causing, rather than taking photos I began sketching the participants and the objects they interacted with (see Figure 6.1). As my sketching was being done alongside my fieldnotes, it provided a bit of anonymity to both my focus and documentation practice because participants were not entirely sure if I was taking notes or drawing, and the subject of my interest was much less apparent in comparison to when I pointed a camera lens at a person, object, or area.

FIGURE 6.1   *View from Director's Desk* (2021), Kyla Tully. Alchemy Film and Arts, Hawick, Scotland. Credit: Author.

While my initial incentive to using drawing as a method of documentation was an attempt to relieve my perceived discomfort of the participants, I encountered several benefits to this approach that kept me returning to it. One such benefit to my incorporation of drawing within my field documentation was the ability to illustrate movement and non-verbal communication within the space. Although there were intensive bursts of conversation and interaction to take notes on throughout the duration of the festival, there were also significant periods of silence during the programme streaming while the staff concentrated on their individual tasks. Drawing became a useful way to document these quieter moments, as I could focus on non-verbal communication between the staff and the physicality of their desk-bound work such as hand gestures and shifting in their chairs (see Figure 6.2). An additional benefit to drawing as a form of field documentation was that it facilitated my engagement with my observational research itself not only during quieter moments of the workday but also as exhaustion set in. Being able to continue documentation in spite of physical and mental exhaustion became crucial over the duration of the festival: with the festival workdays averaging out to 14–16 hours a day, by the third day of the festival the staff members had begun to struggle to string together coherent sentences. Having decided to remain in the field as long as any member of staff was present, this meant that I was at a similar level of fatigue as the festival team. While the coping mechanisms of the staff to stay

FIGURE 6.2 *Shifting, 6PM-7PM* (2021), Kyla Tully. Alchemy Film and Arts, Hawick, Scotland. Credit: Author.

awake and maintain high spirits made for entertaining interactions to document, in particular the increased quantity of inside jokes between staff members, due to exhaustion I struggled to remember names and basic spelling while taking fieldnotes. The reality of this level of fatigue during my fieldwork, commonplace within festival participation (Ruane, 2017), drastically increased the usefulness of drawing as a creative approach to documenting my observations.

The In-Person Festival: Continuing Adjustments to Practice

With the majority of COVID-19 restrictions lifted by mid-April in 2022 (Scottish Parliament, 2022), the twelfth edition of the Alchemy Film and Moving Image Festival was able to occur live and in-person in the spring of 2022. As part of my fieldwork approach, I took a more active role within the production of the festival, working alongside festival staff and volunteers with installing, invigilating, and taking down exhibitions, checking cinema tickets, covering volunteer shifts, delivering lunches, and attending staff meetings. Given that my work schedule with the festival was structured to include tasks that facilitated note-taking, such as more observational roles like invigilation, and included a significant number of breaks throughout the workday, I anticipated that I would be able to carry out my inclusion of drawing within data collection alongside regular fieldnotes much like I had during my first experience of festival fieldwork the year prior. Similar to my previous festival fieldwork, my plans based on this assumption quickly required a shift in plans.

Still-Life Photography

The second deviation from my initial fieldwork plans involved an emphasis on creative photography in place of both documentational photography and drawing. I had previously incorporated photography as a method of data collection with the start of in-person fieldwork in April 2021, but in response to the festival staff's awareness of the camera I limited its use to documenting the field environment with minimal focus on the people themselves within it. Although generally considered a less-intrusive form of field documentation (Barbour, 2014), I found that taking photographs was much more intrusive than my drawing practice. In response to the perceived nervousness of the festival staff around being photographed, as described previously, when I did engage with documentational photography within my fieldwork I focused on photographing items within the office as opposed to people. During my 2021 festival fieldwork, a coffee table within the office's designated "break space" caught my attention in particular: bright red and encircled with armchairs, the table was a frequent informal gathering space for meals and non-work-related conversations during break periods with the festival broadcast. As the festival continued, I grew increasingly interested in the flow of items gathering on and being cleared from the coffee table as a reflection of the wider activities within the work of the festival's production (see Figure 6.3). Due to the pace of the festival, over the course of the day the table would become a gathering place for objects that the staff came in contact with but did not have time to clear away. As such, photographing the table became a way to document characteristics of the nature of the festival production, also framed as the visual culture of the festival workspace (Pink, 2007) in a quick manner without disrupting the flow of work or taking photos of the staff themselves.

As a result, the coffee table became my primary photography focus for the duration of in-person fieldwork from April 2021 to August 2022. However, during the twelfth Alchemy film festival, the first one in-person since the 2020 lockdown, this approach shifted to become my main method of documentation and data generation. As I had opted to take on a more participatory role as part of my festival observations, I found that I was often moving from site

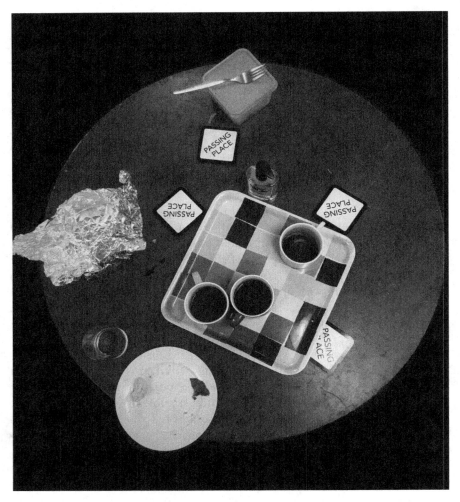

FIGURE 6.3 *Remnants of a Coffee Break* (2021), Kyla Tully. Alchemy Film and Arts, Hawick, Scotland. Credit: Author.

to site far too often to allow for carrying around my materials for my usual note taking and sketching. In addition to this, even in moments where I was in a position to engage in drawing documentation, very few of the festival staff and volunteers were in one place long enough for me to draw and there was such a high volume of visitors to the festival it was difficult to not be engaged with verbally as a recognised festival worker. Throughout all of the commotion and movement, the Alchemy office remained a gathering point for staff who wanted to take a second away from the crowds and as such, the coffee table became a key focus for the duration of the festival as a demonstration of the intensification of the workers' experience and reflection of the tangible aspects of importance within the production of the festival itself (see Figure 6.4).

Given the rapid pace of the festival, I found that focusing my documentation to the coffee table also established a timelapse of sorts that was a point of reflective analysis as well as field documentation. In taking 47 photos over the course of the five days of the festival, I was able to situate them in chronological order to see the development of the festival's pace and intensity over the course of a day as well as the week, as reflected in the pile up and clearance of dishes, the box of baked goods that would diminish over the course of a day, the forgotten programmes, ID tags, rolls of tape, and other necessities that would accumulate and be recovered (see Figure 6.5). The described intuitive sense-making through the identification of patterns of behaviour, as delineated through this particular

FIGURE 6.4 *First Festival Morning* (2022), Kyla Tully. Alchemy Film and Arts, Hawick, Scotland. Credit: Author.

FIGURE 6.5 *Second Festival Afternoon* (2022), Kyla Tully. Alchemy Film and Arts, Hawick, Scotland. Credit: Author.

example of adaptive data gathering, highlights my role within this ethnographic process as "the research instrument" (Barbour, 2014, p. 107), wherein my decision-making within the data collection and generation processes integrated into a reflexive cycle of interest and discovery. While so far this aspect of my position in the research has been explored in relation to the data collection process, its relevance within the analysis of the generated data is a key aspect of the ethnographic approach. As such, the following section will expand on the sense-making process of thematic analysis as it was incorporated into the project.

Between Two Festivals: Developing an Analytical Framework

Thematic Analysis

Throughout the duration of my fieldwork, I saw my use of drawing and photography solely as methods of data collection that I would process alongside my fieldnotes utilising thematic analysis, an approach I felt encapsulated the intuitive nature of analysis within ethnographic research (Coffey, 2018). Reading about thematic analysis was the first time I saw data analysis framed as "an art, not a science" (Braun and Clarke, 2021, p. 9), providing a theoretical justification for the development of my own strategy for categorising data (Coffey, 2018). Although I had formally incorporated this guiding framework before investing in creative methods of data collection, its applicability to both visual and text-based forms of data was compatible with my incorporation of images within and alongside my fieldnotes.

The initial development of my thematic coding process unintentionally occurred while I transcribed my fieldnotes following my first round of festival fieldwork in 2021. Due to the sheer quantity of text-based and visual data that I had generated within this period of fieldwork, I had decided to save my drawings, photos, and typed fieldnotes in separate documents and folders. In the process of dividing these different forms of documentation, I noticed that each creative product could be curated into thematic collections related to their content and context: drawings, maps, and photographs could be categorised by practicalities such as the time of day, or more abstractly by the nature of the composition, such as a time-lapse or a still life, or the context of activity such as a morning meeting or working at computer. While I had initially begun assembling these collections for purely administrative reasons, the process of establishing how best to store the different outputs so they could be easily retrieved served as an initial coding process.

While the metaphor of curation is a conveniently tidy way of encapsulating one aspect of the coding processes of visual data generation and analysis, the contribution of such methods to my overall sense-making and analytical practices is more difficult to verbalise. The analytical vagueness behind more intuitive, visual processes is framed as a common drawback to visual and creative practices precisely because it is difficult to elaborate on the analysis processes in a detailed manner due to the highly personalised and abstract nature of the data (Pink, 2007; Skains, 2018; Mannay et al., 2019). Furthermore, as will be discussed in the following section, the analytical process in my own experience did not occur as a separate and distinct stage within my research, but rather as an embedded factor within my fieldwork.

Clarifications, Caveats, and Considerations

The Entanglement of Collection and Analysis

As previously noted, I have presented my approach to data analysis as a process separate from and subsequent to data collection, with drawing and photography categorised as forms of documentation to be revised within a thematic analytical framework. Yet, these methods, as I utilised them, were deeply enmeshed within both fieldwork and analysis processes. Although I initially understood them to be distinct stages and entered my fieldwork with this expectation, as I began to explain my incorporation of creative methods to my supervisors, research participants, and evaluators following my first round of festival fieldwork, I found it difficult to maintain the categories of "fieldwork" and "analysis" as separate and distinct. I struggled in particular with how to discuss a theme I had noticed while reviewing my collection of photographs and sketches outside the field without detailing the observations that had informed not only what I had chosen to document but how.

In outlining the trajectory of my personal realisation of the complex relationship between processes of data collection and analysis, it is important to clarify that the delay to my understanding of this entanglement does not represent a lack of literature-based guidance or theoretical framing: the texts that guided my research design repeatedly comment on the enmeshed nature of these stages within ethnographic fieldwork. For example, while James Spradley points to an overlap of data gathering and analysis due to a required "constant analysis of utterances" (1979, p. 53) within fieldwork, Karen O'Reilly includes the writing-up stage within the research cycle as "inextricably linked" (2012, p. 186) with both data collection and analysis. However, when I first read these texts early in my research development, I could not see how such concepts applied to my work, as I was attempting to justify the inclusion of both textual and visual creative data and these reassurances centred text-based outputs. As my fieldwork continued over the year between the two festivals and I looked to texts regarding visual data generation and collection (see: Pink, 2007; Leavy, 2020; Ward and Shortt, 2020), I began to recognise not only how applicable this guidance had been all along, but just how interconnected the different stages of my research were.

I have come to understand that the forms of creative practice that I utilised to document my direct observations within my festival fieldwork were embedded with an analytical process that Rachel Gannon and Mirelle Fauchon refer to as "ad-hoc decision-making" (2021, p. 67) related to the composition of my drawings as well as my photographs. Such decision-making is instinctive yet curatorial, a process that is difficult to explain afterwards but feels natural in the moment. While the curatorial aspect is notable within the photographs, this embedded analysis is more explicitly demonstrated within my drawings, my points of interest within the compositions a result of in-the-moment determinations of what to include or exclude. For example, during the streaming of the 2021 virtual film festival I decided to document two of the festival workers who were monitoring the streaming pages (Figure 6.6). A series of choices were made between the initial decision and the final product, such as the different levels of detailing of the two faces and the exclusion of the nearby desks and equipment in relation to the depicted bodies in the space: choices that required a rapid determination of what was important to convey.

FIGURE 6.6 *Difference in Temperatures* (2021), Kyla Tully. Alchemy Film and Arts, Hawick, Scotland. Credit: Author.

The enmeshed relationship between data collection and analysis within my approach to fieldwork is further complicated by the inclusion of thematic analysis and the resulting curated collections, as this frames the creative outputs from my fieldwork both as products of analysis and products to analyse. However, the additional layer of review and revision of these creative outputs was crucial for making connections between themes and observations by forcing me to look at my accumulated data differently. Although the generation of the drawings and photographs were hugely analytical in practice, they required my complete immersion within the field and meant that I was intensely focused on details within my fieldwork. The process of compiling and pairing select photographs and drawings pulled me out of these specificities and allowed me to identify the broader patterns that had not only informed my decision-making within generating my drawings, photographs, and fieldnotes, but were newly present within my selective curations. One of the key observations made from this process was the incorporation of care practices within the organisation's identity and professional practice: such practices were present to varying degrees within the generated photographs and illustrations, such as the bags of sweets sat between computer monitors for the staff to share, the collection of coffee mugs the management team washed every morning, and the plant on the coffee table gifted to a member of staff by a community partner. I had documented these aspects instinctively because in the moment they caught my interest, but it was not until looking at them as a broad collective that I noticed how they all related to a practice of care embedded within the organisation as both a natural occurrence and implicit expectation.

Navigating Creative Approaches in Academic Systems

In discussing the development and application of creative practice within my research I feel it is important to acknowledge the difficult or adversarial aspects of my research process and experience that resulted from external expectations and my own inexperience. While these were not the only challenges I encountered during my research, I emphasise the following points because of their direct link to my inclusion of creative practice and their prevalence within much of my research timeframe. I am confident that if the practices within my presented approach were not intrinsic to how I process information, and if I did not have the enthusiastic support from a selection of supervisors, examiners, and peers, I could not have maintained the inclusion of creative practice within my research.

Many of the challenges I encountered during my research resulted from a lack of prominence of creative methods within academic practice and research: although the utilisation of such methods can generate or illustrate data in a manner more approachable to non-academic audiences (Kara, 2015), I found them to be difficult for academic systems and settings to support or even tolerate. Over the course of my research project, I navigated an absence of academic support for my approach that ranged from explicit discouragement regarding creative practice from institutional leaders to a general lack of guidance on methodology and dissemination. While I received encouragement from practice-based researchers and sociologists at Queen Margaret University, the formal support systems within both my universities such as researcher forums, skills workshops, and thesis writing guidelines were not prepared to assist with creative methods of research. My difficulty in securing academic support for my use of creative methods was further compounded by the particular and exacting nature of key-wording within academic search engines. As such, it took me months to discover the phrasing that linked me to not only a wider network of researchers invested in creative research practices but also the texts that became foundational to my work, namely visual ethnography (Pink, 2007) and illustration research (Gannon and Fauchon, 2021). The time it took to secure these theoretical justifications additionally unnerved my research participants, who were enthused about my creative outputs during my initial fieldwork sessions but soon began to express concern that my research approach would not be seen as valid or "real" research either within or outside academia. I now have the research experience to challenge perceptions of validity and to convey my aims, justifications, and learning, but as a new student engaging with both doctoral research and creative research practice for the first time, this was a significantly isolating experience.

Festivals, Fieldwork, and Care for Self

In her article on the experiences of immersive fieldwork within festival research, Deidre Ruane (2017) notes that festival participants undergo an intensive emotional drop following multiple days of the routine-breaking, highly social and heightened sensory input of festival activities, emphasising that this pattern does not exclude the workers or the researchers within the festival. When planning and beginning my festival fieldwork, my inexperience with festival research meant I failed to take into consideration the likelihood that I would not be immune to the exhaustion of festival participation. My inexperience with conducting research additionally contributed to my negligence in considering my own needs and well-being during my fieldwork experience in general, exemplified by the intensive manner within which I conducted the fieldwork that forms the basis of this chapter. While I made the choice to disregard opportunities for breaks from being actively within the field out of fear of missing valuable data, I did not consider the mental, physical, and emotional toll of being an active observer can be, not to mention over the exhaustive timeframes of festivals. This consideration is not unique to creative practice within fieldwork, as noted by Olga Najera-Ramirez's (1999) observation that "[i]f fieldwork is demanding, conducting fieldwork in a festival setting is especially so" (p. 183), but my utilisation of drawing to both navigate data collection while exhausted and to circumvent my own lack of self-preservation was particular to my fieldwork approach. My lack of self-preservation resulted from my own inexperience with field research outside the incorporation of creative practice, which I attempted to justify through the sheer quantity of fieldwork hours. Although a significant aspect of my need to validate this approach stemmed from a lack of tolerance within academic settings for non-traditional formats of data collection, analysis, and dissemination, I equally failed to prioritise my own needs over the research process.

Conclusions

In framing my approach to festival fieldwork as an expansive process building from participant observation to incorporate creative practice and ultimately integrate thematic analysis, I have offered an illustration of how a formulaic approach to fieldwork can utilise creativity to adapt to the everchanging demands of festival research. While this summary considerably oversimplifies my experience of field research, it highlights the range of opportunities that arise when integrating creative practice into festival research, allowing for the actions of documenting, generating, and analysing data to be tailored to fit a researcher's unique creative skills. In my own research outside the presented examples, my creative approach continually evolved to include additional elements such as crafting maps depicting people's movements within the office, illustrating visual and conversational focus during staff meetings, and creating poetic transcripts of conversations between workers. These continued adaptations to my approach were incorporated in response to the intersection of the demands of my fieldwork with my creative and academic strengths and interests.

Conducting fieldwork within a festival setting means navigating an inherently complex and immersive environment. It is therefore difficult to establish a rigid, all-encompassing framework with regards to data-gathering methods for festival research, as by nature festivals are ever-changing dynamic events wherein standardised approaches can be difficult to maintain. Festival researchers therefore need to maintain a level of flexibility within their fieldwork approach and adapt their methods to the unique rhythms of festival schedules and life cycles. In short, the incorporation of creativity in terms of observational and documentational approaches to festival fieldwork allows researchers to embrace the strange patterns of the festival experience as both a researcher and a participant.

References

Barbour, R. (2014). *Introducing qualitative research: A student's guide* (2nd edn), London: SAGE Publications Ltd.

Braun, V. and Clarke, V. (2021) Conceptual and design thinking for thematic analysis, *Qualitative Psychology*, 9(1), 3–26. https://doi.org/10.1037/qup0000196

Broussine, M. (2011). *Creative methods in organizational research*. London: SAGE Publications Ltd.

Candy, L. (2006) *Practice based research: A guide*. Creativity & Cognition Studios Report. Sydney: University of Technology.

Coffey, A. (2018) *Doing ethnography* (2nd edn), London: SAGE Publications Ltd.

Duffy, M., Waitt, G., Gorman-Murray, A., and Gibson, C. (2011) Bodily rhythms: Corporeal capacities to engage with festival spaces. *Emotion, Space and Society*, 4(1), 17–24. https://doi.org/10.1016/j.emospa.2010.03.004

Gannon, R. and Fauchon, M. (2021) *Illustration research methods*, London: Bloomsbury Publishing.

Kara, H. (2015) *Creative research methods in the social sciences*. Bristol: Policy Press.

Kara, H. (2020) *Creative research: A practical guide*. Bristol: Policy Press.

Leavy, P. (2020) *Method meets art: Arts-based research practice* (3rd edn). New York: Guildford Press.

Mannay, D., Fink, J., and Lomax, H. (2019). Visual ethnography. In: Paul Atkinson, ed., *SAGE research methods foundations*. London: SAGE Publications, Ltd. https://doi.org/10.4135/9781526421036775961

Najera-Ramirez, O. (1999). Of fieldwork, folklore, and festival: Personal encounters. *Journal of American Folklore*, 112(444), 183–199. https://doi.org/10.2307/541948

O'Reilly, K. (2012) *Ethnographic methods* (2nd edn), Oxon: Routledge.

Pauwels L. and Mannay, D. (2020. *The Sage handbook of visual research methods*. London: SAGE Publications, Ltd.

Pink, S. (2007) *Doing visual ethnography* (2nd edn). London: SAGE Publications, Ltd.

Ruane, D. (2017). 'Wearing down of the self': Embodiment, writing and disruptions of identity in transformational festival fieldwork. *Methodological Innovations*, 10(1), 1–11. https://doi.org/10.1177/2059799117720611

Scottish Parliament (2022) Timeline of Coronavirus (COVID-19) in Scotland. *Scottish Parliament Information Centre* [online]. Available at: www.spice-spotlight.scot/2022/05/27/timeline-of-coronavirus-covid-19-in-scotland [Accessed 2 June 2022].

Skains, R. L. (2018). Creative practice as research: A discourse of methodology. *Journal of Media Practice*, 19(1), 82–97. https://doi.org/10.1080/14682753.2017.1362175

Spradley, J. (1979) *The ethnographic interview*. New York: Holt, Rinehart, and Winston.

Suryani, A. (2008) Comparing case study and ethnography as qualitative research approaches. *Jurnal Ilmu Komunikasi*, 5(1), 117–127. https://doi.org/10.24002/jik.v5i1.221

Ward, J. and Shortt, H. (eds.) (2020) *Using arts-based methods of research: A critical introduction to the development of arts-based research methods*. Cham: Springer International Publishing.

7

EXPLORING POSTCARDS AS AN ACCESSIBLE CREATIVE METHOD

Lauren Bouvier

Queen Margaret University, Edinburgh, Scotland

Introduction

Postcards, thematically, in research is not a new or grandiose idea. Researchers' interest has previously focused mainly on the representational visuals blanketing the cardstock. Though previous research remains fascinated by postcards' imagery, their power as a vehicle for data collection requires further development. The postcard is a potentially emotive tool to be used in research, providing a tangible element in an era of digital communication. Postcards bridge generational and cultural boundaries, presenting them as a creative method encompassed in the collective knowledge of how to make use of the common object.

Postcards are defined as an "affordable cultural commodity to be bought, exchanged and collected" (Brownson, 2023, p. 318). One's schematic image of a postcard includes a double-sided cardstock. One side is covered with a picture and the other side is split between a message space and the other half for the mailing address and stamp. A defining feature of the postcard is it does not require an envelope to mail, and also it is an item to collect. Using postcards as a technique for data collection is yet to be further explored. Gugganig and Schor (2020) highlight the limited practice of working with postcards for data collection. They argue that feminist research and linguistic methodologies include limited adoption of them. Indeed, Andriotis and Mavrič (2013) iterate that most of the research is limited to imagery and text with a call to go beyond and explore the multifaceted properties of postcards.

This chapter presents an overview of the postcard's history and navigates how its place in research shifts. A brief review of the current use of postcards in research will then be provided to articulate the brevity of its use. Themes of

DOI: 10.4324/9781032686424-7

nostalgia and storytelling are threaded throughout the following discussion mimicking the object's ability to narrate our personal history (Papadaki, 2006). Then, details will be provided of the process of using postcards as a tool for creative methods and interactions with cultural festival participants. Lastly, a discussion of considerations will be proposed for those contemplating using postcards as a creative research method.

Historical Context of Postcards

In 1870, the British Postcard was invented as a quick and cheap form of communication. These postcards were influenced by the Austria-Hungary design, believed to be the first known postcard in 1869 (Gugganig and Schor, 2020; Tattoni et al., 2021; Postcards, 2022). The use of postcards soared quickly in British society. In 1871, there were approximately 75 million sent across Britain (Postcards, 2022). As the concept grew in popularity, its use escalated immensely during the First World War. As other means of communication grew, such as the telephone, the postcard's role transitioned to a collector's item to commemorate experiences, primarily travelling.

The original designs of British postcards were regulated by the British Empire. Slight changes were made over time to include the capacity for international postage. The original design included the same image and layout. In 1894, the ability to privately publish postcards began to be recognised by the Post Office (Spennemann, 2021). This meant contemporary designs with images could exist. The practice of mailing postcards grew exponentially into the 20th century with over 2.3 million sent in 1904 (Spennemann, 2021). A new language grew out of the customisation of design from the picture, message, and selection of the stamp. The application of elements such as stamps created a new "secret" language using symbolism and placement of such elements to create private messages (Postcards, 2022).

The use of postcards shifted during the First World War. The ease of use allowed for "quick" communication between soldiers and their loved ones. Programmes such as Field Service Cards provided free postage to the soldiers. With the increased use of postcards during the First World War, their popularity further integrated into society. As the war subsided the use of postcards shifted to a means of documenting holidays. The Postcards (2022) said that, for most, buying a postcard reflecting a highlighting picture of the holiday to post home was a key step in personal holiday experiences throughout the 20th century.

The personal expression of experiences laid way into collector habits. The postcard's purpose began to shift with this perspective, once as a communication tool and now as a souvenir. Since postcards are cheap, small, and therefore portable, the card now serves as a tangible reminder of the experiences and further enables the collector's mindset. This identity of a postcard as a souvenir contrasts with perceived mundane activities to validate an extraordinary experience outwith the everyday (Stewart, 1984). Essentially, the power of postcards propels the individual from an event to memory and then fosters a desire to maintain memory with daydreams of escaping back to that moment again (Papadaki, 2006).

With the cultural embrace of technology, the original use of the postcard drifts further away (Symes, 2019). Artistic movements such as Fluxus in the 1960s and 1970s tried to "mail art" to reinvigorate the postcard and connect the art, artist, mail carrier and recipient through, albeit confusing, cross-cultural interactions (Ramkalawon, 2019). The digitisation of communication led to a new digital postcard for those seeking a creative communication tool with a hint of tradition. Other elements such as the speed and cost effectiveness of the postcard are now deemed archaic in comparison to instant messaging.

Researching with Postcards

Current research initiatives focus on the communicative power of postcards. Retroactive research seeks to understand the conversational and historical impact postcards have within society. Present research views postcards as a tool for analysing modern tourism trends. Both practices of postcard analysis often combine the modality of the image (Baldwin, 1988; Hall & Gillen, 2007 as cited in Gugganig and Schor, 2020) and continuous interest in textography (Symes, 2019). Research focusing on the historical value of postcards tends to either focus on the investigation of heritage sights through pictorial evidence (Spennemann, 2021), as ephemera materials (Brownson, 2023), or as a source of conversational and/or heuristic analysis (Wilson, 2020). Innovative research presented by Spennemann (2021) uses published postcards as a document of appearance that creates an interpretative tool for historical landscape and building analysis, only concerned with the images. The postcard is viewed as a design tool to reflect production and image manipulation processes (Spennemann, 2021). The method of analysis balances between a systematic literature review of postcard material of related postcard imagery and tangible artefacts. Like Spennemann's (2021) historical imagery, Arreola and Burkhart (2010) utilise visual imagery on postcards of urban landscapes to map changes within cities.

Spennemann (2021) and Brownson (2023) both critically engage with the concept of postcards as a physical artefact. Waitt and Head (2002), Stevens (2013), and Brownson (2023) continue to base their discussion of postcards as a source of collected ephemera. The Oxford Reference (Oxford University Press, 2024) defines ephemera currently as "things that exist or are used or enjoyed for only a short time; items of collectible memorabilia, typically written or printed ones, that were originally expected to have only short-term usefulness or popularity." Waitt and Head's (2002) research revolves around the analysis of postcards as a tool for circulating and perpetuating Australian frontier myths through the associated pictorial imagery. In contrast, Brownson's (2023) and Stevens's (2013) methodologies focus on archival practice as research, with one specific collection of extensive personal ephemera. The theme of the postcard's practical use as a collector's tool serves as a core theme.

In contrast, research focusing on the modern uses of postcards is directly correlated with tourism studies. Bonarou (2021), Milman (2012), and Corkery and Bailey (1994) correlate the selected photography on printed postcards to reflect the "tourist gaze" in which it represents. Tourist gaze, a term synonymous with Urry's eponymous book (2002, p. 3), refers to "features of landscape and townscape which separate them off from everyday experience." Urry (2002) then details that the tourist gaze is constructed by amalgamating anticipation cues, signs and symbols, and acts of capturing the moment. The tourism sector creates expectations for travellers, and these are then commemorated as a tangible collectible item of their experience. Researchers, such as Tattoni et al. (2021), further discuss how the imagery of postcards reflects an aesthetic expectation that visitors subscribe to, demonstrated through metrics such as sales.

One of the few examples of postcard research exists as a method for pedological research. Framed in Anthropological studies, Gugganig and Schor (2020) review various uses of postcards and their potential relation to other data collection practices such as ethnographic research, a tool for fieldwork, or a reflexive tool. Though the article reflects various implementations, the purpose is to describe but not a review of practical applications. Here, suggestions embrace postcards in classroom settings as an escape from technological platforms and outline the potential for postcards as either tools for data collection, reflection, or fieldwork memoing (Gugganig and Schor, 2020). The article serves as a network for other research databases for unique applications of postcard research. Arguably an exciting review of methods, the article focuses heavily on postcards within academic environments and as a tool for academic reflexivity and communication, particularly in ethnography settings. One of the favoured examples from Gugganig and Schor (2020) is the Dear Data project. Dear Data was started by two researchers, Giorgia Lupi and Stefanie Posavec, who sent each other postcards reflecting personal data back and forth to each other. This autoethnographic project with the ethos of "more humane and to connect with ourselves and others at a deeper level" compiled 52 weeks' worth of postcards with written and drawn elements (Posavec and Lupi, n.d.).

In contrast, traditional modern postcard methods continue to examine the theme of touristic views reflected via the imagery found on the postcards. One critical element of the following articles is the representation of interdisciplinary research. For example, Tattoni et al. (2021) combine environmental/ecosystem studies with aesthetics, also referred to as cultural ecosystems, to review the impact of the two on postcard imagery in the tourist industry framed by Urry's (2002) tourist gaze. The researchers' aim is supported by the concept that "postcards are primarily icons of touristic destinations, and people choose postcards that evoke positive emotions towards those places and promote the desire to travel to them" (Tattoni et al., 2021, p. 2). The researchers combined mapping of the ecological setting to identify the "ideal" view of the naturalistic setting in relation to postcard preference to determine the overall attractiveness of a region in Italy. This theory is supported by previous research that identifies the tourists' desire to purchase postcards with imagery reflective of their preferred landscape representative of the experience (Tattoni et al., 2021). Genre oriented, Tattoni et al. (2021) overlap considerably with photography. Photographic elements of postcards are a key element of the items' associated research. Touristic photography embraces elements of images captured by tourists themselves or photographs used in promotional material such as postcards (Stylianou-Lambert, 2012; Hillman, 2007; Markwick, 2001) and reinforces the associated memories of the place. Stylianou-Lambert's (2012) research grapples with how tourists' photographs are either tools for personal photographic expression or replications of images, such as postcards of the explored setting by comparing photographs uploaded to either location-specific postcards to popular photo-sharing websites.

The theme of picture-specific research continues with Arreola and Burkhart's (2010) analysis of photographic postcards and the visual urban landscape. Their work specifically views photographs as a tool for research methods in which photographic postcards can be one of those applications (2010). Arreola and Burkhart (2010, p. 887) articulate the use of postcards "to capture places of interest or scenes that the photographer thought was representative of the larger place being photographed." Arreola and Burkhart (2010) combine historical postcard studies with modern methods to map the change of urban landscape with the implementation of time series imagery. Simply put, the more an area is photographed, the more likely it will be seen as a postcard representation of the location. This is a theme that continues to be emulated through research approaches. Present postcard research emulates four core imagery perceptions, as summarised by Yu (2018) as relaxing sight-seeing endeavours, enchantment with cities, connections to natural landscapes, and/or historical imagery.

In reflection to both historical and modern framing of postcard research, the focus is primarily that postcards are the objects being studied. A few examples, such as Dear Data, begin to adapt postcards as a tool for data collection. The next section explores an overview of how postcards are implemented as a creative instrument for data collection.

Employing Postcards in Empirical Data Collection

The development of this method emerged from walking through Edinburgh, Scotland, on an errand unrelated to academic life. Tourist shops populate the city centre with racks and racks of postcards beckoning customers, targeting the tourist gaze. Subsequently, they sparked a creative method in the cognitive underbelly of a doctoral candidate. The idea stems from the original purpose, as outlined by Rogan (2005), as a tool for quick, effective, accessible, and nostalgically oriented data collection. The word tool was specifically chosen, as previous research focused heavily on postcards being the subject of research, not the means of acquiring data. Thematically, the use of postcards provides a bridge from the researcher's overall inquiry to the practical element of data collection.

The overall doctoral research inquires how festival attendees remember their festival experiences over a year. The festivals selected are based in Scotland, with a central hub that most, if not all, attendees will pass through to create a commonality between participants to anchor discussions pertaining to the memory of the festival. For this research, the festivals were self-categorised as an arts and cultural festival, taking on various sub-themes. The first festival in which the researcher conducted the postcard method was the Scots Fiddle Festival (SFF) in Edinburgh. Over the course of the three-day festival, over 100 postcards were completed and returned to the researcher. Prior to the festival, meetings occurred with a representative of the festival to review the aims and objectives of the PhD project. Here, the space provided opportunities for the festival representatives to ask questions and communicate their expectations as well. Pre-festival meetings occurred twice, the first as a general conversation in search of approval, the second to iron out the details. The second festival included in the study is CYMERA Festival dedicated to Scotland's sci-fi, fantasy, and horror literature enthusiasts. Steps such as overall approval, email threads, and remote meetings fostered open communication channels. Over 130 postcards were returned during the three-day literary festival.

Preparing for the festival, the necessary materials were purchased including blank postcards, pens, and markers. Furthermore, an upcycled ballot box served as the "post box." In addition to the post box, the researcher created signs to communicate the research on an A3 paper. The poster design also mimicked a large-scale postcard to generate continuity of the research materials for festival attendees. Here, an area of opportunity arises for future academics to add their own flair into the activity. Depending on the demographics, space, and budget, additional items such as stickers to mimic stamps and other craft materials could provide greater engagement. For a festival setting, the addition of these elements did not resonate since the majority of the contributors did not complete their postcards at the table.

The groups observed interacting with the postcards included festival attendees, festival volunteers, presenters/session leaders, market stall workers, bar/cafe staff and the public that continued to interact with the space outside of the festival. Unless specified, the individual postcards include identifiers of who communicated what exact numbers from each group are unobtainable for this research method. For the researcher, each of the groups served as active members of the festival and creators of their own experience and interaction within the space. When interacting with attendees, the researcher asked for anything related to their festival experience to be communicated on the card for the research. Wording such as write or tell were avoided as potential guides of expected communication. Emphasis placed on the words "their" and "experience" created a basis for potential content. If participants asked for expectations, responses dictated that there are no expectations, and anything returned is viewed as "valid" data. Postcards left in zones with minimal engagement from the researcher included the explanation, "Please use this Postcard to share your festival experience for my PhD research." The goal was for festival attendees to communicate their initial experiences at the festivals.

As discussed with each festival, the researcher self-identified as an active researcher at the festival. Ethically, the researcher felt that this decision reflected their personal research values and the festival's requests for a researcher in their spaces. At the Scots Fiddle Festival, this proved to be a vital decision due to the limited space for tabling to occur. CYMERA also happened in the same venue, leading to similar considerations taking place. With a small central cafe serving as the festival hub, the space held everything from ticketing, merchandise, casual seating, market stalls, fundraisers, and the research table. The position of the research table sat between the SFF ticketing table and merchandise, forcing a need for the researcher to be identified to minimise festival attendees' confusion when interacting. At the second festival, the researcher's table was located outside the main theatre, minimising confusion for the attendees about the researcher's role in the festival.

The central location of the "post box" provides ample opportunity for postcards to be returned. Aided by the cafe aesthetic, attendees' interaction with the space supported the postcard method. People floated consistently in and out. With performances in the cafe, attendees could take the postcards and sit down to complete them passively. When leaving the cafe to attend other elements of the festival, the exit passed by the "post box" created a streamlined exercise to return them. From an accessibility point of view, the location of the "post box" and materials were in the most accessible space within the venue. The act of completing a postcard did not require interaction with the researcher, which upon observation, is a preference for attendees who wished to remain completely anonymous or hesitant to interact with an "outsider."

Attendees acquired postcards in three main ways. First, they picked up a postcard from engaging with the research table itself. This often happened while passing between the ticketing booth and merchandise. Folks who interacted directly often did so with an interest in research, a general curiosity, or confusion looking for the ticketing stand. The majority of those who interacted at the table took postcards with them to return at a later point. Second, participants took postcards that the researcher was handing out at peak points in the festival, times which were identified by the festival's staff. The researcher would either stand or manoeuvre throughout the cafe or theatre space. This action was done during the first and second days of both festivals. Lastly, postcards were left on the main seating areas in the cafe on the third day for people to complete at the tables. A major contrast of the third action required the researcher to interact more within the space to collect postcards if not returned, maintain materials, and gather all materials at the end of the day. To communicate the research, little table signs reading, "Please share your festival experience on the postcards" stood alongside the materials.

The researcher's goal in distributing postcards was to interfere as little as possible with the overall festival experience for the attendees. Therefore, passive routes for distributing and collecting were enacted. This meant dialogues with the festival staff aided in identifying prime moments to interact in these spaces. Additionally, the postcards were only in the main hub of the festival where attendees floated through to other events for SFF. In contrast, CYMERA utilised more of the venue space. Therefore, postcards were left in the Gaming Room, Creator's Hall, and Green Room. The Gaming Room and Creator's Hall were identified by the festival team as zones of interest since they are free to all and therefore become spaces for participants to hang out separately from the cafe. Additionally, the Green Room provides space for the authors who may not desire a wander around the venue space. If attendees decided to take the postcards into the other elements of the festival to return later, that decision depended on the whim of the attendee. Some attendees even returned their postcards a day or two after their initial collection.

In addition to postcards, the researcher also wrote active observations in a handheld notebook throughout the event. When talking to festival staff and volunteers, the researcher gained verbal consent to write down any direct quotes about the festival, its operations and history. The observations from the festivals serve as an additional tool for the researcher for future data collection. The process of actively engaging with memo writing also supports later efforts in transcribing the postcards by providing context clues. The memoing process followed Flick's (2014) nine dimensions for descriptive orientation: space, actor, activity, object, act, event, time, goal and feeling. The researcher did an iteration of each of the nine dimensions for each day of the festival to organise thoughts and document changes from each of the three days of the festival. Part of the memo book held space for general quotes and comments, as mentioned above, and catchall spaces for disorganised writing to later be divided into one of the dimensions.

One important aspect of written observations is that some participants within the festival space may be aware of what is being written down. Since the table location sat in a central hub at SFF, writing in the notebook in that zone easily caught the attention of attendees and staff. Therefore, the researcher would often walk and write to minimise the impact and hyper-attention. The process of walking throughout the space also provided the researcher with opportunities to collect tangible materials from the festival and take pictures of related festival signage throughout the event space. Accumulating various source materials is done to support the further transcription and provide context to analyse the postcards. By moving within the festival space, the data table unmanned provided an option for those seeking completely anonymous interactions with the material to participate.

The use of postcards in a festival setting provides one specific example of its practicality as a data collection tool. Postcards provide minimal impact to the overall experience in which the attendees could interact with the material for as long as they wanted. As tangible objects, they easily move throughout space and enable self-reflection at one's leisure during the festival. Therefore, the content provided on the postcards encompasses written, drawn, and other elements of communication. Also, their use reflects the original purpose of the postcard as a cheap, fast, and efficient communication method sparking feelings of nostalgia for those reflecting on their experiences.

Postcard Analysis

The most time-consuming component of using postcards as a research instrument is transcription. Simply, handwritten material is at the mercy of the writer. Meaning, some handwriting is tricky to decipher and requires an awareness of context clues, as if solving a riddle. The researcher kept postcards from each day of the festival separate throughout the entire process. Deciding to organise the postcards in this fashion reflects the memory-oriented element of the research, but also aligns with the memo book sections to support the riddle deciphering. The only direct "alterations" made to each card included an addition of a number to the top corner of each card to coincide with the transcription of each card. The researcher first wrote the transcriptions in OneNote. Using OneNote provided the opportunity to handwrite the notes, but also provided the capability to print the transcriptions for later analysis.

As the collected postcards include both written and drawn elements, a flexible approach for analysis is necessary. Reflexive Thematic Analysis, as presented in Braun and Clarke's *2022 Practical Guide*, was adopted. Braun and Clarke (2022) identify reflexive thematic analysis as the critical interrogation practice of what, how, and why we interact with qualitative data sets to develop themes. Reflexive thematic analysis provides flexibility which helps adapt to the written and drawn elements of the postcards (Braun and Clarke, 2022; Trainor and Bundon, 2021). Trainor and Bundon (2021) draw attention to the perceived flexibility that may present a limitation to thematic analysis and its frequent dismissal as rigorous research practices. Braun et al. (2022) further clarify that flexibility does not mean anything goes, but rather that all the pieces of the puzzle should be of good fit with the philosophical and/or theoretical backbone.

It is vital to note that many academic articles utilise Braun and Clarke's previous iteration of thematic analysis, which has since been updated in their *2022 Practical Guide*, including the rebranding of thematic analysis to reflexive thematic analysis (Trainor and Bundon, 2021). One of the more dramatic developments includes the added sixth phase for thematic analysis (Braun and Clarke, 2022). The sixth phases include data familiarisation, data coding, initial theme generation, theme development and review, theme refining, and the final phase of writing up (Braun and Clarke, 2022). The rounds of data analysis for the postcards provide the grounding for the second phase of the research, which are semi-structured interviews based upon the initial themes. As a continuous process, the analysis encapsulates all data sets, expanding upon each other.

Research Considerations

The use of postcards as a creative method brings it back to its roots as a quick and efficient communication tool. The way people within the festivals interact with postcards is completely up to their own association with their use. To run this method at a festival, or indeed other experiential environments, the researcher needs to ponder the following considerations beforehand:

1. Do the festival attendees know what is expected of them with regard to using a postcard in research?

Considering whether to use this as a tool for data collection, the researcher should reflect on the sum of resources the activity requires. This includes understanding if the "average" festival attendee will know how to interact with a postcard, and, if not, is it possible to educate those that do not? Without knowledge of the original use of a postcard, attendees may simply keep the card as a keepsake for the festival or ignore it altogether. It is a central argument that postcards bridge generational and cultural boundaries for common knowledge, but it does not secure them as common interest. If the attendees are not interested in contributing communicated materials in physical form and prefer digital options, this is an area to explore. With the evolution of technology, the growth of digital postcards provides a solution for the researcher to consider.

2. Is there a central location for the materials to be returned?

The space in which the festival, or any event, is held may also dictate the researcher's ability to run a creative method such as this. Depending on the researcher's intentions, the act of returning the postcards requires an accessible and central location for the duration of the festival may encompass too much scope. For the previously discussed research, the postcard collection sat within the festivals' main hub. Most of the festival attendees interacted with the space and, therefore, were physically central to the materials. Additionally, the festival attendees interacted with the space frequently leading to plenty of opportunities to acquire, write and "post" their cards. If a festival takes place over a series of hubs, the researcher needs to consider the scope of the materials. Would more "posting" points be applicable? Are there resources to check-in with these locations? Is there enough material to cover the allotted space? Would another researcher be helpful to assist?

3. How involved will the researcher(s) be?

These points blur into the next consideration, the positionality of the researcher. There is no set way to conduct this research. A researcher's engagement with the data collection and the setting depends on the theoretical underpinnings of the research along with the selected methodology. Whether there are routes in ontology, epistemology, axiology, or a theoretical framework, considering the researcher's positionality will assist in refining the role.

One area to engage is the researcher's reflexivity. A researcher's reflexivity falls under personal reflexivity as outlined by Finlay and Gough (2003). Finlay and Gough (2003, p. 37) untangle the commonly acknowledged aspect of reflexivity as "an examination of researcher preconceptions and motivations pertaining to the research question(s)." Finlay and Gough (2003) argue that the personal element requires the researcher to situate themselves in their knowledge practices by incorporating the relevant contexts, often identified by interpersonal, institutional, or cultural personal considerations. Braun et al. (2022) further elaborate that researchers are never free from influence and therefore our analysis is shaped directly by assumptions and choices. The incorporation of personal reflexivity into qualitative research was further demonstrated by recent publications (e.g., Braun and Clarke, 2020; Corlett and Mavin, 2017; Dean et al., 2017; Dodgson, 2019; Finefter-Rosenbluh, 2017; Mason-Bish, 2018; as cited in Trainor and Bundon, 2021). Taking time to examine the researcher's role within the space will dictate the actions and potential decisions made. Without this examination, actions made while conducting the data collection may not reflect the values or underpinnings of the researcher.

4. What evaluation methods are the festivals implementing? Is there an overlap?

A key consideration from the stakeholder's point of view is the potential impact the methods may have on the organisations' own evaluation procedure. It is imperative to discuss before engaging with the physical event about research expectations, how it will be used and shared. Some festivals may decide not to move forward with a method such as this due to the correlation it may have to active evaluation efforts and concerns about engagement fatigue for the attendees. This is not the ending point of the conversation however. If communication has evolved in a respectful manner, the festival team may be able to pinpoint other directions and include direct contact with other teams. It is helpful to cover this question within the first meeting with the team to determine if the methods meet expectations.

5. Can the researcher read messy handwriting?

The final consideration for a researcher is one's ability to read and transcribe other people's handwriting. The amount of time it will take to transcribe the cards varies heavily from card to card. Though the content is restrained to the physical size of the card, the number of words people can fit was surprising. The expectation for one to be able to read every single word for the transcription process may not be feasible; and, thus, it may potentially minimise the applicable data analysis tools. Formatted as a simple yes or no question, the researcher should truly engage with the impact the answer may hold. Since the samples of handwriting on each postcard are small, this also currently eliminates handwriting AI (Artificial Intelligence) analysis tools. Both from an ethical point of view and a limited sample to "teach" the AI, the practicality of technological support is currently lacklustre. Considering personal energy reserves, timeline, and overall patience levels before beginning can support the overall success of the research collection.

Conclusions

Postcards as a data collection tool provide a creative method for those fearful of the creative title. Creativity does not always mean the output of an individual, but rather can embrace patterns of thinking to adapt new applications of commonalities. The consideration of a process as being creative is exclaimed as "the producing of something valuable and original by flair" (Gaut, 2003, p. 271). This data collection tool considers both the capabilities of researchers and those completing postcards. People can shock with what they return, sometimes to the point where this researcher was questioning how to find a data analysis tool to connect all the dots. This can stem as a potential limitation of using postcards for research purposes. Not having the capacity to consider different data analysis tools can hinder or exclude elements submitted by the individuals. Another limitation of using postcards is that people take the postcards and fail to return them during the festival. Proper analysis of return rates in experiential settings is an area of opportunity to incorporate into future research.

Further considerations should reflect on the experience of the event or festival. People in attendance may be averse to breaking that experience and moment to complete the postcards. This limitation incorporates previously discussed elements of the researcher's role within the experiential setting and navigating choices to minimise this limitation. In the current axiology that the researcher holds, respecting the desired experience of the attendees supersedes the extra interactions from the researcher.

Additionally, the use of postcards for data collection is an accessible tool to people outside of academia. The decision to utilise postcards was threefold of the ongoing doctoral research. First, is the power of the postcard to evoke memory and nostalgia. As the research proposed focuses on memory studies, this direct connection between the discipline of research and the symbolism of the postcard creates a natural partnership between both. Second, postcards are an instrument for communication that is flexible for a variety of levels of written ability and provides space for individuals to interact creatively if desired. The last principle of using postcards is to review the accessibility of the activity within a festival scene. The goal of the research is to impact the festival experience minimally for the attendees. This means that the activity can be completed quickly and at the leisure of the attendees. Also, postcards are accessible, reflecting the variety of cultural and physical considerations of those in attendance. Given the paucity of this approach in critical event studies, how other researchers decide to incorporate postcards as a tool provides opportunity for future research and exploration.

References

Andriotis, K. and Mavrič, M. (2013). Postcard mobility. *Annals of Tourism Research*, 40, 18–39.

Arreola, D. D. and Burkhart, N. (2010). Photographic postcards and visual urban landscape. *Urban Geography*, 31(7), 885–904.

Baldwin, B. (1988). On the verso: Postcard images as a key to popular prejudices. *Journal of Popular Culture*, 22(3), 15.

Bonarou, C. (2021). The poetics of travel through unravelling visual representations on postcards: A critical semiotics analysis. *Journal of Tourism, Heritage & Services Marketing*, 7(1), 44–53.

Braun, V. and Clarke V. (2020). One size fits all? What counts as quality practice in (reflexive) thematic analysis. *Qualitative Research in Psychology*, 1–25. 10.1080/14780887.2020.1769238

Braun, V. and Clarke, V. (2022). *Thematic analysis: A practical guide*. London: SAGE.

Braun, V. et al. (2022). Doing reflexive thematic analysis. In S. Badger-Charleson and A. McBeath (eds.) *Supporting research in counselling and psychotherapy*. 1st edn. London: Palgrave Macmillan, 19–38.

Brownson, L. (2023). Odds, ends, and archival exclusion: Ephemeral Archives and counter-history in the English country house. *Archives and Records*, 44(3), 308–329.

Corkery, C. and Bailey, A. (1994). Lobster is big in Boston: Postcards, place commodification, and tourism. *GeoJournal*, 34(4), 491–498.

Corlett, S. and Mavin, S. (2017). Reflexivity and researcher positionality. In *The SAGE handbook of qualitative business and research methods*, Vol. 1. SAGE.

Dean, J., Furness, P., Verrier, D., Lennon, H., Bennett, C. and Spencer, S. (2017). Desert island data: An investigation into researcher positionality. *Qualitative Research*, 18(3), pp. 273–289. https://doi.org/10.1177/1468794117714612

Dodgson, J. E. (2019). Reflexivity in qualitative research. *Journal of Human Lactation*, [online] 35(2), pp. 220–222. https://doi.org/10.1177/0890334419830990

Finefter-Rosenbluh, I. (2017). Incorporating perspective taking in reflexivity. *International Journal of Qualitative Methods*, 16(1), p. 160940691770353. https://doi.org/10.1177/1609406917703539

Finlay, L. and Gough, B. (2003). Part II personal reflexivity. In L. Finlay and B. Gough (eds.) *Reflexivity: A practical guide for researchers in health and social sciences.* London: Blackwell Science Ltd, 37–38.

Flick, U. (2014) *The SAGE handbook of qualitative data analysis.* 5th edn. Los Angeles: Sage.

Gaut, B. (2003). Creativity and imagination. In *The Creation of Art*, 148–173.

Gugganig, M. and Schor, S (2020). Teaching (with) postcards: Approaches in the classroom, the field, and the community. *Teaching Anthropology* 9(2), 56–65.

Hall, N. and Gillen, J. (2007). Purchasing pre-packed words: complaint and reproach in early British postcards. In M. Lyons (ed.) *Ordinary Writings, personal narratives: Writing practices in the 19th and early 20th-century Europe*, pp. 101–117.

Hillman, W. (2007). Travel authenticated?: Postcards, tourist brochures, and travel photography. *Tourism Analysis*, 12(3), 135–148.

Markwick, M. (2001). Postcards from malta. *Annals of Tourism Research*, 28(2), 417–438.

Mason-Bish, H. (2018). The elite delusion: reflexivity, identity and positionality in qualitative research. *Qualitative Research*, [online] 19(3), 263–276. https://doi.org/10.1177/1468794118770078

Milman, A. (2012). Postcards as representation of a destination image: The case of Berlin. *Journal of Vacation Marketing*, 18(2), 157–170.

Oxford University Press (2024). *Overview – Ephemera.* Available at: https://www.oxfordreference.com/display/10.1093/oi/authority.20110803095754277 (Accessed 25 April 2024).

Papadaki, Eirini (2006). Narrating personal moments through social images: Postcards as souvenirs of memorable instances and places. In E. Papadaki (ed.) *Narrative, memory & knowledge: Representations, aesthetics, contexts.* Huddersfield: University of Huddersfield, 55–62.

Posavec, S. and Lupi, G. (n.d.). *The project, Dear Data.* Available at: https://www.dear-data.com/theproject (Accessed 4 July 2024).

Postcards (2022). *The Postal Museum.* Available at: https://www.postalmuseum.org/collections/highlights/postcards/ (Accessed 4 July 2024).

Ramkalawon, J. (2019). *The world exists to be put on a postcard, The British Museum.* Available at: https://www.britishmuseum.org/blog/world-exists-be-put-postcard (Accessed 4 July 2024).

Rogan, B. (2005). An entangled object: The picture postcard as souvenir and collectible, exchange and ritual communication. *Cultural Analysis*, 4, 1–27.

Spennemann, D. H. (2021). The evidentiary value of late nineteenth and early twentieth century postcards for Heritage Studies. *Heritage*, 4(3), 1460–1496.

Stevens, N. D. (2013). *Postcards in the library: Invaluable visual resources*. Abingdon: Routledge.

Stewart, S. (1984). *On longing*. Baltimore, MD: John Hopkins University Press.

Stylianou-Lambert, T. (2012). Tourists with cameras: Reproducing or producing?, *Annals of Tourism Research*, 39(4), 1817–1838.

Symes, C. (2019). Something to write home about: A 'textography' of contemporary postcards. *Annals of Leisure Research*, 22(5), 642–660.

Tattoni, C. et al. (2021). The landscape change in the Alps—What postcards have to say about aesthetic preference. *Sustainability*, 13(13), 7426.

Trainor, L. R. and Bundon, A. (2021) Developing the craft: Reflexive accounts of doing reflexive thematic analysis. *Qualitative Research in Sport, Exercise and Health* 13(5), 705–726. https://doi.org/10.1080/2159676x.2020.1840423

Urry, J. (2002). *The tourist gaze*. 2nd edition. London: SAGE.

Waitt, G., & Head, L. (2002). Postcards and frontier mythologies: Sustaining views of the kimberley as timeless. *Environment and Planning D: Society and Space*, 20(3), 319–344.

Wilson, K. (2020). Part I The messages. In K. Wilson (ed.) *Snapshots and short notes: Images and Messages of early twentieth-century photo postcards*. Texas: University of North Texas Press, 18–20.

Yu, H. -Y. (2018). Postcard narratives: A case of Vichy in France. *Tourism Management Perspectives*, 26, 89–96.

8

POSTCARDS FROM THE FUTURE

Researching Audiences at Bad Ischl-Salzkammergut, European Capital of Culture 2024

Barbara Grabher

University of Brighton, Brighton, England

Introduction

'Next stop: Hallstatt' is announced by an overenthusiastic speaker voice while the train moves around a corner and opens the perspective onto the Lake of Hallstatt, its surrounding mountains of the Dachstein glacier and the small village positioned in between the stunning scenery. As the train comes to a halt and doors slide open, waves of new passengers enter the carriage. With luggages stored away and empty seats filled, the bustling crowds settle in for a journey along alpine lakes and mountain ranges. As one of the most frequented routes in the Austrian peripheries, the Salzkammergut-Bahn is famous for its historical significance and contemporary celebration as one of the most scenic routes in the Austrian Alps. This trainline serves as a mode of transportation to get from A to B; but beyond the mere mobility pattern the train journey enables encounters with a region that celebrates the title European Capital of Culture in 2024.

This impression of the train journey is deliberately selected as an introduction to the research context for the project 'Between Culture and Salt'.[1] The initial depiction sets the scene for this chapter as it shares a glimpse into the Salzkammergut-Bahn. Underlying this narrative description lies the interest in the region's ongoing transformation and ambition for change, which is framed by the celebration of the European Capital of Culture title in 2024 and its related event-based regeneration process.

In its 40 years of existence, the European Capital of Culture event framework has become synonymous with urban regeneration and regional development (European Commission, 2010; Bianchini, Albano & Bollo, 2013). The economic, social and cultural regeneration agendas have become defining features in the intention and ambition of applicant cities. Consequentially,

DOI: 10.4324/9781032686424-8

transformation and change are buzzwords in the application process and often reasons for the jury selection of host cities. This transformative potential links the event framework to wider debates of cultural regeneration and allows to think about the event through its impact and legacy (Papanikolaou, 2012; Bianchini & Parkinson, 1993). The event-based transformative ambitions and their related regenerative strategies invite me to consider what actually forms part of a European Capital of Culture event. As host cities conceptualise and approach the European Capital of Culture celebration as a durational project, rather than only a one-off event, various layers of action are entangling in the contemporary understanding of these year-long endeavours. In light of this entanglement, my interest lies less on the flagship cultural activities, which are in the spotlight of public attention; instead, I focus on the dynamics and processes, which act in the background and therefore receive less attention.

In the application and preparation of the event Salzkammergut European Capital of Culture 2024 (SKGT 2024), the key terms of transformation and change are characterising the event as a development opportunity (Heinisch et al., 2019). The inherent event-based regeneration process is strongly driven by socio-cultural values of environmental sustainability. Environment, ecology and climate change are addressed as central concerns, which shape the event process and programme for 2024 (Neuhuber et al., 2019). Hereby, Salzkammergut-Bahn carries enormous importance as sustainable modes of transportation. The authors of the bid book explain:

> In order to respond to the current, but also expected traffic issues [in the region], we initiated a stakeholder group of experts, both from the region and Upper Austria's Government, with the mandate to propose ways of developing a more sustainable and green mobility system for the region. This includes the development of a concept for the enhancement of public transport in the build-up to the title year (and lasting beyond), but also innovative ideas that activate people to use [public transportation] instead of their cars.
>
> *(Neuhuber et al., 2019: 9)*

As communicated in the application documents and related cultural vision 2030 (Heinisch et al., 2020; Neuhuber et al., 2019), SKGT 2024 focuses on this central concern in order to work towards a more sustainable mobility offer and includes within programme cooperations with local and regional decision-makers influencing the public mobility sector.

While I discuss the event-related interests in sustainable mobility in other publications (Grabher, forthcoming), this chapter is dedicated to methodological questions that are provoked by the train journey, its passengers as well as their perspectives for the future. Reflecting upon the data collection process in the pilot study conducted in June 2023, this chapter discusses the innovative and creative methodological approach that drives the research project 'Between Culture and Salt' in its focus on train passengers as audiences of the event-based regeneration process. By provocatively choosing the train and its passengers as the focal point of my study, this chapter concerns with the methodology and methods in rather unusual circumstances for critical event studies. Through conceptual as well as practical perspectives, this chapter questions who are the audiences of the event process of SKGT 2024 and how can these audiences be researched.

The structure and argumentative line of this chapter are two-fold: Firstly, I explore approaches to researching audiences from a conceptual perspective and suggest that not only do we need to know who audiences are but also what audiences are in general. Referring to the widely interdisciplinary debate on audiences, I propose an innovative conceptualisation of passengers of the Salzkammergut-Bahn as audiences of the event-based regeneration process SKGT 2024. Secondly, building on this conceptualisation of audiences, I furthermore discuss the creative research practice in my research with such redefined audiences of event-based regeneration processes. The method 'Postcards of the future' is hereby presented and discussed in regards to context, practices and responses and embedded in a consideration of its limitations and potential.

Conceptualising Audiences for Methodological Purposes

Researching audiences departs from the overwhelming number of disciplines, which concern with the term 'audience'. Reviewing definitions across the fields of media studies, cultural studies, psychology or sociology – to name just a few – it becomes clear that the term is used in a multiplicity of ways without necessarily ever debating the conceptual underpinning of the term in detail (Brooker & Jermyn, 2003; Hay et al., 2018). Going back to the theoretical debates led by Ede (1984), Allor (1988) and Webster (1998) in media/cultural studies in the 1980s and 1990s, the question "What or Who is an audience?" (Ede, 1984: 140) guides my theoretical interrogations of the term.

Research on audiences in event studies generally assumes that "for every event, there is an audience – or group of listeners or spectators expecting to engage with the event" (Mackellar, 2014: 2). Without further questioning this assumed synergy between the event and its audiences, this understanding of audiences is fairly limited. It focuses on the 'event' as a pre-given circumstance which provokes audiences but essentialises hereby how audiences are generated. In the presumed relationship between events and audiences, Mackellar (2014) provides a comprehensive summary of who audiences might be. The author highlights that "audiences are as diverse and complex as people themselves" (Mackellar, 2014: 1) and follows such description immediately with a segmentation of different audience profiles according to the forms of participation with an event: From the distant observer of an event through media channels to the full immersion of an audience member in the happenings. This segmentation of different audiences and their memberships appears to be the dominant approach to the definition of audiences in event studies. In addition to these behavioural categorisations, segmentations of audiences in other fields go even further and influence the field of event studies. When regarding debates of audience development, classifications of audiences by demographic and lifestyle factors feature prominently in research and policy agendas (Hadley, 2021). While these segmentations/categorisations/classifications of audiences respond to the question 'Who is an audience?', the conceptual concern 'What is an audience?' is not yet sufficiently explored. While an event audiences might be simply addressed as the visitors of an event, event-based regeneration processes are much more complex and therefore struggle to pinpoint their 'spectators'. In order to respond to the complexities of such an analogy, I am turning through media and cultural studies to postmodernist, poststructuralist and feminist conceptualisation of audiences.

While published already in the late 1980s, Allor's (1988) conceptual understanding of audiences holds crucial relevance to my conceptual concern of researching audiences. Questioning the theoretical construct of audiences, Allor (1988) argues for a flexible interpretation of audiences. While the author refers to different perspectives, which capture audiences as "labour, the subject in text, the gendered reader, subculture [or] the mass" (Allor, 1988: 228), it is particularly the acknowledgement that audiences "exist nowhere, it inhabits no real space, only positions within analytical discourses" (Allor, 1988: 228) that becomes crucial in my understanding of audiences for the context of event-based regeneration processes. This definition of the non-definition – or, rather: the definition by analytical discourse – is driven by poststructuralist and postmodern epistemologies. Allor (1988) highlights that audiences are nothing more than a constructed unity. By focusing on an audience, the term audiences is defined: Through the analytical focus on event-based regeneration and its relevance to public transportation, the train passengers can analytically be defined as audiences.

This analytical – rather than factual – definition of audiences serves as an entrance point to the conceptualisation of audiences as required for the methodological interest of my study. However, beyond such construction of unity and henceforth identification of an analytical category of audience, my approach to audiences is further defined by the heterogenous relationship between the audiences (i.e. train passenger) and the researched process/object (i.e. the event-based regeneration process). Inspired by the interplay between poststructuralist and postmodern critiques of audiences, I see strong potential in the 'de-centring' of the audiences through an understanding of the 'mass'. While the de-centring approach derives from poststructuralist theories, the notion of the mass is a key interest in postmodernist debates. In both perspectives, the conceptual value of the audiences lies in its discursive existence, which as noted previously is defined by the analytical definition of audiences. However, by de-centring – and therefore de-essentialising audiences as a fixed category of segmentations – the conceptual considerations of audiences can be unfolded (Allor, 1988). Associated with postmodernist interpretations of audiences, Webster (1998) highlights audience-as-mass as a prominent interpretation for media studies and acknowledges this approach as well to be useful for events. While acknowledging the mass as an important concept, Webster interjects that the mass cannot be merely considered on the basis of its vastness or its supposed outcome; rather audiences – as a de-centred mass – require a reading through the lens of agency. This interest in agency is what further drives as well feminist considerations of audiences (Allor, 1988). Building on reader-response theory in literature studies as well as media studies, feminist considerations focus on the positionalities, which are presented in the context of the mass's agency. Therefore, feminist epistemological considerations break down the concepts of the mass into what Allor (1988) highlights as the heterogeneity of positionalities in audiences. Not only is the category of audiences analytically created, but the texture of audiences is driven by agencies of distinct positionalities.

These complex theoretical considerations are necessary in the very particular context, in which I am researching audiences. While event research supposedly identifies audiences by essentialisation and segmentation, the event-based regeneration process and its audiences have a more nuanced definitory relationship. What happens when audiences are not even aware that they are potential audiences? The train journey with the Salzkammergut-Bahn is not depicted as an explicit event participation – let alone a participation in the event-based regeneration process. First and foremost, the journey serves the purpose of mobility through the region. While the event-based regeneration process of SKGT 2024 makes the trainline a key focus of their work in and for the region's future development, the usage of the train (or any other form of public transportation) is independent of event-related participation. This discrepancy is where the research of audiences becomes interesting and methodologically challenging to capture the positionalities of these research participants. As highlighted by Allor (1988), audiences are not a homogeneous category but rather an indefinite group that is descriptively labelled for analytical purposes. In my methodological approach such lack of audience awareness is what makes the research particularly innovative. Rather than working with pre-defined groups of audiences, I am researching a community related to the event-based regeneration process that can barely be captured as audiences at all: the train passengers.[2]

Postcards of the Future: Creativity through Imagination

While the so far presented considerations of audiences contain already some level of originality, my further ambition is to translate this theoretical conceptualisation into a novel research method drawing upon creative practices.

Researching train passengers as the audiences of the event-based regeneration process of SKGT 2024, I developed the method 'Postcards of the future' to enable the imaginations of potential futures in response to the transformative ambitions inherent in the studied event process. The method is driven by the question: What would a postcard of the future of the Salzkammergut look like? While seemingly simple, the context, practice and answers – further outlined in this section – illustrate the complexity of the research practice.

Previous sections already highlighted contextual aspects, which are crucial to the method 'Postcards of the future': In 2024, the region of the Salzkammergut is celebrating the European Capital of Culture title and connects the event process with regenerative strategies for regional developments. This context provides fertile grounds to think about future imaginations for the purpose of this research project (Neuhuber et al., 2019). Beyond these contemporary contextual influences, the method's intentional play with postcards as a research object further refers to the region's historical developments. While the social artefact of the postcard might appear as fairly outdated, it is an important symbol in respect to the regional history in regard to the defining influx of tourism in the 18th and particularly 19th century. Influenced by the natural salt resources in the region, Bad Ischl, as one of the main cities in the region, became a famous destination for wellness tourism. The usage of salt for healing purposes drew the peerage and upper classes of the Habsburg Monarchy to spend their summer months in the city. This substantially altered the region's character and appearance from a rural peasant society to a wealthy, touristic area of political significance (Field Diary, October 2021). Even though the practice of postcard writing is currently on a steady decline, the picturesque depictions and written messages on sturdy cardboard hold a long tradition as a highly influential form of correspondence in the region of the Salzkammergut. As these documents are becoming increasingly attractive collectibles, postcards provide insights into the representations that shaped and continue to shape the Salzkammergut. Due to the spatial restrictions of this paper, I am unable to further dwell on the historical development, relevance of tourism and influence for the region since the 18th/19th century; however, the symbol of the postcard as a central feature of the research method is used as a social artefact to reference the past, present and future perspective of regional development and regeneration.

Next to the explanations of the research context, the method 'Postcards of the future' requires further elaboration. Focusing on train passengers of the Salzkammergut-Bahn as the audiences of the transformative process of SKGT 2024, the research practice of this method is determined by the trainline and the mobility practice of passengers travelling in, through and beyond the Salzkammergut region. As my intention was to work with train passengers in the moment of travel, the approval by the national train services OEBB was essential. The active mobility through the Salzkammergut informed the answers of interview participants making references to either the mobility, the passing scenery, or other passengers on the train. In my pilot study in June 2023, I collected responses from passengers on the train using a random sampling technique informed by purposeful intention. Participants were recruited on a voluntary basis with the power to freely decide on their participation. Potential participants were given information about the research project and asked if they would be interested to answer three questions regarding the future of the Salzkammergut region. Due to the time-sensitivity of train journeys with stops every couple of minutes, the interviews were planned as short semi-structured interviews with three key questions and the option to further probe interview participants for clarification and specification. Any interview was opened with the presentation of a blank postcard already stamped. This presentation of the postcard was accompanied by the question 'What would a postcard of the future of the Salzkammergut look like?'. While initially planned as an act of drawing, the method needed to be adapted to the practicalities of the train journey. Instead of drawing, interview participants preferred to explain their visions – creating therefore a narrated picture for the postcard. This opening question was intentionally difficult and required interview participants to think in an applied manner about their future imaginations for the region. The follow-up question concerned with the ongoing regeneration process of the SKGT 2024 event and invited participants to evaluate the opportunities and challenges of the ongoing event-based regeneration process. The final question was crucial as participants were asked to turn the postcard around and share a wish or a greeting for the future Salzkammergut. The answers to this final question were particularly interesting in regards to the effectiveness of the methods.

Imagining the future of the Salzkammergut and sharing a wish for the region's further development is in itself a rather complex question and in many cases, participants were puzzled by the depth of my queries. The majority of interview participants were careful to respond with great detail. The postcard as a guiding object as well as the train journey was hereby of great help to the interview process. Several participants took the postcard into their own hand and studied its minimalistic features such as paper thickness, address lines or the pre-printed stamp. Others took the time to observe the passing landscape outside the train window before answering my questions. This moment of silence, which I interpret as a moment of contemplation, was frequently followed by an expression of concern regarding the uncertainties that the future might hold. References to war, environmental changes and/or natural disasters were recorded as frequent responses, but similarly the capitalisation of the region, its natural landscape and the inherent exploitation were often referenced. Without wanting to fall into a duality of optimism versus pessimism, I noted that the question of the future was very much a contemplative and serious issue that interview participants did not respond to lightly. The second question regarding the process of the SGKT 2024 and its advantages as well as disadvantages received a lot of queries and questions as awareness of and knowledge about the event-based regeneration process of SKGT 2024 was limited. Throughout the process of data collection, documentation and analysis, I was particularly intrigued by the responses to my final question as a pattern revealed itself through repeating answers. While train passengers were on route to different destinations and had various motives of travel, it is telling that a large majority of respondents used exactly the same phrase in order to express their wish for the future of the Salzkammergut: The German phrase 'Dass alles so bleibt, wie es ist' translates to English as, 'Everything should stay as it is'. This short phrase is loaded with meaning when considering the transformative ambitions of SKGT 2024. The wish inherits the communicated uncertainties regarding future imaginations and takes into consideration the general concern for the region and its fragile landscape. It becomes an important expression of a desire for sustainability and for a future that in its uncertainties is loaded with anticipation.

Outlook: What a Train Journey Can Tell About the Future?

Informed by the regenerative ambitions of the region and its celebration of the European Capital of Culture title in 2024, this chapter seeks to find answers to methodological complexities that require creativity and innovation. My ambition of researching audiences in the context of event-based regeneration is informed by a unique conceptualisation of train passengers as audiences of the event process of SKGT 2024. Researching audiences is not only bound to a particular discipline of research but rather borrows from all kinds of research approaches. The relevance of audiences as a research category and field becomes clear in the plurality of concerns and considerations. As in the research of events audiences are not conceptualised enough, it was necessary to look beyond the boundaries of this disciplinary field and bring various epistemological traditions together to formulate the methodological point that audiences can be researched even if they are not necessarily pre-established. Defined by their heterogeneity, the conceptualisation of audiences is driven through the definitory capacities of an analytical focus on certain processes. Creativity and innovation were not only on a theoretical level driving forces of the conceptualisation of train passengers as audiences of the transformative ambitions of SKGT 2024, but also highly informative for the development of the research practice 'Postcards of the future'. The method uses the social artefact of the postcard and the prompt 'What would a postcard of the future of the Salzkammergut region look like?' to gather imaginations and visions for the region. Playing with symbols of the past to inform the present and envision futures, the haptic element of the postcard served as an essential artefact in the interview. Similarly to this object guiding the conversation, the setting of travelling through a scenic alpine landscape leaves imprints in the responses of interview participants. The context, practice and answers to the method 'Postcards of the future' was used to depict in an insightful way the cause, concern and output of this research practice explicitly developed for the purpose of this research project. In the pilot study in June 2023, I collected 25 short interviews lasting between three and ten minutes. With further fieldwork and data collection planned for 2024, the method requires reflections and adaptations. Hereby, the practicalities of researching on the research location (1), the constraints of random but equally purposeful sampling (2) as well as the different phases of the event process of SKGT 2024 (3) need further discussion.

1 When researching on public transportation, the practical implications of this research location are not to be underestimated. As highlighted previously, my research focuses on train passengers in the moment of moving through the alpine landscape along the trainline of the Salzkammergut-Bahn. This execution is already a compromise as the original intention of the research was to work with users of all kinds of public transportation throughout the region – including ferries, buses and trams among others. Very soon into the pilot study, I had to realise that only one mode of transportation was feasible for this research project. The selection of the train was mainly driven by the comfort of the Austrian trains. Air conditioning, bathrooms and the space to move from one interview participant to another without restricting their travel experience were essential in order to create suitable interview settings. While some bus routes were identified as eventually interesting, the curvy mountain roads and the constrained spaces on buses limited the options on researching passengers in moving vehicles of other public transportation. Furthermore, the decision for the train as the research location was also influenced by the ticket availability, prices and frequency of the train. While interest in ferries and trams continues to be explored, the practicalities of the research location require adaptations in future applications of the research method.

2 Researching on the trainline and with train passengers opens critical questions regarding the chosen sampling technique. In the data collection process during the pilot study in June 2023, I made sure to interview on various days of the week as well as during different times throughout the day. This enabled me to encounter all kinds of train passengers, who were all travelling for diverse motives. However, while this variety in timing might influence the potential encounters, the selection of interview participants needs to be further challenged as randomness and purpose defined the sampling technique simultaneously. As a practical solution to the randomness of my sampling strategy during my pilot study, my focus lay on train passengers, who were sitting in a space, where four chairs faced each other (instead of two chairs facing one direction). In some cases, interviews were conducted while standing but the preference was given to seated passengers. This selection criterion was defined as the seated position enabled better comfort and allowed

me to assume a longer duration of the journey for the interviewed traveller. As a benefit of this random strategy, I was able to interview individuals, couples as well as groups of three or four people to a similar extent. This random sampling technique defined by seating choice was further informed by purposeful strategies driven by demographic factors such as age, gender and language. Since the trainline is frequently used by international tourists visiting world-famous sites of the Salzkammergut region such as the village of Hallstatt, some interviews were conducted in English. The majority of interviews were conducted in German. Hereby, I noted throughout the data collection process that I was biased towards German-speaking train passengers. After several interviews in English with international travellers from the UK, Israel and India, I noticed that these passengers were solely focused on their destination of Hallstatt and lacked awareness for the region of Salzkammergut. As my interview questions required passengers to have a basic understanding of the region as well as the European Capital of Culture event framework, this bias definitely needs further reflections. I suspect that the bias might require adaptations of the questions or a strong reasoning for a more selective sampling technique in future data collection phases.

3 In future planned data collection phases in January, April and June/July 2024, not only the sampling strategy demands further attention but as well the event context of SKGT 2024 needs to be closely monitored. While in the pilot study the event was in its preparatory phase, train passengers expressed very limited knowledge and understanding of the event. Even though awareness of the event process was scarce, it was notable that certain public debates about the organisation of SKGT 2024 influenced the reflections and imaginations of train passengers. I am expecting these influences to become even stronger in the upcoming fieldwork periods as the programme of cultural activities will be fully inaugurated. It will be of interest to see if patterns of responses can be observed and linked to different phases of the event. Depending on research funding, the intention is as well to collect interviews after the event process of SKGT 2024 has officially ended in December 2024 in order to document eventual, immediate impacts of the event and consider its potential legacy for event-based regeneration in this unique research setting and its particular audience voices.

With an interest in unusual audiences of the particular event framework of SKGT 2024, the method 'Postcard of the future' invites for a methodological experimentation for event studies. On the level of conceptualisation of the notion of audiences as well as in regards to the research practice of engaging train passengers of the Salzkammergut-Bahn, creativity and Innovation are the driving forces in the considerations of how such research on transformative ambitions of events can be made possible and enable inspiring and experimental research for the critical study of events.

Notes

1 Funded by the University of Brighton, the research project 'Between Culture and Salt' examines in what way the notion of the Anthropocene holds conceptual and empirical potential for the study of events. Focusing on infrastructures, practices and narratives of the Anthropocene in the event of SKGT 2024, the research project examines the negotiation of environmental sustainability in the context of the European Capital of Culture celebration. The project 'Between Culture and Salt' is currently in progress and has so far secured four ethnographic fieldwork periods in the region of Salzkammergut. The here presented methodology and method have been trialled in a pilot study in June 2023. Further fieldwork periods are planned for 2024 and therefore take place in correlation with the event SKGT 2024. Eventually presented limitations are used as reflection points for future adaptations of the method.

2 It is to be noted that the Salzkammergut-Bahn as well as other smaller trainlines in the region become the location of several art projects and cultural activities that shape again a different, more explicit notion of audiences. One example is the audio trail 'Regional_Express', which allows passengers to learn about the history of the Salzkammergut through five stories (Interview with Artistic Collective, June 2023). Sensitive to the particular environment that the train is travelling through, the audio stories adapt to the different landscapes, stations and general surroundings, telling local stories and allowing therefore the potential audience member to be engaged in this activity through such auditive experience in a rather unusual stage setting defined by the Salzkammergut-Bahn. While such explicit examples of cultural activities exist within the event-based regeneration process of SKGT 2024, I am seeking to capture audiences not in reciprocity to an explicit activity but rather in relation to the transformative process.

References

Allor, M. (1988). Relocating the site of the audience. *Critical Studies in Mass Communication*, 5(3), 217–233.

Bianchini, F., Albano, R., & Bollo, A. (2013). The regenerative impacts of European City and Capital of Culture events. In M. Leary & J. McCarthy (Eds.), *Companion to urban regeneration* (pp. 515–526). Routledge.

Bianchini, F., & Parkinson, M. (1993). *Cultural policy and urban regeneration: The west European experience*. Manchester University Press.

Brooker, W., & Jermyn, D. (2003). *The audience studies reader*. Routledge.

Ede, L. (1984). College composition and communication. *Audience: An Introduction to Research*, 35(2).

European Commission. (2010). Summary of the European Commission conference "Celebrating 25 years of European Capitals of Culture."

Grabher, B. (forthcoming, 2025). Rollendes Vermächtnis. Anthropologische Perspektiven auf infrastrukturelle Veränderung im Rahmen der Europäischen Kulturhauptstadt Salzkammergut 2024. In A. Faerber & B. Schmidt-Lauber (Eds.), *Gesellschaftliche Transformationen durch Grossveranstaltungen*. Transcript.

Hadley, S. (2021). *Audience development and cultural policy*. Palgrave Macmillian. http://www.palgrave.com/gp/series/14748

Hay, J., Grossberg, L., & Wartella, E. (2018). *The audience and its landscape*. Routledge.

Heinisch, S., Christina, J., Kodym, P., Mair, E., Neuhuber, L., & Zednik, H. (2019). *Essenz: Endauswahl 2019*. Bad Ischl.

Heinisch, S., Jaritsch, C., Kodym, P., Mair, E., Neuhuber, L., & Zednik, H. (2020). Kulturvision Salzkammergut 2030. Bad Ischl.

Mackellar, J. (2014). *Event audiences and expectations*. Routledge.

Neuhuber, L., Zednik, H., Kodym, P., Mair, E., & Heinisch, S. (2019). *Bad Ischl-Salzkammergut 2024 European Capital of Culture: Candidate city*. Bad Ischl.

Papanikolaou, P. (2012). The European Capital of Culture: The challenge for urban regeneration and its impact on the cities. *International Journal of Humanities and Social Science*, 2(17), 268–273.

Webster, J. G. (1998). The audience. *Journal of Broadcasting and Electronic Media*, 42(2), 190–207. https://doi.org/10.1080/08838159809364443

9

UTILISING INFORMAL CONVERSATIONS AS A CREATIVE METHOD AT LIVE EVENTS

Leon Davis and Christopher J. Hayes
Teesside University, Middlesbrough, England

Alyssa Eve Brown
University of Sunderland, Sunderland, England

Introduction

Data collection at live events has used a wide variety of creative qualitative and quantitative methods from a range of disciplines in contemporary research. In the twenty-first century, scholars have repeatedly noted how events research has been dominated by quantitative methodologies (see, for example, Draper, Young and Fenich, 2018; Lee and Back, 2005; Yoo and Weber, 2005) and a plethora of secondary research in the field of event studies (see Getz, 2010; Park and Park, 2017). Mair (2012), when noting the lack of rigour in many of the quantitative articles in the field, highlighted that qualitative methodologies were significantly underrepresented in high-impact journals. It was evident by the early 2010s that the event research landscape was lacking studies primarily from a qualitative methodological standpoint. Mair (2012) urged business event researchers to use in-depth qualitative methods, such as ethnographic or discourse analysis, to better understand the meanings that individuals attach to business events to truly progress this important research stream. Finkel and Dashper (2020) noted a 'turn' in events studies research from the mid-2010s onwards, highlighting how event research began to develop from a more critical perspective from cross-disciplinary literatures and cross-fertilising with broader social science approaches and methodologies (cf. Bossey, 2020; Castle et al., 2022; Finkel, Sharp and Sweeney, 2018; McGillivray, McPherson and Misener, 2018; Misener et al., 2015; O'Grady, 2013; Platt and Finkel, 2020; Sharp, 2018). Creative methods have become a way to obtain data in a variety of disciplines, namely the arts and cultural industries (see Kara, 2015, 2023; Van der Vaart, Van Hoven and Huigen, 2018).

DOI: 10.4324/9781032686424-9

Although the use of qualitative research in event studies has increased in recent years, an underrepresented creative qualitative method in events studies is informal conversations. As articulated by Swain and King (2022), initiating a conversation with a person or group of people has been recognised as an integral element of qualitative research for well over 100 years. The method became a popular data collection method in the 1920s and 1930s (see Cressey, 1932; Mead, 1928; Mowrer, 1932; Palmer, 1928; Park, Burgess and McKenzie, 1925; Webb and Webb, 1932; Wirth, 1927). In contemporary research, informal conversations have been used in a variety of studies in other fields, principally since the 2010s (see Angotti and Sennott, 2014; Densley, 2013; Korobov, 2018; Swain and King, 2022; Swain and Spire, 2020; Thomson and Trigwell, 2018). Despite the clear use of the method in other scholarly fields, informal conversations have been infrequently utilised in event studies research.

The aim of this chapter is to make the case for the use of informal conversations as a creative research method when collecting qualitative data at live event spaces. We start by briefly conceptualising informal conversations as a valid standalone method, distinct from the unstructured interview method. To meet the aim, we advance the chapter by presenting three case studies from the respective authors' experiences of collecting data from fans and festivalgoers at a variety of live events – via surveys, interviews, and informal conversations, to highlight the creative way that informal conversations can glean valid and authentic data. This chapter not only explains how informal conversations can be applied in live event spaces, but also explains how the method offers advantages over the use of other qualitative methods.

Conceptualising Informal Conversations

Informal conversations have been referred to in a number of synonyms including 'informal interviewing', 'natural conversations', or have been equated with 'unstructured' interviews (Bernard, 2017; Gray, 2021; Patton, 2002; Zhang and Wildemuth, 2009). However, informal conversations are different to unstructured interviews. Unstructured interviews are informal, in-depth and non-directive (Saunders, Lewis and Thornhill, 2023) and provide the participant with significant control over their contributions, so they can elicit personal and detailed description of participant realities (Sparkes and Smith, 2014). Davis and Boden (2022) described informal conversations as being casual and spontaneous discussions without disclosing a specific agenda. While unstructured interviews have a loose framework, informal conversations are typically free-flowing with no formal structure. Though it is evident that there are clear similarities between the two methods, Swain and King (2022) argued that informal conversations are different to unstructured interviews because unstructured interviews are typically pre-arranged by both parties in terms of time and place, and both parties understand the area they are going to be

TABLE 9.1 Comparison between unstructured interviews and informal conversations

Unstructured interviews	*Informal conversations*
Loosely organised framework informed by a pre-determined topic or agenda	Casual and free-flowing with no formal structure and without the disclosing of a specific agenda
Pre-arranged by both parties in terms of time	Spontaneous discussions in terms of time
Pre-arranged by both parties in terms of location/place	Spontaneous discussions in terms of location/place
Both parties know what they will be talking about	Only the researcher knows the intended topic of conversation

discussing. Opposed to this, we understand informal conversations to be naturally occurring, even though the researcher has arranged to be at the event, they have not agreed times or locations, and the person as part of the sample is not essentially pre-determined. We have comparatively distinguished the two methods in Table 9.1:

Informal conversations are creative because they are fluid and can flow with whatever is happening within the conversation. This allows for more creativity in terms of narrative linked to experiences. The researcher and participant have a dynamic relationship within informal conversations, through their interaction the researcher can interject or add to the participant's narrative, encouraging creative conversation (also see González Viveros, Sierra and Rodríguez, 2020). The lack of formality in a conversation enables and promotes more opportunities for creativity, as opposed to an unstructured interview – which still retains an element of rigidity. We now present three case studies from the respective authors as experiences of collecting data from fans and festivalgoers at a variety of live events – via surveys (Hayes, 2022; Case Study 1), interviews (Brown, 2019; Case Study 2), and informal conversations (Davis, 2020; Case Study 3).

Case Study 1: 2019 Rugby World Cup

Hayes (2022) utilised the survey method in a research project examining the role played by the 2019 Rugby World Cup in shaping visiting fans' travel itineraries, activities, and experiences of the host country, Japan. This method was used as part of a multimodal approach alongside observation, interviews with tourism stakeholders, and document review. The project sought to understand the role of the tournament in the context of the Japanese government's commitment to becoming a 'Sports Nation', one goal of which is to promote tourism development (Ozaki and Kaneko, 2011). The survey element aimed to capture a wide range of visiting fans' experiences, and it is on this method that this case study focuses.

The survey was designed to be completed quickly and efficiently by the participant, recognising that they would be on their way to a rugby match and that the researcher would be holding them up. To this end, in addition to demographic data, the survey was limited to ten questions, and all questions were fitted on one side of A4 paper. The survey combined multiple choice and open-ended questions designed to elicit detailed responses on travel motivations, travel behaviour, and experiences. Survey forms were printed for physical completion and Hayes, while acting as sole researcher, carried multiple clipboards to enable multiple respondents to participate at the same time. The 2019 Rugby World Cup was held in 12 host cities across the country between 20 September and 2 November 2019. For data collection, five cities were chosen where surveys would be conducted: Fukuoka, Kōbe, Kumagaya, Ōsaka, and Yokohama (see Table 9.2 below):

Hayes (2022) was not granted permission to conduct surveys on stadia grounds, which could not have been given by the individual stadia, with whom the author has since engaged with for follow-up interviews, but was controlled by World Rugby, who declined his request. Instead, he positioned himself on public streets leading up to the stadia, specifically those that had been designated as official spectator routes. As well as being included in official maps and event guides, the routes were physically marked out by barriers as well as by volunteers, who were positioned at regular intervals. Local businesses along the routes took advantage of the increased footfall by setting up stalls outside their shops selling street food and alcohol. The atmosphere was carnivalesque, with fans moving as a mass towards the stadium, engaged in conversations, laughing and shouting, and consuming large amounts of alcohol. The carnival or festival atmosphere was further heightened by the provision of entertainments on the routes, with each host city offering something different, including traditional festival floats, musicians and dancers, and opportunities for fans to

TABLE 9.2 2019 Rugby World Cup host city data collection

Host city	Stadium	Data collection dDte(s)
Fukuoka, Fukuoka Prefecture	Fukuoka Hakatanomori Stadium	2 October 2019
Kōbe, Hyōgo Prefecture	Kobe Misaki Stadium	30 September 2019
Kumagaya, Saitama Prefecture	Kumagaya Rugby Stadium	9 October 2019
Ōsaka (Higashiōsaka), Ōsaka Prefecture	Hanazono Rugby Stadium	22 September 2019 28 September 2019 3 October 2019
Yokohama, Kanagawa Prefecture	International Stadium Yokohama	13 October 2019

engage in games and competitions. Although these were liminoid spaces, areas of transition to the stadia where the actual matches would be held, Hayes (2023) found that the routes formed an essential part of the wider event space and experience.

Potential respondents were 'called out to' as they passed Hayes (2022) and asked for a few minutes of their time. Surveys were filled out by hand on paper forms by either the respondent or by Hayes. Generally, non-native speakers of English preferred to give their answers verbally. An unintended consequence of conducting the surveys in person was that at times the interactions bore a closer resemblance to semi-structured interviews. Even in the case of multiple-choice questions, respondents often elaborated upon their answers, providing additional details and contextual information that Hayes (2022) noted in the margins. Collected survey data was entered into a spreadsheet manually before being imported into NVivo for analysis. After the data was cleaned and incomplete surveys were removed, there was a total of 115 valid surveys.

Case Study 2: Live UK Music Festivals

Brown (2019) explored the festivalgoer and their experience at UK music festivals. The main objectives of the study were to identify socio-demographic and psychographic characteristics of UK music festivalgoers, to determine what festivalgoers value in their UK music festival experience and to discover the extent to which festivalgoers' socio-demographic and psychographic characteristics determine the value of experience attributes (also see Brown and Sharpley, 2019; Brown, 2022; Brown, 2023; Brown and Pappas, 2023). A mixed method approach was required in order to ensure the depth, breadth and validity of the results. The study was designed around three phases that collectively sought to elicit the perspectives of festival organisers and festivalgoers through qualitative, semi-structured, face-to-face interviews, and the generation of quantitative data through an online survey aimed at festivalgoers. Table 9.3 below highlights the research methods adopted at each stage of the study:

TABLE 9.3 The methods that Brown used to collect data at festivals during the three phases of research

Phase of research	Quantitative research methods	Qualitative research methods
Phase I: Festival organisers		Semi-structured interviews (exploratory)
Phase II: Festivalgoers	Online survey (exploratory)	
Phase III: Festivalgoers		Semi-structured interviews (explanatory and exploratory)

As the aim of this chapter is to focus on data collection with the live event space, this case study will now specifically focus on the Phase III research. Phase III comprised of on-site, face-to-face, semi-structured interviews with festivalgoers. With both an explanatory and exploratory focus, the festivalgoer interviews were conducted in order to support and build upon the previous research, and to allow the researcher to delve deeper into the perspective of festivalgoers. Conducting the interviews on-site at the music festivals allowed for conversations to flow, building up a connection between the interviewee and interviewer and allowing for probing for more information and further clarification in the exploration of the festivalgoer experience. This qualitative data collection technique sought to examine the 'lived' experience, rather than focusing on the evaluated experience from previous methods in the study.

The questions were divided into two sections, collecting socio-demographic information about the festivalgoer along with their evaluations and opinions regarding their experience at UK music festivals. This information was collected to support and explain the quality and value of the UK music festival experience. Questions were asked in order as per the interview guide while allowing for further questions to be added to probe further or clarify any responses. All interviews were audio recorded with permission from participants, transcribed verbatim and thematically coded and analysed. The interviews lasted between 4 and 62 minutes (averaging 15 minutes) and included 1–5 participants per interview, conducted on-site at three UK music festivals during 2015. Access and permission to attend the music festivals to interview festivalgoers on-site was provided by the festival organisers. The details of the three festivals attended are provided in Table 9.4.

These festivals were selected through convenience sampling and accessibility as the festival organisers offered to help support the researcher by providing tickets and permission to undertake the research on-site at their festival. These festivals predominantly attract those with preferences towards rock or metal music, hence limiting the scope of the research. However, attendance at additional festivals was not financially viable. Nevertheless, many of the festivalgoers participating in the interviews on-site had previously attended a variety of other festivals which were acknowledged and utilised in the data analysis stage.

TABLE 9.4 Festival locations in the UK

Festival	Date	Location
HRH (Hard Rock Hell) United	12–15 March 2015	Haven Hafan y Mor Holiday Park, Pwllheli, Gwynedd, Wales
Download festival	12–14 June 2015	Donnington Park, Donnington, Derbyshire, England
Leeds festival	28–30 August 2015	Bramham Park, Leeds, England

A total of 43 interviews with 124 participants were conducted across the three festivals. Both random and convenience sampling were used as the researcher approached festivalgoers without any structured method other than seeking out those that were considered to be more likely or willing to participate. This included approaching festivalgoers while they were relaxing away from any of the main stages. This also ensured a better recording of the interview.

For the interviews at HRH United, the socio-demographic question categories had been previously printed on paper for the interviewee to complete in order to respect the comfort of potential interviewees; it is documented that some respondents may feel awkward or uncomfortable verbally answering questions regarding annual income, gender and other personal questions (Locke and Gilbert, 1995). However, it became apparent that this was not practical owing to the weather and potential issues with privacy and storage. Therefore, it was decided that, at the other festivals, socio-demographic questions would be posed verbally and recorded. Anonymity and confidentiality remained as no personal details that could be associated directly to the participants were included in the interview.

Limitations of Surveys and Semi-structured Interviews at Live Events

To present informal conversations as the most appropriate method to collect data from fans or festivals at live events, in this section we highlight some of the limitations that emerged from the methods employed in Case Studies 1 and 2 and the challenges they presented to the researchers.

In Case Study 1, Hayes (2022) found that although he was administering a survey, respondents were providing rich, qualitative data through conversation, which could not be adequately captured within the rigid structure of the survey. Indeed, although the survey asked open-ended questions, respondents wrote their answers in note form and yet provided much more detailed information to him verbally. While the survey data was still valuable, on reflection semi-structured interviews may have been able to capture a greater amount of information from respondents.

One of the major issues and limitations of the survey method faced by Hayes (2022) was the difficulty of recruiting respondents. While he was able to collect enough responses for the data to be usable, the sum of 115 valid surveys was the combined total across seven days split between five stadia. When attempting to solicit survey responses, he often found that the passing rugby fans would ignore him or even change direction and increase the distance to prevent him from asking for their participation. Some fans also expressed frustration at being asked to participate in a survey. O'Grady (2013), when discussing EDM (electronic dance music) festivals, describes this as 'intrusion' by researchers. She argues that interrupting festivalgoers to discuss their experience 'destabilises it and threatens to collapse it entirely' (2013, p. 35). This is consistent with other literature in both tourism and events studies. For example, John Urry's seminal theory of the tourist gaze posits that tourists take on behaviours while engaged in tourism that differ from their everyday behaviour and that this affects how they perceive what they see and *gaze* upon while on holiday (Urry and Larsen, 2011). Engaging in tourism, including travelling to attend an international sports event, is ultimately a break from everyday life, allowing the individual to focus on leisure activities. In attempting to ask people to participate in the survey, Hayes (2022) was interrupting their tourist gaze and disrupting the event environment. It is therefore understandable that many rugby fans would not have been interested in participating in a survey. However, a semi-structured interview may have also had the same effect of pulling the respondent out of the event mood and atmosphere, potentially affecting their experience of the rest of the day. It is in contexts such as this that unstructured interviews or informal conversations may offer a solution.

Brown (2019) chose to conduct semi-structured interviews because there was an element of informality whereby the researcher could ask additional questions or direct the interview towards something specific the participant has responded with (see Adhabi and Anozie, 2017). However, Brown (2019) found some key limitations when using semi-structured interviews as a form of data collection at the live music festivals. Some respondents were naturally biased in their opinions. For example, festivalgoers are having an enjoyable experience, they are less likely (whether consciously or not) to disclose or discuss negative experiences (also see Boyce and Neale, 2006). Similarly, the opposite occurred if a festivalgoer was having a negative experience, and, as a consequence, they did not refer to previous positive experiences. It was found that interviewees were more likely to be polite in an attempt to adhere to social norms, and may have just agreed with Brown or said what they believed she wished to hear.

Due to the power dynamics between the researcher and the participant, the semi-structured interview process is more formal, and the balance is structured towards the interviewer leading the interview. Due to these formalities, it is less likely that a researcher can glean honest and accurate data. Brown found that when a rapport was established during the interview, and the participant realised that Brown was also an avid festivalgoer, the interviews essentially morphed into informal conversations. It was at this juncture that Brown gained the most data.

As the interviews conducted were often with more than one individual, another limitation that could be considered with interviews is the potential influence of inter-participant dynamics. Frey and Fontana (1991) asserted that the social dynamics of group members can stimulate expression and elaboration, however, it is also more common in group interviews for individuals to be stifled or dominated by one or two group members. While group interviews are more efficient and reserve resources by interviewing multiple people in the same time-frame, Frey and Fontana also warned against the higher production of irrelevant data as participants may distract one another or re-direct conversations away from the research purpose. However, in order for Brown to conduct interviews with festivalgoers at the festival site, the success-ful participation of individuals sometimes relied on interviewing groups rather than isolating individuals from their social circle which could have negatively impacted on their festival experience and the honesty in their responses (if they agreed to participate).

Case Study 3: Live PDC Darts Events

The previous section analysed some of the limitations faced in the previous two case studies when collecting data from fans and festivalgoers using survey and semi-structured interview methods. This final case study explains the pro-cess of how Davis (2020) conducted informal conversations at live Professional Darts Corporation (PDC) darts events in multipurpose arenas. Davis examined how darts fans' performances and creation of the atmosphere at live darts events have been the main reason for the rapid global transformation of professional darts in the twenty-first century (also see Davis, 2022; Davis, 2023; Davis and Gibbons, 2023). The collection of data for the study occurred across the 2016, 2017, and 2018 PDC darts seasons (Table 9.5):

During the data collection, Davis was granted 'access all areas' to live PDC tournaments around the world. With this rare opportunity, he was able to fully explore how the fans perform at all live darts events across the PDC circuit. By the conclusion of the 2018 PDC darts season, Davis (2020) had collected the data necessary where the overall study had reached the point of saturation (see Hennink and Kaiser, 2022) and no new findings were being revealed at any of the live PDC events attended.

Similar to the other case studies presented, Davis (2020) utilised an eclectic range of qualitative, ethnographic methods (non-participant observation, semi-structured interviews, informal conversations and visual methods) to collect the necessary data for the objectives of the study. The data collection was not a one-off, but an ongoing process that entailed several stages during visits to various live PDC events. With a darts event lasting between one and twenty days, there was the opportunity to attend events in repeated measure to collect additional data over a period of one to three days. While a multimodal approach was taken to collect data, the primary methods used to glean data from the live event spaces were informal conversations with darts fans within the multipurpose arenas (n=80); and the semi-structured interviews conducted with the PDC (current and former) players, administrators and management (n=30).

The sample of participants consisted of both males and females,[1] over the age of 18. Fans were approached randomly: no pre-selection process occurred. Of those that Davis (2020) spoke to, 24 were PDC 'members' (a PDC member

TABLE 9.5 The premier live PDC Darts events between 2016 and 2018 which Davis attended

Event	Location	2016 season	2017 season	2018 season
Unibet Masters (January)	Arena MK, Milton Keynes	✓	✓	✓
Players Championships (Each month from Feb toNov)	Barnsley Metrodome/ Various venues	✓	✓	✓
Betway Premier League (February–May)	Various arenas across the UK, Dublin, Rotterdam (Netherlands) and Berlin (Germany)	✓	✓	✓
Coral UK Open (March)	Butlin's Resort, Minehead, England	✓	✓	✓
US Masters (July)	Tropicana Hotel, Las Vegas, USA	NOT HELD	✓	✓
BetVictor World Matchplay (July)	Winter Gardens, Blackpool	✓	✓	✓
Unibet Champions League of Darts (September)	Motorpoint Arena, Cardiff	✓	✓	✓
PartyPoker World Grand Prix (October)	Citywest Hotel, Dublin	✓	✓	✓
Singha Beer Grand Slam of Darts (November)	Wolverhampton Civic Hall	✓	✓	✓
William Hill PDC World Darts Championship (December/January)	Alexandra Palace, London	✓	✓	✓

is someone who had paid an annual membership which allows members to watch all PDC events online and purchase tickets for some of the PDC televised tournaments in a priority sale period ahead of the general sale tickets); 38 were not members but had attended a PDC event before, and 18 were first-time attendees, though all first-time attendees stated that they had watched the sport of darts on the television before. The characteristics of the fan sample are presented in Table 9.6:

The aim of the informal conversations conducted with the fans was to gain their experiences and emotions when attending a darts event. This was to try and obtain data linked to the aim of Davis' (2020) doctoral study, which centred upon the critical role of prosumer fandom at live darts events, and how overt demonstrations of darts fandom in the live arenas helped foster a rapid transformation of the PDC version of the sport. In regard to ethics, consent

TABLE 9.6 Characteristics of the PDC fan sample – 80 fans

Characteristics of the fan sample	Numbers	Percentage (%)
Male	50	63
Female	30	37
Age	>35 (46)	57
	<35 (34)	43
PDC members	24	30
Not a member but attended a PDC Event before	38	47
First-time attendees	18	23

was implied in different ways. While Davis (2020) asked for verbal confirmation that they could have a conversation with the fan, it was also noted that within the fine print in the terms and conditions of tickets for live PDC darts events, the recording of persons or perspectives would occur before, during and after an event. Therefore, the confirmation was essentially embedded within the ticket transaction. However, if the fan did not want to participate or speak, Davis agreed that he would not use their points.

The best time period to speak to the fans was prior to the darts matches starting, or between matches. The main reason that discussion was avoided while a match was in play was that there are certain moments in a darts match that become very emotive, and the fans' responses may have been unclear or unfocused, such as if a lengthy question was asked when the match was at a pivotal moment (for example at the end of a leg, a set, or if a player had a chance to complete a nine-darter). The fan may have responded with half an answer or forgotten the point of the question, meaning a sub-question would have had to be asked and this could have increased the length of the conversation.

A key step was to decide where the informal conversations would be conducted. The multipurpose arena was chosen because it was within the live event space that the fan would portray their darts fandom. With the issues regarding fan typologies (critiqued by the likes of Dixon, 2016), rather than focusing on a specific type of fan to interview, Davis (2020) was open to speaking to any type of fan and moved through the arena to ensure he spoke to a variety of fans. This kept his position neutral and ensured the sample was consistent. This helped to avoid bias in searching for fans wearing fancy dress (for example) as Davis required input from all fans to understand the diverse perspectives or viewpoints of the live event.

Most observers will try to develop a system in which they can record their responses (see Harari et al., 2016). It was understood that logging responses would require a pen, paper, or a book/clipboard in a highly active environment, which would have been more obvious to the participants close to Davis' position in the event areas could have heightened their reaction and sense of perspective, thus their attitude to engage may have changed (as seen in Case Study 1). Davis

(2020) did not audio record any informal conversations on a dictaphone or smartphone, as he felt this moved towards the interview method, and respondents can provide stilted answers or become nervous when being audio recorded. Immediately following the conversation, he typed up the conversation notes into the *Notes* application of his smartphone in the live event setting.

For Case Study 3, the collection of data with the fans can be established as informal conversations in a number of ways: the way in which Davis approached fans spontaneously in the multipurpose arena; the casual and free-flowing conversation, which typically lasted on average between 1 and 5 mins; and that only Davis knew the intended topic of conversation as he approached a fan. The timeframe available to conduct a conversation with the fan in the natural PDC darts arena left no practical time to build a relationship – a rapport was created, but with no depth: when analysing responsive interviewing, the relationship that is created is supposed to last over a sustained period and often outlasts the period of research (Rubin and Rubin, 2012). This was not possible with the nature of the setting and the need to move among the fans to obtain data. There was no way the fan could be treated as a 'partner' rather than a 'subject of research', which is what Rubin and Rubin (2012, p. 38) outline as a key element of the interviewing technique.

On reflection, a key to informal conversations being one of the most valid and creative methods when collecting data at live events was the location. Taking participants out of the live event setting to conduct interviews or focus groups can lead to protracted answers, refusal to engage with the researchers, or persons just saying 'anything' to return to the actual event experience. This is particularly apt when fans are in queues or stationed in certain areas such as disabled viewing platforms or hospitality sections. They will converse in these areas in an informal conversational manner, but do not want to be moved from their position. Added to this, recording the conversations appeared to make fans uneasy or nervous, so they would become less receptive to responding to many questions, and any unstructured interview would lead to more closed responses and the discussion would be very staccato. Informal conversations were more fluid and fostered a deeper range of perspectives being provided by participants, while also encouraging other fans to add to the conversations, adding more context.

Conclusion

The aim of this chapter was to promote a greater use of informal conversations in qualitative research. The informal conversation method has specific advantages in the live event setting that are beneficial for researchers in the field as opposed to other methods. This chapter argued that informal conversations can be considered to be a more effective method than the likes of surveys or interviews in live event settings and create more authentic data than the likes of unstructured interviews in the live event space. We presented three case studies as experiences of collecting data from consumers at a variety of live events, via surveys (Hayes, 2022), interviews (Brown, 2019) and informal conversations (Davis, 2020). It was key to highlight the benefits and the issues with conducting surveys and interviews at live events, to further explicate why informal conversations are the most naturalistic and valid method of data collection in these settings. The final case study presented the process of how informal conversations can be conducted and the process of how to log data in live event settings.

Like many creative methods, there are certain methodological issues linked to conducting informal conversations regarding validity, authenticity and ethics that must be considered by researchers before conducting the conversations. As this method is emerging within the field of event studies, these issues have not yet been fully explored, and require further consideration. However, by presenting these case studies and our processes in this chapter, we believe that using informal conversations as a qualitative method is one of the most creative ways to gain insightful data from fans and festivalgoers in live event spaces. Future research could explore the use of informal conversations as a qualitative method in other event spaces or analyse the use of informal conversations from an interdisciplinary perspective. Researchers could also expand on the power dynamics between researchers and participants when collecting qualitative data and strategies that can be used to gain valid and authentic information.

Note

1 Gender which they identified as, to meet the requirements of the UK Government Equality Act (2010). It was explained that they did not have to identify this if they did not want to.

References

Adhabi, E. and Anozie, C.B. (2017) 'Literature review for the type of interview in qualitative research', *International Journal of Education*, 9(3), pp. 86–97. https://doi.org/10.5296/ije.v9i3.11483

Angotti, N. and Sennott, C. (2014) 'Implementing 'insider' ethnography: Lessons from the public conversations about HIV/AIDS project in rural South Africa', *Qualitative Research*, 15(4), pp. 437–453. https://doi.org/10.1177/1468794114543402

Bernard, H.R. (2017) *Research methods in anthropology: Qualitative and quantitative approaches.* Lanham, MD: Rowan and Littlefield Publishers.

Bossey, A. (2020) 'Accessibility all areas? UK live music industry perceptions of current practice and Information and Communication Technology improvements to accessibility for music festival attendees who are deaf or disabled', *International Journal of Event and Festival Management*, 11(1), pp. 6–25. https://doi.org/10.1108/IJEFM-03-2019-0022

Boyce, C. and Neale, P. (2006) *Conducting in-depth interviews: A guide for designing and conducting in-depth interviews for evaluation input.* Watertown, MA: Pathfinder international.

Brown, A.E. (2019) *Is it just the music? Towards an understanding of festival-goers and their experience at UK Music Festivals.* [Unpublished thesis]. University of Central Lancashire.

Brown, A.E. (2022) 'Is it just the music?: Understanding the atmosphere in festivalgoers experience at British rock music festivals'. In R. Sharpley (Ed.), *Routledge handbook of the tourist experience.* Abingdon: Routledge, pp. 301–314.

Brown, A.E. (2023) 'Cocreation and engagement: What festivalgoers want in the UK rock festival experience', *Event Management*, 27(2), pp. 201–216. https://doi.org/10.3727/152599521X16367300695690

Brown, A.E. and Pappas, N. (2023) 'Added value and music events: A festivalgoer perspective', *Annals of Leisure Research*, 26(1), pp. 117–139. https://doi.org/10.1080/11745398.2021.1878378

Brown, A.E. and Sharpley, R. (2019) 'Understanding festival-goers and their experience at UK music festivals', *Event Management*, 23(4–5), pp. 699–720. https://doi.org/10.3727/152599519X15506259855733

Castle, C.L., Burland, K. and Greasley, A. (2022) 'Attending live music events with a visual impairment: Experiences, accessibility and recommendations for the future', *Arts and the Market*, 12(2), pp. 164–179. https://doi.org/10.1108/AAM-04-2022-0015

Cressey, P.G. (1932) *The taxi-dance hall: A sociological study in commercialized recreation and city life.* Chicago: The University of Chicago Press.

Davis, L. (2020) *The critical role of prosumer fandom in the spectacle of PDC darts.* [Unpublished thesis] Teesside University.

Davis, L. (2022) 'Don't stop the party: Exploring the tools used by fans to create atmospheres at live PDC darts events', *Managing Sport and Leisure*, pp. 1–21. https://doi.org/10.1080/23750472.2022.2105252

Davis, L. (2023) 'Stand up if you love "The Darts" – Understanding some of the catalysts responsible for the rapid transformation of PDC darts in the 2000s', *Sport in History.* https://doi.org/10.1080/17460263.2023.2175029

Davis, L. and Boden, B. (2022) 'Analysing the landside passenger experience during the 2022 UK airport delays', *Fourth International Aviation Management Conference 2022*, Dubai, (UAE), 21 November–22 November. IAMC. https://www.eau.ac.ae/media/1672/iamc_2022_proceedings.pdf

Davis, L. and Gibbons, T. (2023) "We can't participate like this at football, can we'? Exploring in-person performative prosumer fandom at live PDC darts events', *Journal of Consumer Culture*, 23(4), 1036–1053. https://doi.org/10.1177/14695405231168971

Densley, J. (2013) *How gangs work: An ethnography of youth violence.* Palgrave: Macmillan.

Dixon, K. (2016) 'Fandom'. In E. Cashmore and K. Dixon (Eds.), *Studying football.* London: Routledge, pp. 44–63.

Draper, J., Young, L. and Fenich, G. (2018) 'Event management research over the past 12 years: What are the current trends in research methods, data collection, data analysis procedures, and event types?', *Journal of Convention and Event Tourism*, 19(1), pp. 3–24. https://doi.org/10.1080/15470148.2017.1404533

Equality Act. 2010. https://www.legislation.gov.uk/ukpga/2010/15

Finkel, R. and Dashper, K. (2020) 'Accessibility, diversity and inclusion in events'. In S. Page and J. Connell (Eds.), *The Routledge handbook of events*, 2nd edn. London: Routledge, pp. 475–490.

Finkel, R., Sharp, B. and Sweeney, M. (2018) *Accessibility, inclusion, and diversity in critical event studies.* London: Taylor and Francis.

Frey, J.H. and Fontana, A. (1991) 'The group interview in social research', *The Social Science Journal*, 28(2), pp. 175–187.

Getz, D. (2010) 'The nature and scope of festival studies', *International Journal of Event Management Research*, 5(1), pp. 1–47.

González Viveros, J.M., Sierra, V. and Rodríguez, C. (2020). 'Nurturing creative confidence through narrative conversations', *The International Journal of Design Education*, 14(4), 79–91. https://doi.org/10.18848/2325-128X/CGP/v14i04/79-91

Gray, D.E. (2021) *Doing research in the real world*, 5th edn. Thousand Oaks, CA: Sage Publications.

Harari, G.M., Lane, N.D., Wang, R., Crosier, B.S., Campbell, A.T. and Gosling, S.D. (2016) 'Using smartphones to collect behavioral data in psychological science: Opportunities, practical considerations, and challenges', *Perspectives on Psychological Science*, 11(6), pp. 838–854. https://doi.org/10.1177/1745691616650285

Hayes, C.J. (2022) 'Gaikokujin ragubī fan kara mita kyōto – ragubī wārudo kappu 2019 nihon taikai no kankyaku no kankō katsudō wo chūshin ni' [Kyoto through the eyes of foreign rugby fans: Tourism activities during the Rugby World Cup 2019], *Kyōto furitsu gaku rekisaikan kiyō*, 5, pp. 93–120.

Hayes, C.J. (2023) 'Placemaking in the periphery: Leveraging liminoid spaces for host promotions and experience creation at the Japan 2019 Rugby World Cup', *Tourism and Hospitality* 4(2), pp. 214–232. https://doi.org/10.3390/tourhosp4020013

Hennink, M. and Kaiser, B.N. (2022) 'Sample sizes for saturation in qualitative research: A systematic review of empirical tests', *Social Science and Medicine*, 292, 114523. https://doi.org/10.1016/j.socscimed.2021.114523

Kara, H. (2015) *Creative research methods in the social sciences. A practical guide.* Bristol: Policy Press.

Kara, H. (2023) *The Bloomsbury handbook of creative research methods.* London: Bloomsbury Publishing.

Korobov, N. (2018) 'Indirect pursuits of intimacy in romantic couples everyday conversations: A discourse analytic approach', *Forum Qualitative Sozialforschung/Forum: Qualitative Social Research*, 19(2). https://doi.org/10.17169/fqs-19.2.3012

Lee, M.J. and Back, K.-J. (2005) 'A review of convention and meeting management research 1990–2003: Identification of statistical methods and subject areas', *Journal of Convention and Event Tourism*, 7(2), pp. 1–20. https://doi.org/10.1300/J452v07n02_01

Locke, S.D. and Gilbert, B.O. (1995) 'Method of psychological assessment, self-disclosure, and experiential differences: A study of computer, questionnaire, and interview assessment formats', *Journal of Social Behavior and Personality*, 10(1), pp. 255–273.

Mair, J. (2012) '*A review of business events literature*', *Event Management*, 16(2), pp. 133–141. https://doi.org/10.3727/152599512X13343565268339

McGillivray, D., McPherson, G. and Misener, L. (2018) 'Major sporting events and geographies of disability', *Urban Geography*, 39(3), pp. 329–344. https://doi.org/10.1080/02723638.2017.1328577

Mead, M. (1928) *Coming of age in Samoa: A psychological study of primitive youth for western civilisation.* New York: Harper Perennial.

Misener, L., McGillivray, D., McPherson, G. and Legg, D. (2015) 'Leveraging parasport events for sustainable community participation: The Glasgow 2014 Commonwealth Games', *Annals of Leisure Research*, 18(4), pp, 450–469. https://doi.org/10.1080/11745398.2015.1045913

Mowrer, E.R. (1932) *Family disorganization: An introduction to a sociological analysis.* Chicago: University of Chicago Press.

O'Grady, A. (2013) 'Interrupting flow: Researching play, performance and immersion in festival scenes', *Dancecult: Journal of Electronic Dance Music Culture*, pp. 18–38. https://dj.dancecult.net/index.php/dancecult/article/view/353

Ozaki, M. and Kaneko, F. (2011) 'A history of post-war sport policy in Japan and the United Kingdom', *Hitotsubashi Journal of Social Studies*, 43(2), pp. 81–102. https://www.jstor.org/stable/43294559

Palmer, V.M. (1928) *Field studies in sociology: A students' manual*. Chicago: University of Chicago Press.

Park, R.E., Burgess, E. and McKenzie, R. (1925) *The city*. Chicago: University of Chicago Press.

Park, S.B. and Park, K. (2017) 'Thematic trends in event management research', *International Journal of Contemporary Hospitality Management*, 29(3), pp. 848–861. https://doi.org/10.1108/IJCHM-09-2015-0521

Patton, M.Q. (2002) *Qualitative research and evaluation methods*. Thousand Oaks, CA: Sage.

Platt, L. and Finkel, R. (2020) *Gendered violence at international festivals: An interdisciplinary perspective*. Abingdon: Routledge.

Rubin, H.J. and Rubin, I.S. (2012) *Qualitative interviewing: The art of hearing data*, 3rd edn. Thousand Oaks, CA: Sage.

Saunders, M., Lewis, P. and Thornhill, A. (2023) *Research methods for business students*, 9th edn. Harlow: Pearson Education Limited.

Sharp, B. (2018) 'Volunteering and wellbeing: A case study of the Glasgow 2014 Commonwealth Games volunteer programmes'. In R. Finkel, B. Sharp and M. Sweeney (Eds.), *Accessibility, inclusion, and diversity in critical event studies*. Abingdon: Routledge.

Sparkes, A. and Smith, B. (2014) *Qualitative research methods in sport, exercise and health from process to product*, 1st edn. Abingdon: Routledge.

Swain, J. and King, B. (2022) 'Using informal conversations in qualitative research', *International Journal of Qualitative Methods*, 21. https://doi.org/10.1177/16094069221085056

Swain, J. and Spire, Z. (2020) 'The role of informal conversations in generating data, and the ethical and methodological issues they raise', *Forum Qualitative Sozialforschung/Forum: Qualitative Social Research*, 21(1). https://doi.org/10.17169/fqs-.Art10,21.1.3344

Thomson, K.E. and Trigwell, K.R. (2018) 'The role of informal conversations in developing university teaching?', *Studies in Higher Education*, 43(9), pp. 1536–1547. https://doi.org/10.1080/03075079.2016.1265498

Urry, J. and Larsen, J. (2011) *The Tourist Gaze 3.0*. Thousand Oaks, CA: Sage.

Van der Vaart, G., Van Hoven, B. and Huigen, P.P. (2018) 'Creative and arts-based research methods in academic research: Lessons from a participatory research project in the Netherlands', In *Forum Qualitative Sozialforschung/Forum: Qualitative Social Research*, 19(2), p. 30. https://doi.org/10.17169/fqs-19.2.2961

Webb, S. and Webb, B. (1932) *Methods of social study*. London: Longman Green.

Wirth, L. (1927) 'The Ghetto', *American Journal of Sociology*, 33(1), pp. 57–71. https://doi.org/10.1086/214333

Yoo, J. and Weber, K. (2005) 'Progress in convention tourism research', *Journal of Hospitality and Tourism Research*, 29(2), pp. 194–222. https://doi.org/10.1177/1096348004272177

Zhang, Y. and Wildemuth, B.M. (2009) 'Qualitative analysis of content'. In B.M. Wildemuth (Ed.), *Applications of social research methods to questions in information and library science*. London: Libraries Unlimited. pp. 1–12.

10

WHEN HORROR AND LOCAL STORIES MEET THE ARCHIVES

Participatory Events in the North of Ireland

Laura Aguiar
Ulster University, Derry, Northern Ireland

Bronagh McAtasney
Northern Ireland Screen, Belfast, Northern Ireland

Introduction

This chapter examines two (free) filmmaking events and the participatory creative approach taken by the authors in their creative outreach roles for Northern Ireland Screen and partner organisations to reach out to non-traditional audiences of archives – young and cross-border people.[1] *The Horror!* was a week-long film camp that connected 13–15 year-olds with film archives and filmmaking techniques in 2021. The *Northwest Film Challenge* was a two-week online film challenge that saw first-time and amateur filmmakers creatively reuse archives and make films for a film festival in 2023.

Through our case studies, we demonstrate how participation and creativity can be powerful audience development tools and how events delivered within professional settings can be fertile grounds for subsequent scholar research to evaluate the strengths, limitations, and impact of events. We argue that practice-based reflective approaches can offer a creative method to look back at the event design and delivery processes and draw learnings from these.

Before proceeding, it is important to define what we mean by 'practice-based', as this is just one approach among various methods of conducting creative practice research. Within the academic landscape, 'learning through doing' has acquired several monikers, including 'practice-led', 'arts-based', 'participatory action research', 'practice as research', and 'research-led practice' (Smith and Dean, 2009; Nelson, 2013; Leavy, 2017; Skains, 2018; Kara, 2020). While discussions on epistemologies, terminologies, and paradigms are still in development, the myriad of terms highlight how transdisciplinary creative practice has

DOI: 10.4324/9781032686424-10

become and also how scholars are coming out of silos to generate insights "whether through the act of creating artistic works or through their subsequent documentation and theoretical exploration" (Smith and Dean, 2009, p. 2). For the purposes of this chapter, we have used the term 'practice-based' which encompasses research that derives from practice and is expressed in conventional word-based formats (Nelson, 2013, p. 10).

Although both events were delivered outside of an academic context by the authors,[2] we kept a journal with notes of meetings, documentation, and reflections as the events were delivered. As will be discussed later, journals can be creative tools for data collection in practice-based reflective research. As Lyle Skains observes, reflection can be dependent on memory and when conducted after the creative project (rather than during or as close to it as possible), it "can be an unfortunately fallible method", and may fail "to offer insights into the cognitive processes of creation" (Skains, 2018, p. 87). Therefore, we draw on our notes as well as on participant feedback surveys to carry out our analysis of the two events.

'Participatory' is another keyword here and also a term that has been used to mean many different things. In media projects, for instance, Katerina Cizek notes that there is now a multitude of methodologies, with each "exploring new forms and new ways of telling stories in terms of the mechanics of it, and the technology" (Miller, Little and High, 2017, p. 36). Therefore, the levels of participation in an event can vary and attendees can get involved in different ways, from co-creating content with the facilitators but leaving the technical work to the professionals, to going full DIY ('do it yourself'). As will be seen later, our participatory approach evokes action, agency and shared learning and gives attendees full control over the production and editing of their stories.

As we discuss next, this is not the most common outreach approach by archives, but it is in line with the 'community turn' that archives have been experiencing since the 1980s. We focus on this discussion now, and then analyse the methodology employed when delivering *The Horror!* and *The Northwest Film Challenge* and share some reflections and 'think points'. By bringing archives and participatory filmmaking debates into the field of Event Studies, and conducting a *posteriori* reflective analysis, we hope to demonstrate how professional practitioners can contribute to academic debates around issues of accessibility, creative (and meaningful) engagement, and the impact of events.

The Participatory Archives

Archives have a long history and over the centuries, their roles have evolved significantly, transitioning from storage and preservation centres to the main places for capturing, preserving, sharing, and memorialising our everyday lives (Giannachi, 2016, p. 76). Since the 1980s, the traditional perception of archives as rigid, bureaucratic institutions responsible for preserving official history has been undergoing a transformation. Archives now offer a more fluid perspective of history that better captures the diversity of the societies that create them (Popple, Prescott and Mutibwa, 2020, p. 1).

The archives of today come in many shapes and sizes: audio-visual, written texts, photographs, sound recordings, postcards, medical records, websites, social media posts, to name a few. This dynamic perspective is bringing about a fundamental shift in the way we capture and curate collective memories. It is also reshaping our conception of archives, their operational principles, and the individuals involved in their management. Furthermore, activities such as genealogy are fostering a deeper sense of involvement and community identity and digital catalogues are becoming increasingly prevalent, facilitating civil society's remote access to archives.

In line with the wider heritage sector, archives are also experiencing a "community turn" which is re-evaluating the roles of users (Grau, Coones and Rühse, 2017). Community-based archives (those established by and within communities rather than governments) are springing up and users who are helping identify, digitise, and archive a nation's history through online crowd-sourcing (Giannachi, 2016, p. 144). Consequently, these shifts are leading to a re-evaluation of the intrinsic value of archives and are bringing new challenges, namely heightened awareness of the need to identify exclusions in collections and fill gaps, growing demand for new digital services, and new models of digital preservation and curation (Giannachi, 2016; Grau, Coones and Rühse, 2017; Popple, Prescott and Mutibwa, 2020).

It should be evident through this brief overview how archives are in the process of contestation, construction, and reconstruction. There is a shift, albeit gradual, from being static repositories primarily catering to a select few, towards evolving into inclusive spaces of experimentation which are accessible to a broader audience (Giannachi, 2016; Benoit and Eveleigh, 2019; Popple, Prescott and Mutibwa, 2020). We hope to demonstrate here how *The Horror!* and the *Northwest Film Challenge* are good case studies of how archives can utilise creative methods in event design and how subsequent reflections can provide insights for researchers interested in incorporating participatory methods into their own projects.

Northern Ireland Screen

Northern Ireland Screen is a government agency, funded by the Department of the Economy and Department for Communities. It is committed to creating a viable and sustainable film industry in Northern Ireland and such commitment extends across all aspects of film production including skills and education. Their current strategy *Stories, Skills & Sustainability* places storytelling at the heart of what the agency seeks to do.[3] This strategy forms the focus for the

Heritage & Education department of Northern Ireland Screen. Within this department, a team of cataloguers, curators, and engagement and education staff process thousands of films from a wide source of donations (private collections, independent filmmakers, the Ulster Television archive and more). The department engages the public with the film heritage of Northern Ireland via the Digital Film Archive (DFA),[4] public engagement, curatorial events and in liaison with schools, colleges and universities. This also includes programmes to create new film which will in turn be added to the archive.

As a relatively young society, with a large rural population, Northern Ireland's film archive is relatively small compared to other parts of the United Kingdom, and the country does not have an official moving image archive. This means that Northern Ireland Screen does not have a dedicated archive storage facility and most films are retained by the owners of the film with only digital copies being kept by Northern Ireland Screen. The one exception is the archive of Ulster Television (1959–2015) with their physical files being stored at the country's official archives PRONI (Public Record Office of Northern Ireland).

In addition, the archive tends to be urban-based (mostly within the capital, Belfast) and in terms of private collections, somewhat limited to economically advantaged communities. However, through outreach and engagement, the department seeks to capture the stories of all parts of Northern Ireland society. This includes welcoming donations of films from many sources, a dedicated digitisation programme and facilitating the creation of new films with under-represented groups, such as rural communities, women, the LGBTQIA+, disability, and international communities. These new films are then added to the DFA, such as the ones created during the two case studies we will examine now.

The Horror!

The Horror! was a week-long filmmaking camp that connected 15 young people, aged 13–15, with the DFA in the summer of 2021. The camp was co-delivered with creative media hub the Nerve Centre and PRONI and was one of the 30 outreach projects delivered under a wider programme called *Making the Future.*

Funded by the European Union's PEACE IV Programme, *Making the Future* (2018–2021) was a cultural programme by Nerve Centre, PRONI, National Museums NI and the Linen Hall Library. The programme brought people of diverse backgrounds and ages together to use archives to explore the past, learn new skills and improve community relations. Northern Ireland Screen partnered with PRONI on various projects and *The Horror!* was one of them.

The aim of *The Horror!* was to attract young people to the archives. When surveying the literature on heritage engagement, it is visible that PRONI and Northern Ireland Screen are not alone when it comes to poor youth engagement. Réka Fogarasi Musso traced several reasons including: time and money limitations; culture not regarded as a priority; non-appealing offers; do not see their values, identity and objects represented in such places; lack of public transport; and staff limited capacity and skill set to creatively attract this audience group (Fogarasi Musso, 2023, p. 16). Young people, writes Graham Black, want "active experiences, have higher expectations from what is on offer and are less willing to accept poor quality" (Black, 2012, p. 38).

With this in mind, we used horror filmmaking as a (fun) hook to attract young people to the archives and adopted a film camp approach to maintain sustained engagement over five consecutive days. We chose to focus on the Spence Brothers film collection which contains low (or zero) budget films made by amateur filmmakers Noel and Roy Spence. This collection covers over fifty years of film history, with film subjects ranging from crafty leprechauns, space creatures to Rockabilly Rebels, and Frankenstein's monster.[5] This collection was chosen to get young filmmakers to think about the art of filmmaking, especially how special effects technology has evolved and how our rich film traditions must be preserved and made accessible to future generations.

The camp was free to attend, lunch was provided, and participants were recruited via an online open call. Most workshops took place at the Ulster Folk Museum,[6] near Belfast, from 10 am to 3 pm, with each day dedicated to a particular skills-building activity:

- **Day 1: Introductions to the Archives** – we started the film camp at PRONI and after some ice-breakers, we took the participants on a behind-the-scenes tour to see how audio-visual archives are stored and preserved. They were also introduced to the Spence Brothers collection and we screened some of their shorts for inspiration.
- **Day 2: Filmmaking Workshops** – we moved to the Ulster Folk Museum and introduced them to the art of filmmaking. We split them into groups of four and gave them the task of creating a one-minute non-dialogue horror film. The groups wrote the script and storyboards for their films.
- **Day 3: Makeup and Acting Workshops** – we worked with external facilitators, Connie McGrath and Rob Crawford who taught them basic special effects make-up and acting techniques, respectively.
- **Day 4: Filming Day** – we spent the day filming across the Ulster Folk Museum. McGrath returned to help participants with their make-ups.
- **Day 5: Editing Day** – we used the last day to capture the final footage and to edit the films.

The Nerve Centre provided iPads for the filming and editing and the three partner organisations provided staff support: Northern Ireland Screen's Bronagh McAatasney was responsible for selecting and providing the archival material. Laura Aguiar and Jude Mullan were the main filmmaking facilitators from the Nerve Centre. Laura was also the creative producer for the project and, together with Bronagh and PRONI archivist Lynsey Gillespie, was responsible for designing the film camp event and delivering it.

As seen above, we also worked with external facilitators who provided skilled workshops in acting and special effects make-up. However, we took a participatory approach to filmmaking and made sure the young participants went completely DIY (do-it-yourself), *i.e.* they scripted, storyboarded, filmed and edited their own films. Upon completion, a launch event at the historic Strand Cinema in Belfast was organised for participants and guests.[7]

The Northwest Film Challenge

Northern Ireland Screen has its headquarters in Belfast and although it engages with rural audiences consistently through its outreach programmes, people based in the northwest, particularly in cross-border areas, such as counties Donegal and Derry, remain under-targeted. To address this gap, Northern Ireland Screen partnered with the Rathmullan Film Festival, a voluntary-led festival based in Donegal, which is run on a pro-bono basis by Laura.

The Northwest Film Challenge was a two-week online event and took place in January 2023. The Challenge gave aspiring filmmakers based in Donegal and Derry access to selected archival material and permission to creatively reuse them. The filmmakers received filmmaking training via Zoom and each was tasked with producing a three-minute short film repurposing the archives for the festival. 12 people signed up for the project and we used an online survey to capture the participant profile and plan the workshops accordingly:

- Ages: 18 to 60+.
- 50/50 gender split (Female and Male).
- 80% based in county Donegal, 20% based in county Derry.
- Occupations include genealogists, researchers, students, IT professionals, and artists.
- 55% considered themselves first-time filmmakers and 45% have made amateur films before.
- Access to equipment: almost 50/50 split between smartphones only and film equipment.
- Editing experience: most have used editing software before, but some were editing for the first time.

The format for this event was inspired by the *48 Hour Film Project* which is a global event that takes place in over 45 countries throughout the year. Since 2001, the event has brought filmmakers together in-person to respond to a brief and make films in two days.[8] As we wanted to target people who were geographically spread out from each other, encourage first-time filmmakers to participate and to get people to creatively reuse archival material, we adapted the 48-hour format to suit our needs and aims.

The event took place over two weeks with four online sessions (two full Saturdays and two weekday evenings) and was facilitated by the authors, Lynsey Gillespie and filmmakers Camilla Meegan and Kieran Kelly (Póca Productions). As with the above project, each session offered particular skills-building activities and we focused on smartphone filmmaking as participants were less likely to have access to professional equipment and software:

- Session 1 (Saturday) – Introduction to the project, to the archival material, and to each other, and guest talk by film scholar Dr Ciara Chambers about creative reuse of archives.
- Session 2 (Monday) – Pre-production workshop with Póca Productions where the participants learned how to script, storyboard and prepare for production.
- Session 3 (Wednesday) – Filming and sound recording workshop with Póca Productions where they learned how to use their phones to create audio-visual content.
- Session 4 (Saturday) – We used the morning to catch up with the participants and Póca Productions delivered an editing workshop in the afternoon.

Participants were given one week to complete and submit their films and one-to-one online technical support was also offered if they needed help with the filming or editing. A few weeks later, the films premiered at a dog-friendly screening at a local bar during the 2023 edition of the Rathmullan Film Festival.[9]

Reflecting on Our Participatory Practice

Whilst these two training events were delivered within a professional setting, they provide a well-founded laboratory for reflective research by those who were directly involved in delivering them. As mentioned earlier, the authors partnered to co-design and deliver both projects: Bronagh in her capacity as the Access and Outreach Officer for Northern Ireland Screen and Laura in her role as the creative producer for PRONI/Nerve Centre and the Rathmullan Film Festival.

We draw here mostly on journal notes we kept when planning and delivering *The Horror!* and the *Northwest Film Challenge*. While both projects asked participants to fill out evaluation forms upon completion, we could only use feedback for the latter project. As the *Making the Future* project has ended and Laura is no longer employed by it, we do not have access to *The Horror!* forms due to The General Data Protection Regulation (DGPR).

Nevertheless, our journal notes provide important insights into our changing and developing understanding of both events. In her informative overview of creative research methods, Helen Kara highlights how journaling (and project documents) can be useful sources of data gathering (2020, p. 173). In contrast to formal writing formats, they generally embrace nonlinear thinking and lack specific guidelines or rules, enabling professionals and researchers to experiment with diverse writing styles and incorporate visual elements like sketches and doodles. Therefore, as Uwe Flick notes, their usefulness lies in capturing "experiences, ideas, fears, mistakes, confusions, breakthroughs, and problems" that emerge during a project (Flick, 2009, p. 297).

However, through our reflective research, we have discovered that while journaling can foster creativity and spontaneity, it also raises concerns regarding rigour and validity. Journal entries are inherently subjective and reflect the personal perspectives, biases, and experiences of the author. While there is a well-documented cross-disciplinary debate on the benefits of reflexivity in research (see for instance Schön, 1984; Etherington, 2004; Alvesson and Skoldberg, 2009; Kara, 2020) – and we are strong supporters of it – we recognised its limitations. Firstly, due to the personal focus, journals may fail to adequately capture the broader context or complexities of a given topic and, as such, they may provide only a narrow perspective and overlook important factors or variables relevant to the research inquiry. Secondly, unlike structured research methods such as surveys or interviews, journaling typically lacks a systematic approach to categorising, coding and interpreting entries consistently, which may lead to subjective interpretations and unreliable conclusions.

Despite the above limitations, in writing this chapter we found our journals to be helpful tools for subsequent reflection on roles, impact of the project upon personal and professional lives, our relationships with participants (and our perception of the impact we may be making in their lives), and on our feelings about what was happening during the project. However, we also found them to be insufficient as a standalone research method and it was helpful to have access (though partial) to the participant feedback surveys so that our findings had rigour and broader perspectives. In the following, we break down our reflective analysis into the following sections: What & Who, How, When, and Why.

What & Who – Designing the Events

Both events were about celebrating the power of archives and enabling people to be inspired by or creatively reuse them. They were also about audience development and widening the partner organisation's reach: while *The Horror!* enabled Northern Ireland Screen and PRONI to engage with young people, *The Northwest Film Challenge* enabled Northern Ireland Screen and the Rathmullan Film Festival to engage with cross-border audiences.

Therefore, when designing the events, it was important to start with the careful selection of archival material and the activities for participants to take part in. As mentioned earlier, during *The Horror!* the young filmmakers used the Spence Brothers collection as an inspiration to make horror films. As important as introducing them to these amateur filmmakers and teaching them filmmaking techniques, was getting them to think about the role, the value and the ethics of archives. As archivist Rick Prelinger points out, "we have a new generation of especially younger media authors arising, who have no sense that intellectual property laws exist, or that content is property and that they should really even deal with that" (Curran Bernard and Rabin, 2008, p. 289). Hence the importance of events such as *The Horror!* film camp: it not only makes history more engaging to young audiences, but it also teaches them how to ethically re-imagine this history.

For one of the *Northwest Film Challenge* participants, the "free use of the footage cause it's normally covered in red tape" was regarded as the highlight of the event (Participant Feedback, 2023, n.p.). These 'red tapes' are well documented and "finding, using, and licensing archival images and sound can be daunting, even to experienced filmmakers" (Curran Bernard and Rabin, 2008, p. 5). In addition, the extension of copyright terms, skyrocketing licensing costs, limited digital access, sheer volume of collections, not knowing where to start from, or even the thought that 'archives are not for me' have been regarded as reasons for poor engagement with archives and demonstrate the importance of events such as ours in facilitating access (Curran Bernard and Rabin, 2008; Stevens, Flinn and Shepherd, 2010).

Participants were given access to 15 clips from Northern Ireland Screen's Ulster Television Archive collection and permission to creatively re-use them as they wished. These clips were selected by Bronagh and were chosen because they focussed on the geographic area of Northern Donegal and county Derry in Northern Ireland. They were a deliberately wide-range of films including news reports and magazine-style stories on folklore and history. During the event, we reinforced their responsibility as content creators and the need to be respectful to those who created the archives they were reusing. It was important to make them aware of the dangers of taking archives out of their original context, namely: offer anachronistic interpretations and judgements; loose important historical, social, or cultural information and context; infringe on privacy; or perpetuate stereotypes or cultural insensitivities.

We were pleased to see that all filmmakers approached archive reuse with critical thinking, sensitivity to context, and a commitment to ethical practices while being very creative. Their different levels of reuse blew us away and their films varied in approach, from using clips as inspiration to weaving them into new narratives, poignant documentaries and fictional tales, showcasing both community figures and rural life.

How – Online vs In-Person

Lynn van der Wagen and Brenda R. Carlos list seven elements that are 'designed' when planning events, namely the theme of the event; the creative use of the venue (layout); venue décor; technical requirements; staging; entertainment; and catering (2004, p. 26). While *The Horror!* was an in-person experience, we opted to go completely online for *The Northwest Film Challenge*. Participants for both projects were recruited via an open call via the partners' social media channels.

Both authors had experience delivering online training events during the lockdowns and found that the virtual format was the most suitable when seeking participation of people located geographically far from each other, as was the case with the cross-border target audience for *The Northwest Film Challenge*. As seen previously, we were able to recruit people from both Donegal and Derry who perhaps would have not taken part in the project had it taken place fully in-person in either county. However, participant feedback revealed that most wished there was at least one in-person session where they could engage in practical workshops and "hone the precious points of the story telling" (Participant Feedback, 2023, n.p.).

By contrast, having delivered both in-person and online film camps for young people before and during the pandemic for *Making the Future*, Laura had found that in-person engagement allows participants to build stronger connections with the archives and the filmmaking learning is maximised as there is equal access to adequate technology and possibility of group work. The venues for *The Horror!* – PRONI and the Ulster Folk Museum – and the length of time in each were also carefully planned: while the one day at PRONI enabled participants to immerse themselves in the archives, the four days at the museum offered the adequate space for filming, with many buildings and outdoor spaces at the participants' disposal.

Indeed, the COVID-19 pandemic brought many conversations around the benefits and limitations of online and in-person events. As Rafie Cecilia notes, this challenging time proved that "remote participation is not only possible, but actually works" and if remote engagement was often "labelled in the past as a fantasy or as difficult to achieve", it became the only feasible way of running events during the pandemic (Cecilia, 2021, p. 5). Film festivals and heritage organisations such as archives and museums harnessed the web's power to expand their audience base and widen participation by disadvantaged groups in society (Smits, 2021; Crooke et al., 2022).

Moreover, as archives can be "(deliberately) off-putting and intimidating places and as such the physical set-up impedes participation" (Stevens, Flinn and Shepherd, 2010, p. 71), online events enable people to engage with archives where they feel most comfortable – at their homes. This is an important barrier breaker. It is also a more accessible and affordable way of attending events:

participants do not have to spend money to travel to the venue and they make it work around personal and professional commitments. For event organisers, it is a much cheaper venture as there are no travel or catering costs to cover for staff or guests and you have access to a wider pool of facilitators.

However, online events also have limitations, particularly in relation to access and use of digital technology. For *The Northwest Film Challenge*, we were dependent on people's access to equipment and this was uneven: three participants owned professional film equipment and nine relied on their mobile devices for filming and editing. Whilst most participants had access to editing software such as iMovie and DaVinci Resolve, many were editing for the first time.

Furthermore, having experienced and first-time filmmakers in the group made the workshop facilitation challenging particularly given the tight project schedule. We had to provide one-on-one support for the less experienced filmmakers and this proved to be more time consuming than anticipated. Also, some participants, particularly the first-time filmmakers who used mobile devices, struggled to achieve certain visual or audio effects and had to overcome limited storage space, battery issues, sensor sizes and ergonomic features. Consequently, some films lacked the polished cinematic quality expected in professional filmmaking, resulting in uneven aesthetic standards. Delivery of the workshops in-person could have facilitated better support and ensured equal access to professional equipment, enhancing overall technical quality.

However, as the event was more about the process rather than the product, we were all pleased with what the participants achieved, particularly given the short space of time. Whilst one participant highlighted how the project gave him "the confidence to make a short movie about the Derry Walls using equipment to hand", another noted how the event created "a great entry point into film making" and showed "how easy it can be to get started" (Participant Feedback, 2023, n.p.).

Thinking carefully about digital technology is also important when delivering in-person events. For the *Horror!*, we used iPads, tripods and boom microphones for filmmaking. Although project partners Nerve Centre made professional film cameras available for us to use, we opted to use iPads as they are more kid-friendly, *i.e.* participants can easily move them around, use the same device for filming and editing, and if they break them, iPads are cheaper to be fixed/replaced than professional cameras. However, it must be noted that the camera quality of an iPad is nowhere near the quality of a professional camera and by making this choice we were favouring process, *i.e.* their engagement with archives and learning how to make films, rather than the product, *i.e.* the film. When films hold equal or greater importance than the filmmaking process, iPads may not offer the desired quality. Our experience highlights that when designing film camps and challenges it is important to think carefully about whether the chosen digital technology is the right one for the project and the effects of this choice (Miller, Little and High, 2017, pp. 30–31).

When – Scheduling

The Horror! took place over five days, from 10 am to 3 pm, with a lunch break in between. Having run other youth projects, we found that working with two-hour blocks provided enough time for hands-on activities without losing young people's focus. Equally, starting at 10 am was ideal as it was not too early and finishing by 3 pm was necessary as their attention span starts to dwindle. The week-long film camp format is also a great way of sustaining engagement from start to finish and we did not lose participants along the way.

Both authors had experience running online projects during the COVID-19 lockdowns and their varied lengths and formats (and subsequent learnings) informed our approach for *The Northwest Film Challenge*. The project took place over two full Saturdays, from 11 am to 4 pm, with two two-hour workshops and a lunch break in between. These were complemented by two one-hour evening sessions during the week. When reviewing participant feedback, it is noticeable that most found this tight schedule "time efficient" and that it "forced them to make something" and to learn "a great deal of relevant information in a short space of time while also allowing everyone to get to know one another a bit" (Participant Feedback, 2023, n.p.). Although some participants found it challenging to fit the tasks around other family and work commitments and had wished there was more time to complete them, one participant captured our rationale well when they questioned "whether doing it over a longer period would make it easier or would risk losing momentum" (Participant Feedback, 2023, n.p.).

As tight as it is to make a film in two weeks, particularly for first-time filmmakers, event feedback demonstrates that the learning outcomes were achieved. For one participant, the project has "made the film making process a whole lot less daunting and accessible" while for others it has motivated them to continue making films (Participant Feedback, 2023, n.p.). One participant noted how the filmmaking skills acquired during the project will benefit their career and another noted that it has made her "want to do more [and] link it in with my love of storytelling, local interest, and social history" (Participant Feedback, 2023, n.p.). Offering the participants the opportunity to launch their films at the festival was another incentive and one participant observed how exciting it was "be motivated towards our event at the film festival" (Participant Feedback, 2023, n.p.).

The two events demonstrate that tight schedules can work, but these need to be well planned and managed, and participants need to be supported along the way and have something to work towards so that they feel motivated to engage from start to finish. The DIY participatory filmmaking approach also played an important role in sustaining consistent engagement throughout. In both events, participants had complete creative control over their projects and were able to write, shoot, and edit their films according to their vision while working to fulfil their respective briefs. While the cross-border filmmakers were able to tell stories they felt passionate about or interested in bringing to life, the young filmmakers expressed their creativity and brought their imagination to life on screen.

In both cases, the DIY participatory approach allowed the filmmakers to find creative solutions to overcome technical and logistical challenges as well as experiment with different techniques, styles, and storytelling approaches without the pressure of commercial success or having to achieve a certain professional quality. The sense of ownership over their work and accomplishment in both events was evident. The films produced by them are testament to their determination and creativity. Therefore, our experience illustrates how the Film Camp and Film Challenge formats can be two effective event models to not only engage people creatively with archives and widen an organisation's audience reach, but it is also a gratifying and valuable avenue for creative expression and skill development.

Why – Impact

In terms of impact, both events helped break down barriers of access to Northern Ireland Screen's archives and also functioned as important audience development tools for partners Rathmullan Film Festival, PRONI, and the Nerve Centre.

In a 2001 study of arts organisations in the United States, McCarthy and Jinnet identified three ways in which participation can be increased: diversifying, broadening, and deepening (Bladen et al., 2023, pp. 388–389). Diversifying participation involves attracting people who would not normally attend a particular event and, as a result, organisations may benefit from finding new sources of revenue and more support for cultural innovation. Broadening, in turn, means attracting more people (from a pool of likely attendees) to an event and strengthening revenue streams and cultural innovation. Deepening participation, subsequently, is about increasing loyalty which, subsequently, may lead to audience spending and extended support for cultural innovation (Bladen et al., 2023, p. 389).

Given the short duration of both events and their not-for-profit nature, both projects focused on the first strategy – diversifying and reaching out to new audiences, namely young people and cross-border communities. Partner organisations also benefited from this strategy, but the benefits went beyond reaching out to new audiences. By working together on both projects, all parties involved were able to harness each other's available resources (technical, skills and financial) and learn about different methods of engagement: while Northern Ireland Screen and PRONI learned how film camps can offer an accessible (and fun) way into archives, the Rathmullan Film Festival and Nerve Centre were able to experiment with different ways that filmmakers can work with archives.

For us, as event coordinators, both events offered us the opportunity not only to experiment with different forms of participatory storytelling, but also to reflect on our own practice, think about what we value in our work, why we do it, how we do it and the benefits, limitations and challenges for all parties involved. By opening up authorship and focusing more on the process than on the product, the benefits of this type of engagement are visibly not just organisational but are also personal. Chatterjee and Noble's lists of positive effects can also be applied to events such as ours: "reduced social isolation; opportunities for learning and acquiring news skills; calming experiences, leading to decreased anxiety; increased positive emotions, such as optimism, hope and enjoyment; increased self-esteem and sense of identity…" (cited in Fogarasi Musso, 2023, pp. 1–2).

Conclusion

As Rick Prelinger rightly observes, archives have "got a long history, but I think we've only begun to see its potential" (Curran Bernard and Rabin, 2008, p. 147). Our case studies from the North of Ireland illustrate how creative event formats, such as a participatory film camp and film challenge, can harness the potential of archives.

We concur with Helen Kara that taking a creative research approach is more than 'simply finding answers to questions', but it is very much about 'enabling us to see and understand problems and topics in new ways' (2020, p. 18). As Event Studies is a multidisciplinary field in nature, often drawing theory, knowledge, methodologies, and methods from many established disciplines, such as management and tourism (Getz, 2007, p. 353), we hope that we have demonstrated how archive and participatory film scholarship, professional creative practice and practice-based reflective research can be combined to generate insights in relation to how events are designed, managed and evaluated.

We would like to conclude with some 'think points' in relation to the participatory event practice and reflective research framework we adopted and how this can be particularly useful when designing and delivering events for new audiences and subsequently reflecting on them:

Participatory Creative Events
- Being open to new ideas, tools, methods, and types of relationships is a fundamental part of any participatory endeavour.
- Do not underestimate the time required to build trust and relationships. It is essential to take time to discuss expectations, availability, and roles.
- Participatory events give attendees a sense of ownership and authorship when working towards producing something together, such as films. It is important to have from the outset a clear goal in mind and well-defined guidelines so that everyone can move towards achieving that goal.

- Online and In-person projects have strengths and limitations. Online works well when reaching people who are geographically apart and is a more affordable type of event. In-person allows for more in-depth engagement and better access to adequate equipment. Refer to the event aims, target audience, resources needed, etc when deciding what format to use.
- Our case studies show that short length is great for keeping momentum, ensuring commitment throughout, and getting the 'work done'. However, the rushed nature means that less time can be spent on ensuring the quality of the outputs. Hence the importance of deciding early on which one is more important: process or product.
- Be mindful of people's uneven access to technology, digital skills, and confidence levels when designing events.
- The possibilities brought by digital technology are tempting, but make sure to choose the right technology for the project. Smartphones can be more effective than professional cameras when the aim is to introduce people to the art of filmmaking, break down barriers and widen access. Technology must be a tool for engagement not a barrier.

The Reflective Research

1 Professional contexts are great laboratories for subsequent research. They provide 'real world' case studies and lessons for future practice and research.
2 Precisely because professional contexts are not necessarily research contexts, journaling allows practitioners to capture all the nuances, the messiness, the thoughts, and reactions during all phases of the projects. If it were not for our journals, our reflective analysis would have been quite limited.
3 The creative power of journaling is better harnessed when it is complemented by other methods, such as interviews and surveys. Employing a mixed method approach increases the likelihood of capturing diverse contexts and complexities during categorisation, coding, and analysis. As a result, this ensures that the research findings maintain rigour, validity, and reliability.
4 Make sure you conduct participant feedback surveys and that you do it in a way that you can easily access it if circumstances change. Our analysis of *The Horror!* would have been enriched had we been able to analyse the feedback forms from that project.
5 When engaging in reflective research, analyse everything: what worked well but also what did not, the in-betweens, silences, absences. We concur with Miller, Little and High that central to our practice and reflective work "is a shared sense of urgency to rethink our capacity to take our work public as cultural producers, advocates for social change, and researchers" (2017, p. 14).

Notes

1 Northern Ireland Screen is the national screen agency for Northern Ireland and it promotes the development of a sustainable audio-visual production industry as well as preserve and make accessible the region's moving image heritage.
2 The authors' roles in the projects include Access and Outreach Officer at Northern Ireland Screen (Bronagh McAtasney) and creative producer at partner organisations Rathmullan Film Festival and Nerve Centre/PRONI (Laura Aguiar).
3 See Northern Ireland Screen's Business Plan (2022–23): https://shorturl.at/eotIU.
4 The Digital Film Archive (DFA) is a free public access website and contains hundreds of hours of moving image titles, spanning from 1897 to the present day. For more, see: digitalfilmarchive.net.
5 For more, see: https://digitalfilmarchive.net/collection/the-spence-brothers-22.
6 The Ulster Folk Museum is an open-air living museum with 170 acres recreating the rural way of life in the early 20th century. For more, see https://www.ulsterfolkmuseum.org.
7 The films are available online: https://makingthefuture.eu/news/spence-brothers-archives-inspire-young-horror-filmmakers.
8 See: https://www.48hourfilm.com/.
9 The films can be watched online: https://digitalfilmarchive.net/collection/rathmullan-film-festival-2023-the-northwest-236.

References

Alvesson, M. and Skoldberg, K. (2009) *Reflexive Methodology: New Vistas for Qualitative Research*. London: Sage.

Benoit III, E. and Eveleigh, A. (2019) *Participatory Archives: Theory and Practice*. London: Facet Publishing.

Black, G. (2012) *Transforming Museums in the Twenty-first Century*. London: Routledge.

Bladen, C., Kennell, J., Abson, E. and Wilde, N. (2023) *Events Management: An Introduction*. London: Routledge.

Cecilia, R Rafie. 2021. COVID-19 Pandemic: Threat or Opportunity for Blind and Partially Sighted Museum Visitors? *Journal of Conservation and Museum Studies*, 19(1):5, 1–8. https://doi.org/10.5334/ jcms.200

Crooke, E., Farrell-Banks, D., Friel, B., Jackson, H., Hook, A., Maguire, T., and McDermott, P. (2022). *Museums and Community Wellbeing: A Report of the Museums, Crisis and COVID-19 Project*. Ulster University.

Curran Bernard, S. and Rabin, K. (2008) *Archival Storytelling: A Filmmaker's Guide to Finding, Using, and Licensing Third-Party Visuals and Music*. New York: Routledge.

Etherington, K. (2004) *Becoming a Reflexive Researcher: Using Our Selves in Research*. London: Jessica Kingsley Publishers.

Flick, U. (2009) *An Introduction to Qualitative Research*. London: Sage.

Fogarasi Musso, R. (2023) *Museums, Wellbeing and Young People An Exploration into Museum Wellbeing Activities Tailored to Young People*. MA Museum Practice and Management. Derry: Ulster University.

Getz, D. (2007) *Event Studies: Theory, Research and Policy for Planned Events*. Oxford: Elsevier.

Giannachi, G. (2016) *Archive Everything: Mapping the Everyday*. Cambridge: Massachusetts Institute of Technology.

Grau, O., Coones, W. and Rühse, V. (2017) *Museum and Archive on the Move*. Berlin/Boston: Walter De Gruyter.

Kara, H. (2020) *Creative Research Methods: A Practical Guide*. Bristol: Policy Press.

Leavy, P. (2017) *Handbook of Arts-Based Research*. New York: Guilford Publications.

Miller, L., Little, E. and High, S. (2017) *Going Public: The Art of Participatory Practice*. Vancouver: UBC Press.

Nelson, R. (2013) *Practice as Research in the Arts: Principles, Protocols, Pedagogies*. London: Palgrave Macmillan.

Popple, S., Prescott, A. and Mutibwa, D. H. (2020) *Communities, Archives and New Collaborative Practices*. Bristol: Bristol University Press.

Schön, D. A. (1984). *The Reflective Practitioner: How Professionals Think in Action*. New York: Basic Books.

Skains, R. L. (2018) "Creative practice as research: Discourse on methodology". *Media Practice and Education*, 19:1, 82–97.

Smith, H. and Dean, R. T. (2009) *Practice-led Research, Research-led Practice in the Creative Arts*. Edinburgh: Edinburgh University Press.

Smits, R. (2021). *European Film Festivals in Transition: Film Festival Formats in Times of COVID*. Report for Thessaloniki International Film Festival.

Stevens, M., Flinn, A. and Shepherd, E. (2010) "New frameworks for community engagement in the archive sector: From handing over to handing on". *International Journal of Heritage Studies*, 16:1–2, 59–76.

Van Der Wagen, L. and Carlos, B. R. (2004) *Event Management For Tourism, Cultural, Business, and Sporting Events*. Indiana: Pearson.

11

CO-CREATED RESEARCH OR CO-CREATED CHAOS? HANDING THE RESEARCH REIGNS TO LOCAL COMMUNITIES

Evaluating the Social Impact of the Tour de Yorkshire

Neil Ormerod

Universidade do Algarve, Faro, Portugal

Introduction

This chapter draws on the knowledge gained from five years of collaborative and co-creative research to evaluate the social impacts of several major sporting events in Doncaster, UK. Through the presentation and critique of two methods case studies, this chapter demonstrates how rich social impact data can be collected through co-creative research design and the creative application of new and traditional research instruments. Within this context, co-creation serves a dual purpose, enabling the collection of social impact data, whilst simultaneously supporting collaboration between host communities, event organisers and other stakeholders to enhance the social impacts of event portfolio programmes.

Whilst there is no consensus regarding the definition of co-creation, this chapter draws on the definition by Nicholas et al. (2019) who define co-creation (within a research context) "as an approach to research that values the expertise and perspectives of those likely to be affected by the work, and those who utilise insights from the work" (p. 355). Turning to the other key concept of this work 'social impact', the International Association for Impact Assessment's definition of social impact underpinned the programme of research in Doncaster:

> Specifically, a social impact is considered to be something that is experienced or felt in either a perceptual (cognitive) or a corporeal (bodily, physical) sense, at any level, for example at the level of an individual person,

DOI: 10.4324/9781032686424-11

an economic unit (family/household), a social group (circle of friends), a workplace (a company or government agency), or by community/society generally. These different levels are affected in different ways by an impact or impact causing action.

(Vanclay et al., 2015: 2)

A key aspect of co-creative research is the importance of understanding local dynamics, this includes both what unites communities as well as understanding potential divisions – e.g., ethnic, political, and other tensions. As this chapter will explain, knowing communities well is the key to accessing different community groups, navigating challenges to community engagement, and maximising social impact benefits.

Many community settings, notably cities and towns, are now 'major event hosts' due to the growth of event funding policies globally at national, state, and regional scales (Ormerod and Wood, 2020). For policymakers, hosting major sporting and cultural events is an attractive proposition, primarily for reasons of their perceived positive economic impact from tourist expenditure, their ability to showcase destinations, and their use as a 'soft power' communication platform (Grix and Houlihan, 2014). Likewise, many communities welcome the hosting of major events for economic and social reasons. For example, such events can provide an economic boost to local businesses and generate new employment opportunities. They also provide a focal point around which local people can come together to celebrate their community and culture with visitors (both physically and virtually) (Finkel, 2009).

Despite these potential benefits, host community social and environmental impacts from major events are often overlooked in preference to measuring the immediate (direct) economic impacts or capturing tourist event satisfaction (Wood, 2005). Reliance on this narrow view of event impacts for justifying investment in major events is now regarded as incomplete and outdated, evidenced by pointed critique and increased academic research into the social impact benefits and legacies of the Olympics, FIFA World Cup, and other large-scale events (Rowe, 2012; Rogerson, 2016; Byers, Hayday and Pappous, 2020).

Consequently, closer attention is now being placed on the social impacts of major events and the methods by which they can be monitored and evaluated. This shift in event impact thinking mirrors a broader trend for emphasising community-oriented public policy which has seen the terms 'social innovation' and 'co-creation' enter the parlance of policymakers, researchers, and consultants (Nicholas et al., 2019). Whilst it is easy to dismiss these terms as buzzwords, engaging with such popular or 'magic concepts' (Pollitt and Hupe, 2011; Voorberg, Bekkers and Tummers, 2015) can bridge the research-practice gap by providing a common language for achieving shared objectives.

By extension, efforts to bridge the research-practice gap have also led to a re-evaluation of the constraints associated with traditional top-down 'researcher as expert' approaches (Wilson and Hollinshead, 2015). Specifically, these actions have focused on how to better engage host-populations in research activities and the opportunities for developing co-created studies. The key benefit of rejecting top-down approaches in favour of disruptive and co-creative methods is that they centralise dialogic ground-up collaboration to achieve greater access to research populations (Wilson and Hollinshead, 2015; Ivanova, Buda and Burrai, 2021).

The case study evidence presented in this chapter is underpinned by these principles. When meaningfully applied, co-creation has multiple benefits, including strengthened stakeholder relationships and informed intervention design. Similarly, when applied to an event evaluation context, co-creation offers new possibilities for developing creative research methods and for applying traditional research methods in creative ways.

Successful and sustainable contemporary events, therefore, require a symbiotic relationship between event organisers and host communities as key stakeholders, based on an understanding of mutual benefit. From a research perspective, a logical extension for approaching social impact monitoring and evaluation is to engage and involve local people more deeply in the research process in a spirit of collaboration underpinned by the theory of co-creation (Jull, Giles and Graham, 2017).

Handing the research reigns to local people has many advantages and brings new possibilities for understanding community social impacts, however, it also presents challenges such as the need to invest additional time and resources to provide training and other support to enable local people, often with no previous experience, to conduct research-related activities. Whilst, these aspects must be carefully considered and addressed for the successful delivery of co-created research, collaborating with local people also empowers communities to take control of their social impact benefits by providing opportunities to build relationships and improve event outcomes.

Furthermore, social impact interventions such as supporting older people to access an event or supporting community events around a major event often need longer periods of engagement to manifest as medium- and long-term impacts, and thus require a different, approach to monitoring and evaluation. This latter aspect is particularly important for recurring events or where communities are repeatedly involved in an event portfolio programme (Ziakas, 2014).

The co-created methods described in this chapter have been designed, developed, and refined through engagement with local people to collect social impact data relating to community engagement with the Tour de Yorkshire cycle race. Since 2018, residents in Doncaster have been instrumental in evaluating the social impacts of several high-profile sporting events, including two editions of the Tour de Yorkshire cycle race, the UCI Road World Championships, and several Women's Red Roses Six Nations rugby matches.

Hosting and evaluating these events provided an ideal opportunity for collaboration between local government event organisers, host communities, and academic researchers. Examples of co-created community research involvement include conducting resident-to-resident questionnaire surveys, coordinating focus groups, and collecting data from community groups using a creative event visitor book method.

It is important to acknowledge, that without this level of community engagement it would not have been possible to gather the depth of data that has been obtained from these events. It is this invaluable local knowledge of people, places, connections, tensions, and barriers that brings a research advantage for better understanding the social impacts of major sporting and cultural events. From a creative methods perspective, this work demonstrates the importance of considering research creativity from a broad perspective, one that recognises both new methods *and* the opportunities for the creative use of traditional research instruments, such as surveys, to meet co-creative research objectives.

Case Study: The Tour de Yorkshire Cycle Race

The Tour de Yorkshire cycle race (hereafter TdY) took place for five successful editions from 2015 to 2019 and was promoted as a legacy event following the high-profile hosting of two stages of the 2014 Tour de France Grand Depart in Yorkshire. The four-day event attracted high-profile cyclists and international cycling teams and was organised by the regional tourism body Welcome to Yorkshire and Tour de France organisers ASO. The event had clear tourism objectives of showcasing Yorkshire to the world and was estimated to have generated almost £60m for the regional economy in 2019 (Lomax, 2019). Although subsequent editions in 2020 and 2021 were cancelled due to the Covid-19 pandemic and the future of the race was put on hold due to the collapse of Welcome to Yorkshire into administration in 2022, there is hope that the race can be reinstated in a new format in 2024 (Hammond, 2022).

Doncaster Council's (hereafter, the Council) involvement in the race began when Doncaster hosted a stage finish in 2018 and a stage start in 2019. These events formed part of a wider and evolving event portfolio strategy which complemented their commitment to community health and exercise through Doncaster's designation as a Sport England Local Delivery Pilot location. As such, the Council was interested in leveraging high-profile publicly funded events to produce social benefits for host communities. Pertinently, this longer-term view looked beyond economically important but short-term tourism objectives, by acknowledging the vital role that communities play in supporting sustainable event portfolio strategies.

The Council's approach involved working with communities to support community-led events and activities that would take place alongside the TdY with the aim of enhancing *personal wellbeing, community cohesion*, and *civic pride*. Their belief in this approach stemmed from their experience of hosting of the Olympic Torch Relay in 2012. During this event it was observed that communities had come together and made considerable effort to support the event. This public display of community support sparked the Council's enduring interest in conducting research to understand if and how an event portfolio strategy can be leveraged to benefit communities.

Overview of Tour de Yorkshire Social Impact Research

The 2018 TdY study comprised a broad-based research project to assess social impact in six Doncaster communities. This involved engaging with 28 key stakeholders and 690 residents from six geographically and socioeconomically diverse Doncaster communities located along the 2018 TdY route. Specifically, the research included the following communities: Bennetthorpe, Conisbrough, Hatfield, Hooton Pagnell, Mexborough, and Stainforth. Data collection within the communities involved a variety of methods including:

- Resident event survey (444 participants)
- Post-event resident-to-resident survey (221 participants)
- Key stakeholder phone interviews (18 participants)
- Physical activity expert interviews (10 participants)
- Physical activity resident focus groups (25 participants)

Combined, these methods focused on 'measuring' the qualitative impacts of the TdY, focusing on community wellbeing, sense of civic pride, sense of community spirit (social capital) and physical activity levels. The collected data was then analysed to produce average 'barometer' scores, providing a visual reference for current performance in these areas and a baseline for assessing future impacts of the event.

Importantly, for the creative methods focus of this book, these methods included trialling a post-event resident-to-resident survey that involved working with local people to co-create and conduct a survey that would provide insight from each of the six communities. This creative *by residents, for residents*, approach placed communities at the heart of the research and aligned the evaluation with the community objectives of the Council's event portfolio approach. This method is returned to later in the chapter (Method 1) where it is described and critiqued in greater detail.

The study findings revealed that within the surveyed communities, residents were generally very satisfied about the local impacts of the TdY, with 93% of respondents describing their experience of the TdY as very positive or positive. However, the study also revealed that:

Different individuals and groups in the Doncaster community have different capacities, opportunities and aspirations for how much they engage in local events.

Specifically, the findings highlighted that seven target groups (Table 11.1) would benefit from additional support to increase engagement with the TdY.

In response, the Council introduced a 'Micro-grant' scheme among other actions intended to provide practical and financial support to community groups to support their involvement in future large-scale sporting events.

Drawing on the findings of the 2018 study, the Council decided that the 2019 TdY study should target some of the groups shown in Table 11.1 with specific interventions to support their involvement in the event. Two of these interventions focused on providing better support to community event organisers (Group 1) and addressing the issue of accessibility for older people and those with mobility and other accessibility needs (Group 2). For this latter group, practical issues such as accessing the event, not having somewhere comfortable to sit, and a lack of nearby refreshments and toilet facilities were identified as significant barriers to participating in TdY community events. Targeting this group was also considered important for addressing broader societal challenges such as social isolation and loneliness through facilitating greater community engagement. The interventions combined a newly developed Micro-grant scheme with partnership working to create community events that could welcome and comfortably host elderly people and those with mobility issues.

TABLE 11.1 Identified target groups to support engagement in the TdY

1	**Community event organisers** who would appreciate a greater level of support for delivering their community activities to improve or scale-up what they do.
2	**Older people and others with access needs** who require additional practical support to engage with spectating and community activities in comfort.
3	**Young people/teenagers** who were not catered for to some extent in the design and delivery of community events organised alongside the race.
4	**School/pre-school children** who in some cases were unable to engage with the event due to practical restrictions within schools/nurseries such as staff availability and supervision ratios.
5	**Casual event 'browsers'** who do not normally engage with community events but venture out for occasions such as the TdY. This presents a rare opportunity for local community projects and service providers to try and engage with these 'hard to reach' groups.
6	**Local businesses** on the TdY route (some) who felt they could contribute more to the event in a variety of ways if the right approach and practical support to facilitate their engagement were in place.
7	**BME groups** in some communities who highlighted that with some practical support, the TdY could be used to celebrate and raise awareness of the cultural diversity in communities.

The Micro-grant scheme, with a maximum limit of £200 per application, was introduced following the recommendation that community event organisers should be supported in their efforts to hold associated community events around major public events such as the TdY (McCombes et al., 2018). The Micro-grant scheme was designed to be easy for community groups to access with a simple application process that could be completed by email or post. This process was also supported by direct community engagement from a Council representative. Importantly the scheme was not designed to finance the event, its purpose was to incentivise and support local event organisers to enhance their events, and thus maximise the social impact benefits.

For example, Micro-grants can be awarded to community groups with no requirement for them to be formally constituted organisations and can be used for things such as simple refreshments e.g. tea/coffee, seating, and arts/crafts materials for event decoration. It should also be noted that the scheme does not provide cash grants, instead, items are purchased on behalf of, and delivered to the community groups. A related benefit of this approach is that it increases direct engagement between the Council and community groups, providing opportunities to enhance existing communication channels and open new ones with communities. It also removes the need for groups to have accounting and auditing processes in place which would be prohibitive for non-formalised groups. In total, 18 Micro-grants from a total of 21 submissions met the criteria for funding. From the 18 awarded, four were selected as social impact case studies for evaluation (Table 11.2).

To evaluate these events a novel 'visitor book' method was developed and combined with organiser interviews to understand the social impact of these community events and attendees' engagement with the TdY. When developing this new method, an important emphasis was placed on ensuring as far as possible that the method would not interfere with the participants' enjoyment of the event. Afterall, the focus of the intervention was to generate positive social impact and the evaluation of this should not negatively affect the experience. The visitor book approach along with a reflective discussion of its value is presented in the section titled: Method 2.

Method 1: Resident-to-Resident Survey

Method Overview

Serving two interrelated research purposes, the post-event resident-to-resident survey was primarily intended to capture social impact data to ascertain levels of community engagement and residents' perceived benefits of the TdY in relation to aspects of personal well-being, civic pride, and community cohesion. Secondly, by recruiting local people to conduct the data collection, the survey served as an initial trial of the Council's collaborative and co-creative approach

TABLE 11.2 Overview of community events

Location	Event activities	Target group
Askern Library Library and community hub.	• Arts and crafts decoration by regular library groups including the Dementia support group. • Refreshments and get-together before race.	Event open to all residents/visitors but involved community groups such as the Dementia support group.
Askarne Smile Day care centre in Askern for older people and adults with learning difficulties.	• Decoration e.g. flag making. • Picnic for day care clients. • Gazebo purchased through Micro-grant scheme to provide shelter whilst watching the race. • Fundraising bottle tombola	Askarne Smile clients Decoration included artwork by primary school children who attend the centre as part of a scheme to bring older and younger people together.
Renew 127 Faith-based community centre in Bentley linked to Bentley Baptist Church.	• Decoration e.g. window dressing, knitted bunting, bike decoration and TdY themed baking. • Refreshments and get together before, during and after race. • Micro-grant purchases included seating for watching race.	Event open to all but with a focus on older people, and casual event browsers. Although faith based, Renew 127 is a community hub and is open to all.
Toll Bar TARA Resident association	• Decoration e.g. knitted bunting, bike decoration, children's artwork, and baking. • Refreshments and activities before during and after the race. Including children's activities and fundraising collaboration with The Royal British Legion. • Some refreshments and decorations were purchased via Micro-grant scheme.	Event open to all but with a focus on families and children's activities.

to event evaluation. Through this 'test and learn' approach, it was intended that robust co-creative methods would be developed to evaluate the Council's evolving event portfolio strategy. This forward-thinking approach demonstrates that event evaluation does not need to be the preserve of academics or consultants, it can also be co-created through collaboration with local communities.

The survey involved the recruitment of 10 *Community Influencers* to work as researchers in the six communities shown in Table 11.3. For some locations *Community Influencers* worked in pairs to collect the data. *Community Influencers* were remunerated for their work with cash payments or shopping vouchers (value £200) of their choice. In total, the survey gathered 221 responses from residents eight weeks after the event.

Method Approach

Pre-Event

The first step in developing the co-creative research approach involved getting to know the *Community influencers*. To do this, the Council provided the research team with a list of individuals who were known to organise community activities in the six locations. The *Community Influencers* were then contacted to explain the purpose of the study and to invite them to be part of the evaluation team. The research team then arranged to meet the recruited *Community Influencers* in their communities around two months before the TdY at a place of their choosing. This enabled the researchers to get to know the *Community Influencers* and find out more about their plans for community events to celebrate the TdY. Following this meeting, the research team provided detailed written information about the survey and followed up with a phone call to answer any questions the *Community Influencers* may have. This also provided an opportunity to obtain finalised information about the community events which would take place.

TABLE 11.3 Overview of collected surveys by area

Area	Number of surveys	%*
Bennetthorpe	25	11
Conisbrough	48	22
Hatfield	56	25
Hooten Pagnell	22	10
Mexborough	42	19
Stainforth	28	13
Total	**221**	

* Percentages rounded to nearest whole number.

During the Event

Although the *Community Influencers* were not involved in conducting research until after the event, the research team made a point of visiting the *Community Influencers* on the day of the TdY to see and experience their community events. This was considered an important part of the co-creative approach, as support should be reciprocated between the research team and *Community Influencers*. It also enabled the *Community Influencer(s)* to introduce the research team to other members of the community. This approach helped pave the way for the post-event survey as the research team could explain more about what the survey was about and answer any questions potential respondents may have.

Post-Event

The day after the TdY, two members of the research team re-visited the *Community Influencers*. This visit had a dual purpose. The first was to gather the *Community Influencer's* views on the TdY, their specific community event, and the Micro-grant scheme. This took the form of a recorded semi-structured interview in a public location chosen by the *Community Influencer*. The second purpose was to provide survey materials and training to the *Community Influencer* in advance of them conducting the post-event survey. It also provided an opportunity to discuss the survey approach and address any questions or queries.

The survey was then conducted by the *Community Influencers* eight weeks after the event over a period of two weeks. In most cases, surveys were left with residents and then collected at a predetermined date and time. This in-person approach had the benefit that the *Community Influencers* could explain the purpose of the survey and answer any questions potential respondents may have, hopefully leading to an increased response rate. During this time, the research team maintained weekly contact with the *Community Influencers*, in addition to being available via phone or email to respond to any issues that arose during the survey period.

Although the post-event survey followed a convenience sampling approach, *Community Influencers* were encouraged (as far as possible) to consider the demographic balance of the survey responses with the aim of collecting responses from a broad demographic mix of residents. Specifically, the survey comprised of 14 questions which were derived from existing theoretical frameworks, namely the New Economics Foundation (NEF) five drivers of wellbeing, the Warwick-Edinburgh Mental Well-being Scale (WEMWBS) of subjective personal wellbeing, and an influencer behavioural change framework which represents a simplification of the Social Ecological Model. For further details of the methods used please see (McCombes et al., 2018).

Analysis

Overall, our *Community Influencers* were invaluable in facilitating greater access to a wide range of residents, enabling good-quality data to be gathered from all six communities.

Analysis of the resident-to-resident survey involved descriptive analysis of the data and the generation of community 'barometer' scores for the measures of community wellbeing, sense of civic pride, and sense of community spirit (social capital). For more details of the analysis conducted please refer to (McCombes et al., 2018).

Lessons and Limitations

Working with inexperienced researchers inevitably presents challenges from a data collection perspective. However, the biggest challenge encountered with the resident-to-resident survey related to delays in receiving the completed surveys. Whilst this challenged the *Community Influencers*, this issue would likely have been more profound if experienced but non-local researchers had been used instead.

Other challenges included some *Community Influencers* struggling to fit their research obligations around their existing time commitments. Whilst these challenges did cause minor delays to the data collection phase, neither proved insurmountable. Moreover, they need to be considered in relation to the alternative approach of using experienced contracted researchers with no local knowledge. It should also be remembered that working with local people brings additional benefits for future research, notably the ability to build valuable network connections. Nevertheless, we would advise researchers considering this type of approach to carefully consider the level of training, incentives and time commitment required, so that this information can be clearly communicated from the beginning when recruiting local researchers.

Method 2: Community Event Visitor Books

Method Overview

To gain an in-depth understanding of the impact of community Micro-grant interventions on resident engagement with the 2019 TdY, it was decided that the study required an inclusive and accessible method of collecting data from residents attending Micro-grant funded local events. The aim here was to understand residents' live event experiences without intruding on their participation. For this reason, traditional methods such as interviews, focus groups and questionnaires were rejected as being too intrusive to the event experience.

To address the issue of event intrusion, the idea of a visitor book to record attendee comments was put forward as an interesting and creative way of doing this. Furthermore, this approach built on the success of working with *Community Influencers* to conduct the post-event TdY resident-resident survey in 2018 (Method 1). An added benefit of this approach was that the visitor book could be given back to the community groups after analysis as a memento of their event participation. The books were individually labelled and closed with a ribbon matching the TdY event colour scheme.

Method Approach

Pre-Event

The first stage in the co-creation process involved visiting the event organisers at the community event venue. This enabled the research team to meet the event organisers and explain the purpose of the study and why they would like the community group to be involved. It also enabled the researchers to see the event space and understand how the event would take place. The visitor book idea was then discussed with each organiser, enabling them to ask questions or raise concerns. The proposed approach received positive feedback, with all event organisers committing to help complete the data collection. Ethical approval was then sought and granted by the research team's institutional ethics committee prior to conducting the research.

In the lead up to the event, the research team kept in regular contact with the community organisers regarding the arrangements for the study, such as dropping off the visitor books the day before the event. This enabled the research team to check that the organisers were happy with the arrangements and address any final questions or queries.

During the Event

On the day of the event, the research team visited each community group at least once to experience the community event and check how the visitor book was working. Whilst this was recognised as an important aspect of supporting the event organisers, it was decided for reasons of minimising intrusion that it was unhelpful to have a member of the team at each event for the full event duration. This also provided space for the event organisers to run their event and manage how they circulated the visitor books. Whilst an important aspect of the method was having the event organiser on-hand to manage the data collection, the visitor books included clearly displayed information about the study, including ethics approval and contact details if respondents had any questions about the study. Respondents were also encouraged to express their thoughts freely within the books about the day and TdY but were asked to consider the following three questions when leaving comments:

- What does experiencing the Tour de Yorkshire in (name of location) mean to you personally?
- What do you think the Tour de Yorkshire means to your community?
- How has (name of specific community group) helped you to be a part of the Tour de Yorkshire?

To ensure that the questions were always visible when participants were writing their comments, the questions were printed on a card that was attached to the top of the book.

Post-Event

After the event, the visitor books were collected from the event organisers. In one case, one book was posted back due to logistical issues of collecting it. In this case, recorded delivery was paid for by the research team. The books were then thematically analysed and then posted back to the community groups.

Analysis

Overall, the four visitor books captured 58 comments from across the four community events. The analysis involved systematically coding each visitor book and subsequently organising identified codes into themes (Braun and Clarke, 2006). These were then reviewed and revised by the research team to ensure they were a good reflection of the complete dataset.

Table 11.4 shows the key themes identified from the visitor book comments. In total six themes were identified. Although it should be noted that many of the themes and respondent comments overlap. For example, although the theme of 'excitement and enjoyment' is more prominent within comments from Askern Community Library and Askarne Smile day centre, it does not imply that attendees of events at Renew 127 and Toll Bar TARA did not enjoy the day, rather their comments relating to enjoyment were more strongly associated with community action activities such as decorating the venue and running the community event.

Furthermore, respondents at all the events regarded the TdY to be a special occasion and possibly a once-in-a-lifetime opportunity to experience the TdY in their community. This perspective was often coupled with comments that articulated the importance of place importance/pride for their community. In many cases, this sense of pride can also be strongly linked to community engagement and the TdY being a positive event which brings the community together.

TABLE 11.4 Visitor book themes for the four communities

Community Groups			
Askern Library	*Askarne Smile*	*Renew 127*	*Toll Bar TARA*
	Accessibility		
Community action	Community action	Community action	Community action
Excitement/ enjoyment	Excitement/ enjoyment		
		Gratitude	
Place importance/ pride		Place importance/ pride	Place importance/ pride
Special occasion	Special occasion	Special occasion	Special occasion

Excitement/enjoyment was also found to be linked to seeing the enjoyment of others, notably children. Gratitude was identified as a further theme across many of the events but was particularly highlighted within comments made by attendees at Renew 127. In this context, gratitude was found to mainly refer to respondents expressing thanks for bringing the TdY to their community. Attendees were also extremely grateful to the event organisers for their efforts in making the day a success. Comments from the Askarne Smile event also emphasised the importance of addressing accessibility needs. Without the support of the Askarne Smile Centre, including dedicated staff and a transport bus, these attendees would not have been able to experience the TdY in person.

Lessons and Limitations

Although the visitor book approach proved very successful as a creative data collection method, resulting in the collection of a wealth of in-depth qualitative data, it is not without its limitations. A principal limitation of the approach is that the format may discourage individuals from leaving negative comments, leading to a positive data bias. Specifically, although the comments are anonymous, due to the nature of the book format they are visible to others, and respondents may be deterred from leaving a negative message if they see that lots of positive messages have already been written. However, this tendency was mitigated to an extent by researcher visits to the community events during the data collection to observe and talk to participants about their feelings towards the TdY. Post-event feedback was also sought from the organisers through follow-up interviews, with all stating that the approach had been successful and that they had enjoyed being part of the study.

Co-Created Research or Co-Created Chaos?

The title of this chapter alludes to the challenges of not just *involving* local people in social impact research but extending this approach with the aim of working *with* local people to co-create and evaluate social impact interventions. As has already been discussed, handing the research reigns to local people in this way has many advantages and brings new possibilities for understanding community social impacts through closer engagement. In turn, this creates opportunities to develop specific interventions to enhance the social impact benefits of major events. However, from a research perspective, it also presents challenges such as the need to invest additional time and resources to provide training and other support to enable local people, often with no previous experience, to lead research-related activities.

To answer the principal question of whether *co-created research results in co-created chaos?* the findings from five years of collaborative and co-created research in Doncaster demonstrate that community involvement in event evaluation supports a collaborative environment which then enables specific community-focused interventions to be developed to enhance the social impact benefits of major events. When applied to an event portfolio approach the benefits are multiplied, as the repeated cycle of host community engagement with events provides an opportunity to develop longer-term complementary social impact interventions alongside the events programme. However, the successful application of this approach requires greater resources and sustained community engagement.

Turning attention to the two method case study examples of how local people can be engaged creatively in the evaluation of large-scale events. The experience from developing and trialling Methods 1 and 2 reveal the importance of the following aspects (Think Points), which should be considered when planning co-creative research approaches using new and traditional data collection methods. For additional information and examples regarding approaches to maximise the social impact of major events, please see (Ormerod et al., 2023).

Think Points

Supporting Host Communities is the Key to Leveraging the Social Impacts of Major Events

In the context of hosting major cultural and sporting events it is very easy for community impacts to be overlooked in preference of a focus on attracting tourist expenditure. This outlook fails to recognise the important need for sustained host community support to successfully implement event portfolio strategies. Conducting event evaluation in a co-creative way not only generates research insight it also builds connections between host communities and event stakeholders. These connections then provide the foundations for developing evidence-based social impact interventions that can be trialled and evaluated within an event portfolio programme.

Leverage the Power of Community Events

The social impacts of major events can be enhanced by leveraging the power of associated community events. However, for success, these need to be developed in collaboration with host communities, they also need to be resourced, implemented and evaluated effectively. In summary, these associated community events form social impact bridges that facilitate engagement between host communities, event organisers and other stakeholders.

Collaborate, Then Co-Create

Supporting local people to evaluate the social impact of events within their communities requires a clear and sustained commitment from the researcher(s) to the collaboration. This provides the foundations for co-creating event evaluation approaches. The timescale for engaging with communities to begin the process of co-creating and conducting research activities should be carefully considered. This is to ensure that sufficient time is allocated for building working relationships between the researcher(s) and the community.

A good starting point is to identify connections between people and places. Of particular importance is identifying *Community Influencers*, individuals and or community groups who are active in their community. Typically, these people will be well-known community figures already involved in organising local activities and events. It is also important to identify community resources (such as village halls or sports clubs) as these can be helpful gateways for accessing and researching the community. Whilst this process undoubtedly takes longer than the alternative approach of contracting research expertise, it is important to highlight that long-term benefits for both the researcher(s) and the community can be realised when lasting research partnerships are forged. This is particularly true where multiple evaluations take place across an event portfolio.

Let Local People Lead the Way

When thinking about event evaluation and the use of creative methods it should be remembered that local people are best placed to understand the needs and challenges of hosting and evaluating events in their communities. Therefore, conducting community-based research is much easier if local people are involved due to their community connections enabling greater access to potential respondents. The two creative methods case studies presented in this chapter highlight the effectiveness of working with *Community Influencers*. *Community Influencers* are already engaged in community activities aimed at improving where they live, so it makes sense to work with like-minded people and benefit from their knowledge to co-create approaches that can capture event impacts. In Doncaster, this approach has even led to one community forming its own events team.

Value and Incentivise

Conducting community research is time consuming and hard work even for individuals who regularly dedicate their time to community activities. Therefore, it is essential that co-creative research approaches are properly resourced to support and reward this work. Reward can take many forms, ranging from incentives through to direct payment for the work carried out. Trials in Doncaster involved a mixture of cash and shopping voucher payments alongside the award of Micro-grants to support specific community events. It is also important to remember that individuals such as *Community Influencers* will wish to be recognised in different ways. In Doncaster, several preferred a donation to support future community activities over a personal payment.

Training, rewarding, and treating *Community Influencers* as integrated members of the research team helps ensure event evaluation success. Collecting event data can be daunting, even when *Community Influencers* know their community well. To make it easier, event evaluation approaches should be designed using the EAST framework of (Easy, Accessible, Social and Timely action) (Social Change UK, n.d.).

Combining this with a personal touch approach to communication and training also works best. A great way to start is for the research team to meet with *Community Influencers* where the event is taking place. It is also important to involve *Community Influencers* when disseminating the results of the event evaluation, showcasing their involvement from start to finish. Ideally this should include a public dissemination event where the results can be shared with the community. Such an event also provides an opportunity for the research team to publicly thank the community, and in particular, the *Community Influencer(s)* involved in the research.

Acknowledgement

The author's contribution to this book is financed by National Funds provided by FCT – Foundation for Science and Technology through project UIDB/04020/2020 with DOI 10.54499/UIDB/04020/2020 (https://doi.org/10.54499/UIDB/04020/2020).

References

Braun, V. and Clarke, V. (2006) 'Using thematic analysis in psychology', *Qualitative Research in Psychology*, 3(2), pp. 77–101. https://doi.org/10.1191/1478088706qp063oa

Byers, T., Hayday, E. and Pappous, A. (2020) 'A new conceptualization of mega sports event legacy delivery: Wicked problems and critical realist solution', *Sport Management Review*, 23(2), pp. 171–182. https://doi.org/10.1016/j.smr.2019.04.001

Finkel, R. (2009) 'A picture of the Contemporary Combined Arts Festival Landscape', *Cultural Trends*, 18(1), pp. 3–21. https://doi.org/10.1080/09548960802651195

Grix, J. and Houlihan, B. (2014) 'Sports mega-events as part of a Nation's soft power strategy: The cases of Germany (2006) and the UK (2012)', *British Journal of Politics and International Relations*, 16(4), pp. 572–596. https://doi.org/10.1111/1467-856X.12017

Hammond, G. (28 July, 2022) 'Tour de Yorkshire to be replaced with new-look event in the region from 2024', *The Yorkshire Post*. Available at: https://www.yorkshirepost. co.uk/sport/other-sport/tour-de-yorkshire-to-be-replaced-with-new-look-event-in-the-region-from-2024-3785252 (Accessed: 27 November 2023).

Ivanova, M., Buda, D.-M. and Burrai, E. (2021) 'Creative and disruptive methodologies in tourism studies', *Tourism Geographies*, 23(1–2), pp. 1–10. https://doi.org/10.1080/14616688.2020.1784992

Jull, J., Giles, A. and Graham, I.D. (2017) 'Community-based participatory research and integrated knowledge translation: Advancing the co-creation of knowledge', *Implementation Science*, 12(150), pp. 1–9. https://doi.org/10.1186/s13012-017-0696-3

Lomax, C. (10 July, 2019) 'Tour de Yorkshire boost to economy', *The Ilkley Gazette*. Available at: https://www.ilkleygazette.co.uk/news/17760615.tour-de-yorkshire-boost-economy/ (Accessed: 27 November 2023).

McCombes, L., Ormerod, N., Wood, E. McKenna, J., Morris, J. and Christensen, A. (2018) 'Maximising local benefits from the Tour de Yorkshire in Doncaster: Social impact assessment findings and recommendations for Doncaster Council'. [Online]. Doncaster Council, pp. 1–112. Available at: https://getdoncastermoving.org/uploads/maximising-local-benefits-of-the-2018-tour-de-yorkshire-in-doncaster-(sept-2018).pdf?v=1642701792 (Accessed: 27 November 2023).

Nicholas, G., Foote, J., Kainz, K., Midgley, G., Prager, K. and Zurbriggen, C. (2019). 'Towards a heart and soul for co-creative research practice: A systemic approach', *Evidence & Policy*, 15(3), pp. 353–370. https://doi.org/10.1332/174426419X15578220630571

Ormerod, N., McCombes, L. Fletcher, T. McKenna, J. Rawson, J. Jenkins, G. and Wood, E. (2023) *Gameplan A guide to maximising the social impacts of big events.* [eBook] Doncaster, UK: Doncaster Council. Available at: https://getdoncastermoving.org/gameplan

Ormerod, N. and Wood, E.H. (2020) 'Regional event tourism funding policies: A strategic-relational critique of current practice', *Journal of Travel Research*, 60(4), pp. 860–877. https://doi.org/10.1177/0047287520913631

Pollitt, C. and Hupe, P. (2011). 'Talking about government: The role of magic concepts', *Public Management Review*, 13(5), pp. 641–658. https://doi.org/10.1080/14719037.2010.532963

Rogerson, R.J. (2016) 'Re-defining temporal notions of event legacy: Lessons from Glasgow's Commonwealth Games', *Annals of Leisure Research*, 19(4), pp. 497–518. https://doi.org/10.1080/11745398.2016.1151367

Rowe, D. (2012) 'The bid, the lead-up, the event and the legacy: Global cultural politics and hosting the Olympics', *British Journal of Sociology*, 63(2), pp. 285–305. https://doi.org/10.1111/j.1468-4446.2012.01410.x

Social Change UK. (n.d.) *Using the EAST Framework: Understanding What Drives People to Make Decisions is Key to Changing Their Behaviour.* Available at: https://social-change.co.uk/files/Social_Change_UK_Using_the_EAST_framework.pdf (Accessed: 27 November 2023).

Vanclay, F., Esteves, A.M., Aucamp, I. and Franks, D. (2015) *Social impact assessment: Guidance for assessing and managing the social impacts of projects.* [Online]. Fargo ND: International Association for Impact Assessment. Available at: https://www.iaia.org/uploads/pdf/SIA_Guidance_Document_IAIA.pdf (Accessed: 27 November 2023).

Voorberg, W.H., Bekkers, V.J.J.M. and Tummers, L.G. (2015). 'A systematic review of co-creation and co-production: Embarking on the social innovation journey', *Public Management Review*, 17(9), pp. 1333–1357. https://doi.org/10.1080/14719037.2014.930505

Wilson, E. and Hollinshead, K. (2015). 'Qualitative tourism research: Opportunities in the emergent soft sciences', *Annals of Tourism Research*, 54, pp. 30–47. https://doi.org/10.1016/j.annals.2015.06.001

Wood, E.H. (2005) 'Measuring the economic and social impacts of local authority events', *International Journal of Public Sector Management*, 18(1), pp. 37–53. https://doi.org/10.1108/09513550510576143

Ziakas, V. (2014) 'Planning and leveraging event portfolios: Towards a holistic theory', *Journal of Hospitality Marketing & Management*, 23(3), pp. 327–356. https://doi.org/10.1080/19368623.2013.796868

12

ACTION RESEARCH IN CROSS-CULTURAL THEATRE MARKETING

A Dual Role as Practitioner and Researcher

Fan Wu

University of Applied Sciences Utrecht, Utrecht, Netherlands

Introduction

Events encompass various forms, and a common characteristic shared by events and ceremonies is that "they are designed to mark and celebrate a unique moment in time and to differentiate one time from another and one place from another" (Silvers, 2012, p. ix). In this regard, theatre, as a performing art that evolved from ritual ceremonies, exemplifies the essence of events. Theatre productions staged in different cultures amplify the sense of experiencing a "unique moment" for the participating audience. To stage a theatre production is to organise an event: creating a collective space for something to happen and for the participants to share a collective memory. Existing studies on and off the stage of the theatre have applied different methodologies, but the voices from the participants – both the production and marketing team and the audience members – have not been engaged in the discussion, not to mention in the cross-cultural context. Action research as a method provides a possibility to bridge industrial practice and academia in audience understanding and marketing strategy.

There has always been a gap in audience understanding, both in theatre marketing practices and in academia (Wu, 2018; Heim, 2010; Bennett, 1990; Reason, 2004), even though the important role the audience plays is well acknowledged. "Can theatre exist without an audience? At least one spectator is needed to make it a performance" (Grotowski, cited by Bennett, 1990, p. 1). Richard Schechner, Victor Turner, Jane Goodall, and other practical and theoretical theatre researchers consider the audience "a tangibly active creator of the theatrical event" (Bennett, 2013, p. 9). Caroline Heim (2010) believes there are myriad ways, "vocally, physically, emotionally and perceptually" (p. 1),

DOI: 10.4324/9781032686424-12

for audiences to contribute to the whole process of performance, especially post-show. Additionally, Rosanne Martorella (1977) expressed the weight of audiences and patrons by acknowledging that "they express their interest by purchasing tickets and making contributions" (pp. 356–357) even before they buy the ticket. All these statements value the importance and contribution of audiences to theatres, from the attempt to be an audience to sitting in the auditorium until after the performance. However, the reality is that there is limited empirical research dedicated to audiences (Reason, 2004). The understudy of the audience in academia does not mean that the theatre event stakeholders neglect their audience, the fact that an after-performance survey is a routine action for the theatre venues shows the value of the audience for the theatre venue. However, neither the numerous audience surveys in practice nor the limited empirical audience research in academia has managed to reveal a deeper understanding of the theatre audience, such as the segments, motivations, or experiences. The little communication between practice and academic research has not contributed to changing the current situation. Action research, in this research context, led by an academic researcher, bridges a communication channel for the industry and the academic to exchange understanding of the audience via daily operations, contributing to the construction of common knowledge to improve practice and further research.

This chapter critically examines the author's experience as an action researcher in cross-cultural theatre marketing in the UK from 2014 to 2018. Action research, simply put, is a methodology centred around "learning by doing" (O'Brien, 1998), which has garnered increasing attention in the study of social phenomena (Checkland and Holwell, 2007). The five-year experience of actively engaging in marketing Chinese theatre productions in the UK not only offers first-hand insights into the application of this methodology but also yields practical and theoretical outcomes derived from these "actions" initiatives within the industry. Through a series of "plan-act-observe-reflect" processes carried out in various settings, including festivals (e.g., the Edinburgh Fringe Festival), commercial performances in the West End, and collaborative educational events, this paper reflects on the original practice of action research in cross-cultural marketing within the theatre industry. The extended collaboration afforded by action research effectively bridged the gap between the industry and the academia regarding audience profiles, motivations, experiences, culminating in the synthesis of novel insights from their actions. Notably, collaborations between cultural and commercial entities were found to significantly enhance audience engagement for inter-cultural theatre events in the UK. Furthermore, as the researcher delved deeper into their engagement with practitioners, they observed that communication gaps extended not only between industry and academia but also, more problematically, across various sectors within the industry itself. These included disparities between national subsidised institutes and smaller cultural organisations, among cultural entities and commercial institutes, and among regional, national, international, and foreign theatre institutions. Action research, as an innovative methodology, affords the researcher a dual role, enabling them to observe, reflect upon, and distil lessons learned from practice to academia and vice versa.

Building upon this reflection, this chapter aims to validate the efficacy of this innovative methodology in theatre marketing practice and research while also providing a practical "how-to" guide to facilitate collaboration between researchers and practitioners, fostering knowledge sharing and problem-solving. Drawing from five years of practical experience as an action researcher within the industry, the researcher advocates for increased collaborative projects utilising action research methodology within the theatre industry and events sector. Such initiatives aim to systematically address the challenges associated with knowledge transformation between practice and academia.

Action Research and the Application

The methodology employed in the study of theatre participation has predominantly favoured quantitative research methods, particularly in the context of marketing studies (Ginters, 2010). Surveys represent one of the most commonly used techniques for comprehending the theatre audience by both practitioners and researchers. Nevertheless, as asserted by Walmsley (2011), quantitative methods have yet to convincingly demonstrate "a true synthesis of motivation" as they fall short in elucidating "the behavioural and emotional meaning of unmet needs" (p. 4), a crucial aspect for understanding and analysing audiences' oriented pursuit of theatre. Moreover, Walmsley (2015) notes a methodological shift in audience study from marketing and metrics towards anthropology and discovery. This shift frequently involves academics and arts workers acting as facilitators and conduits to cultural value and meaning. Tedlock (1991) makes analogous statements about cultural anthropology, proposing that the receptionist of a gallery or museum possesses the resources to be the best anthropologist studying the audience or visitors to the institution. In other words, working in creative events provides a unique position to study the audience and their behaviours during the event or cultural activity. To comprehend the audience and their participating experience, qualitative research – anthropology being one such approach – aligns with the requirement, and action research is an effective method to provide practical and academic perspectives in the creative event setting. Action research is deeply rooted in the anthropology approach.

Anthropology, as defined by Ingold (2008), is "a practice of observation grounded in participatory dialogue" (p. 87), and "a field of nomothetic science" (p. 70), in contrast to ethnography, which is idiographic and descriptive. Ingold (2008) endorses anthropology as a philosophy, stating that "it is not a study of at all, but a study *with*" (p. 82, original italics), and argues that anthropologists "do their thing, talking and writing in and with the world" (p. 88). We have been unable to study the unknown world from the armchair, ever since Malinowski's (1922) suggestion that the ethnographer must be able to "grasp the native's point of view, his relation to life, to realize his version of his world." Researchers should attain "human understanding" through learning to "think, see, feel and sometimes even behave as a native" (Malinowski, 1922, p. 25 cited by Tedlock, 1991, pp. 69–70). The world, Ingold (2008) insists, is "what we think *with*" rather than "what we think about" (p. 83). Regarding the participatory experience understanding of creative events, especially in a cross-cultural context, unless researchers engage with audiences and practitioners in the industry, converse with them, listen to them, think and take actions with them, they will never fully understand either existing or potential audiences and how to take efficient actions to engage them in theatre events. In this project, the position as a working member of the team as well as a participant provides the researcher with a unique lens to study the cross-cultural interaction and engagement of the creative event, further contributing to the marketing strategy for forthcoming events.

Denscombe (2014) defines action research as a research strategy rather than a research method. Action research is a term used to describe a "spectrum of activities" (Cunningham, 1993, p. 4) that focuses on "research, planning, theorizing, learning, and development" (Cunningham, 1993, p. 4). The aim of this research strategy is to conceive the research and learning process as a long-term relationship with a social issue/problem. Sanford (1981) describes the process of research as "analysis, fact-doing, conceptualization, planning, execution," followed by more findings and evaluation, and this process is repeated until the studied issue is solved. This definition of the repeated process/circle echoes the definition of action research by Kurt Lewin (1946). Lewin was the first to coin the term "action research," and he defines it as "comparative research on the conditions and effects of various forms of social action and research leading to social action" (Lewin, 1946, p. 35) and as "a spiral of steps, each of which is composed of a circle of planning, action, and fact-finding about the result of the action" (Lewin, 1946, p. 38), and in the practice of this research, each case the researcher participated followed the following four steps: planning, acting, observing, and reflecting.

Lewin (1946) posited that psychology, sociology, and cultural anthropology should collaborate on social issues, and action research is the culmination of this integrated approach to social research. Although Lewin never systematically articulated his views on action research, a few themes stand out (Argyris, Putnam, and Smith, 1985): it involves change experiments on real problems in social systems, focuses on a particular problem, and seeks to provide assistance to the client system; it incorporates iterative cycles of identifying a problem, planning, acting, and evaluating; it includes re-education; it challenges the status quo from the perspective of democratic values, which requires effective re-education; and it aims to contribute to basic knowledge in social science and social action in everyday life. The emphasis of action research, stressed by Lewin, lies in the continuities between the activities of science and the activities of learning in the action context, "the mutually reinforcing values of science, democracy, and education, and the benefits of combining science and social practice" (Argyris, Putnam, and Smith, 1985, pp. 7–8). Also, the central concerns of "the practice of intervention" and the distinctive feature of action research involve "engagement with client systems" (Argyris, Putnam, and Smith, 1985, pp. 7–8), which aligns with Ingold's (2008) definition of anthropology working with the world. Specific to participatory action research (PAR), Heron's (1996) definition makes the link clear: "action research is doing research 'with' people rather than undertaking research 'on' people or 'about' people" (cited by Yu, 2004, p. 121). This is exactly what Ingold (2008) insists about the anthropological research spirit: work and think with people instead of on or about them.

The core attitude of action research guided the practice and the research process of the UK–China theatre projects between 2015 and 2019 and onwards. In practice, action research is associated with social change and committed to social justice; the researcher participated in conducting the research as well as working for the improvement of the community (Bell, 2010). In cultural and creative industries, participatory research seeks to relocate the power dimension between the academic as an expert in control and the community members, transforming it so that community members take the role of driving and shaping the research (Finkel and Sang, 2016). In the five-year-long practice in the industry, the researcher did not attempt to relocate the "power dimension" as a researcher, instead she immersed herself in the community as a genuine working member with the theoretical knowledge and the cumulated practical industrial experience to reshape the practice of intercultural theatre marketing with the community.

The practice as a member of the production and marketing teams in three different Chinese theatre productions in the UK over five years provided the researcher with a unique position to plan, act, observe, and evaluate in different live event scenarios. The experience of working and thinking *with* practitioners in the creative industries has led to a better understanding of the challenges of marketing foreign productions and potential strategies through multiple rounds of action-reflection cycles during the five-year period of rooted herself in the creative industry community.

The three Chinese theatre productions the author took action with are *Richard III* in Shakespeare's Globe Theatre (London) by the National Theatre of China; *Poker Night Blues* at the Edinburgh Fringe Festival (Edinburgh) by a private Chinese theatre company; and China National Peking Opera Company's UK tour in 2015 and the following four years performance projects. In 2015, the three productions happened one after another; the action-reflection cycle from the earlier project impacted on the planning stage of the following one, and these three cycles constructed the PhD thesis of the researcher, and the theoretical analysis from the evaluation and reflection from the practice in 2015 initiated the planning stage of the following four-year Peking Opera UK tour project, which is the key case study in this chapter. All three productions were performed in Mandarin with English subtitles and aimed to attract the local British audience. From the production's perspective, the three cases in 2015 include three different theatre typologies: *Richard III* is a Shakespearean spoken drama, *Poker Night Blues* is a piece of physical theatre, and Peking Opera is a traditional Chinese musical performance with dancing.

Although all three productions are from China and use Mandarin for dialogue, the cultural familiarity of the three productions, as Carlson (1990) defines it, is different (see Figure 12.1) to the local audience. The first production is a Chinese version of a famous Shakespearean play. For a British audience, the Chinese stage traditions are still culturally "foreign," but it builds upon the familiar Shakespearean story, which locates it between levels 5 and 6.

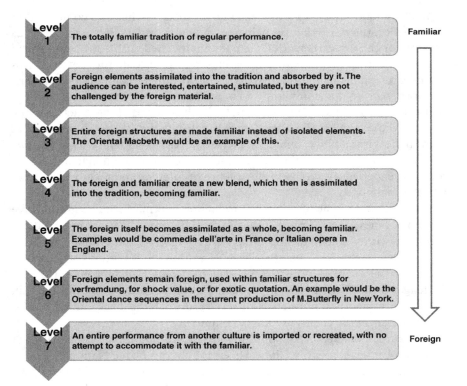

FIGURE 12.1 Levels from culturally familiar to the culturally foreign.

(Based on Carlson, 1990).

The reason for this location is that the Chinese cultural elements and theatrical expression remain foreign; however, the foreign elements are assimilated with the familiar Shakespearean story, making the whole experience of the play relatively familiar.

The second production, *Poker Night Blues*, shares similarities with the first to some degree (located at level 4). The combination of a well-known Western masterpiece (adapted from *"A Streetcar Named Desire"* by Tennessee Williams) with Chinese stylised physical expression makes the experience closer to the familiar than the foreign for the audience. At the same time, the special international and avant-garde festival context (the International Edinburgh Festival Fringe) makes the cultural fusion less foreign for the audience.

The third production, the Peking Opera tour is entirely traditional Northern Chinese in terms of story, narrative style, stage design, cultural background, and performing tradition, leading to the most foreign experience of the three cases (level 7). The varied cultural familiarity of these three productions provided different contexts for the researcher to action with different teams and different sections in the theatre industry and to observe the audience of Chinese theatre in the UK in different settings. These diverse action-reflection cycles enhanced the theoretical reflections of the researcher's practical actions.

The three productions in 2015 built up a linear process of three action-reflection circles: the practice and research with *Richard III* inspired the planning and acting of *Poker Night Blues* in Edinburgh, and the reflections from actions of the first two productions guided the Peking Opera tour in 2015. In the following four years (2016–2019) of China National Peking Opera Company's performance and related educational events in the UK, the researcher was deeply involved in producing and marketing practice (see Figure 12.2) with the knowledge of a researcher. Action research as a method had been applied in daily practice in each event during the period, with reflections and evaluations from the previous action-reflection cycles. The evaluations and experiences from the three different projects with varied levels of cultural foreignness not only contributed to the academic theories in cross-cultural theatre audience understanding and marketing strategy but also to the practical knowledge in working in the theatre industry as a practitioner. Consequently, the research had applied action research in the following four-year Peking Opera UK tour project with more confidence in planning, acting, observing, and reflecting as well as in working *with* the community on proposing the potential solutions to the challenges. Hence, more changes had been proposed and implemented through the four-year practical project, and before the COVID-19 global pandemic, marked certain impact in the industry. But the evaluation and reflection from this action-reflection cycle on the theoretical level have not yet been systematically written and published. This chapter is the first attempt to reflect on the four-year action research project in which the

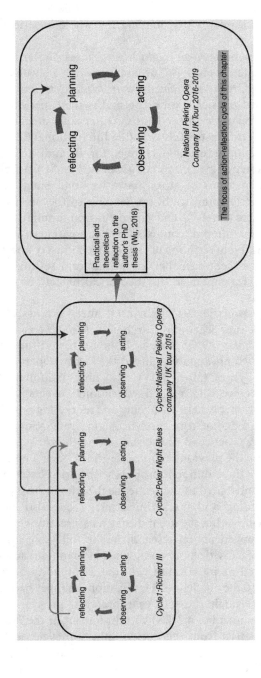

FIGURE 12.2 Flow chart of the action-reflection cycles of this project.

researcher initiated the planning to tackle one of the most difficult practical challenges of intercultural marketing in theatre events: how to reach out to the right audience segments.

Confronting the Challenge with the Community

The Role of the Researcher in the Team

Bringing the role of a researcher to the practice, the author and the producing company of the China National Peking Opera Company in the UK reached an undocumented agreement for the author to join the team as a freelancer and, after submitting the PhD thesis, as a full-time employee. The producing company itself is newly established with the aim of presenting Chinese performing arts, particularly traditional cultural heritage, to the UK market and eventually expanding into the European market. The key members include the producing director, K, who is strongly connected with Peking Opera performing companies in China, and producer B, who has experience in the entertainment industry in the UK (see Figure 12.3). The researcher's role in the team was agreed upon as follows:

Daily work: Taking on the role of an international producing assistant to bridge the Chinese performing company with the British market, including coordinating with theatre venues and designing marketing campaigns.

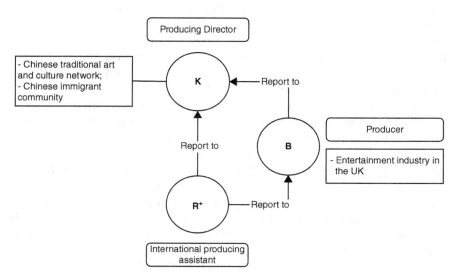

FIGURE 12.3   Key roles in the participated company (*Researcher).

As an expert: Proposing and supervising the marketing strategy, including the target audience, digital marketing contents, and educational events.

As a researcher: The author had the freedom to take notes of her work, including internal meetings, meetings with stakeholders (anonymity), observations of the performance and the events. Irregularly, the researcher brought her findings to the team to propose new solutions for the challenges (not related to financial issues) observed.

The role as a colleague instead of an external expert provided an immersed position for the researcher to reflect on the challenges from the real theatre event scenario and confront them with the community – the cross-cultural theatre industry – and eventually sum up the solutions from the practice. This chapter will reflect on how the researcher worked with the community to confront the challenge. There were difficulties during communication internally as well as with partners in the industry, and more importantly, there were inspirations for all the stakeholders to move forward in future practice and research in audience understanding and marketing strategy.

Identify the Audience

Before taking actions with the three Chinese theatre productions, some audience segments that might be interested in Chinese performance were interviewed to pre-test audience awareness and gauge their opinions of foreign productions. The reflections upon these interviews contributed to the plan for the first case, *Richard III*, as the action-reflection cycle requires, and the same for the next two cases. In summary, 40 interviews were conducted, including 55 interviewees (informal short conversations were conducted with more people, but their information is not included; however, their opinions contribute to the findings) from the three productions in 2015. The theoretical analysis of the observation and reflection from the practice contributes to the following four-year Peking Opera project (see Figure 12.2).

From the first three practices in different event scenarios with different cultural content, the audience profile for Chinese theatre in the UK has been sketched. The demographic details from the interviewees offer a skewed profile of the attendees of Chinese theatre in the UK: middle-aged or above, highly educated, professional, and often working in the cultural industries. In other words, they represent typical theatre-goers in the UK (Wu, 2018). In the Peking Opera performance in 2015, along with the theatre-goers, there were a significant number of Chinese immigrants (first and second generations) in different age groups who normally came with family members (including non-Chinese) and friends (Wu, 2018).

To segment the audience further, the lifestyles of the interviewees were reflected to enrich the understanding of the audience. Using lifestyle factors, also called psychographics, is considered a more variable and dynamic approach to audience segmentation than traditional divisions such as socioeconomic characteristics (Kotler and Scheff, 1997). Lifestyle segmentation is based on the idea that people do what they do because it fits into the kind of life they live or want to live, leading to a focus on the audiences' activities, interests, values, opinions, and the like (Kotler and Scheff, 1997).

The lifestyles of the audience for Chinese theatre in the UK reflect a shared interest in theatre and foreign cultures. The common lifestyle factors of the audiences include strong interests in arts, cultural events, and cross-cultural travel. To be specific, the majority of the attendees interviewed are theatre-goers who love theatre in general and attend arts events regularly. Also, if they can afford it, they tend to seek out new theatrical and cultural experiences. Moreover, as theatre-goers, they would try to experience local performances when travelling in a foreign culture (Wu, 2018). The features of the attendees match the audience segmentations identified by The Audience Agency (2017): Metroculturals – prosperous, liberal, urbanites interested in a very wide cultural spectrum; Commuterland Culturebuffs – affluent and professional consumers of culture; and Experience Seekers – highly active, diverse, social, and ambitious, engaging with arts regularly.

In other words, audiences for Chinese theatre in the UK are open to foreign cultures and love to travel to foreign countries whenever they have the opportunity. Instead of being "the snob" (Peterson and Kern, 1996), the audience who is willing to engage with Chinese theatre in the UK, from the perspective of cultural sociology, are more "the omnivore" (Roose, Van Eijck, and Lievens, 2012). Omnivorousness, defined by Peterson and Kern (1996), is a reflection of openness to other cultures and the weakening of both social and cultural boundaries. Peterson (1992) applies the term to audience lifestyle and states that the audience is omnivorous for cultural productions, which he calls "cultural omnivores." In Maguire's (2015) book, cultural omnivores are cultural consumers whose cultural consumption tastes include both high-brow and popular genres. A similar argument of cultural openness is suggested by Roose, Van Eijck, and Lievens (2012): "A more open personality," they believe, "is likely to engage more in both diverse and high-brow cultural behaviour" (Roose, Van Eijck, and Lievens, 2012, p. 494). Roose, Van Eijck, and Lievens (2012) conclude from their empirical research that this omnivorousness is part of a cultural lifestyle, and the openness related to "trying new things and enjoying diversity" is characteristic of cultural omnivores. In the cross-cultural engagement context, the cultural omnivores in the UK who are open to diverse cultural events are more willing to try the novel cultural experience. The observation and reflection from the three participated action-reflection cycles, the British audience who attended the Chinese theatre events took the activity as a statement of their identities as cultural omnivores (Wu, 2018).

The demographic and lifestyle portrait of the audience from the three action-reflection cycles in 2015 provides the target audience segment for the Peking Opera performance in London in the following four years. The clear identification of the audience and further the motivations for their participation in foreign theatre events assisted the author in proposing new outreach strategies to the team in the company and eventually taking actions with them.

Doubt and Support: Working Together

The author presented observations about the audience for two contemporary Chinese theatre productions and the first Peking Opera performance to the team: traditional theatre-goers, cross-cultural travellers, and Chinese immigrants, especially those with families. The team was in doubt; both K and B believed that as a traditional Chinese performance, the Chinese immigrant community was the natural key segment.

For K, previous experience in organising Chinese community events convinced him that immigrants longed for authentic cultural activities. The findings from the first Peking Opera performance also agreed with this experience; for Chinese immigrants, one of the key motivations for attending was "cultural homecoming" and the "nostalgia" from the performance (Wu, 2018). However, among the Chinese immigrant community, there were more familiar audiences (aged 30s–40s) who came with younger generations. They did not need the sense of "cultural belonging" themselves, as Peking Opera was too traditional and Northern-culture-oriented. Instead, they considered it an authentic cultural event, wanting their children, born outside of the homeland, to find their "cultural roots" through participation in these events. Compared to the "old Chinese immigrants," the Chinatown community, the new immigrants, known as "the educational immigrants" (Chen, Tajeddini, Ratten, and Tabari, 2019), were more motivated to "pay" for cultural events for educational purposes for their children. The discussion with K did not entirely convince him about the sub-segmentation of the Chinese community, but he agreed to take action on targeting the new immigrants while he focused on his familiar community. With the project unfolding, K realised that the Chinese old immigrant community was not used to the concept of paying for a "community cultural event," which the China National Peking Opera Company's UK tour clearly was not.

For the experienced commercial event producer B, targeting British theatre-goers for a traditional Chinese opera performance was mistargeted and commercially risky. Even English-spoken Shakespearean productions could flop in the West End; how could a traditional Chinese opera performance, the most foreign cultural production, attract the picky London theatre audience? The interview notes from the previous three cases did not completely dismiss the doubt but convinced her to try, albeit with a limited budget in marketing and PR campaigns.

Eventually, the second year of the five-year UK tour project (2016) initiated the targeted audience segments: regular British theatre-goers, cross-cultural theatre travellers, and, in the current context, those who had travelled to China would be the target, along with new Chinese immigrants. Audience development continued in the following four years, and the strategy of reaching the targeted audience was developed over the years based on the agreed-upon audience segments.

The first year of the Peking Opera project relied on a PR campaign (articles in top newspapers and traditional media buying, e.g., posters in London underground stations) to attract the general public and word of mouth in the Chinese community. It did work to a certain degree but with a high cost to push the performance information to the general public. The following four years faced the challenge of a limited budget in PR and marketing and aiming to achieve a higher box office. The specific audience portrait proposed by the researcher to the company helped build an efficient marketing strategy to deliver the information to the right audience.

The motivations of theatre-going were another concept that the researcher brought to the team to justify the educational events co-organized with other public institutes as a promotional campaign. The financial pressure on the producing company, a private company, made the management team (K and B) cautious about non-profitable activities and naturally doubted the author's "business sense" due to the "researcher mindset." Through working with the team throughout the projects and providing practical suggestions and a hands-on professional attitude, the identity as a "researcher" had been slowly transformed into "international producer" and a key member of the team, especially from the third year of the project. Consequently, the theoretical knowledge that the researcher brought to the practice had been better valued within the company.

Cooper-Martin (1991) considers live performance events to be experiential services, meaning services consumers expect to "experience and enjoy" through consumption. In other words, Cooper-Martin believes that to "experience" and "enjoy" are the underlying motivations for experiential consumption. To some degree, audiences go to the theatre for experience and enjoyment, as with many other experiential services, but the distinction between a theatre experience and other types of experiential services makes the motivations for attendance much more complicated and nuanced than simply experience and enjoyment.

Understanding why audiences are motivated to attend a theatre production is one of the key topics of audience research. Kotler and Armstrong (2008) define consumer motivation as the need that directs people to seek satisfaction of their desires. Desires and needs motivate audiences to take action, which, to some degree, explains theatre attendance behaviours. The desires and expectations of theatre-going, as existing research shows, are emotional, intellectual, social, edutainment, escapist, aesthetic, self-esteem enhancement, novelty, and hedonism (Walmsley, 2011; Swanson, Davis, and Zhao, 2008; Nicholson and Pearce, 2001, etc.). Motivations for theatre attendance are complicated, and people are not motivated by just one thing. The drivers of theatre-going overlap rather than being mutually exclusive. For Chinese theatre-going, it is even more so. The summary from the first three action-reflection cycles indicates that the motivations for the audience participating in the Chinese theatre event in the UK are new experiences, risk and artistic quality, aesthetic enjoyment and nostalgia, cultural inheritance and education, family cohesion, and social motivation (Wu, 2018).

To explain the motivations further, risk and artistic quality are strongly related to cultural foreign productions. For theatre productions, which are intangible experiences, quality is difficult to judge in advance, unlike durable goods, and no refund or compensation is possible (Throsby, 1990; Colbert, 2003). Attending a foreign theatre production is more risky for the audience, as Throsby (1990) argues. For regular theatre-goers, they seek new experiences, but some assurance of artistic quality is essential to motivate them. Peking Opera as a completely foreign production, the assurance of the artistic quality of the performance comes from the performance company of China National Peking Opera Company and, more importantly, the cultural institutes the audiences are familiar with. In the theatre event context, the theatre venue provides a certain guarantee for the regular theatre-goers due to familiarity as well as the artistic reputation of the cultural institute.

Based on this understanding, the researcher proposed to work with the venue in audience outreach.

The theatre venue did not expect the request and had the same doubt about targeting regular theatre-goers as K and B. The marketing and event team from the venue was not convinced at the beginning; "our regular audiences are interested in contemporary dance, not traditional opera." "But they also love productions from foreign cultures, like traditional Indian dance," the researcher and B challenged their judgement based on our knowledge of the West End industry. Eventually, the venue introduced the Peking Opera production to their audience base through newsletters, social media posts, and posters in the venue to deliver the event information to their audience members. From conversations with the venue's marketing team over the five-year collaboration, they had mentioned that it has also been a learning curve for them, especially refreshing their understanding of the audience: new experiences from foreign productions are welcome. Through the broader inclusion of international productions, Peking Opera was one of them, the venue also enhanced the reputation of the artistic quality among the general theatre-goers and their audience base.

The motivations of cultural inheritance and education combined with artistic quality led to the proposal of series educational events from 2017. The company was hesitant due to the budget until the researcher successfully pitched the events to the British Library. Collaborating with the British Library in educational events not only helped the theatre event reach a broader audience base but also ensured the artistic quality from the collaborative organisation. The knowledge-sharing nature of the British Library has a big base of audience who is interested in foreign culture, as well as families with children who are interested in general educational events in relation to diverse cultures, including educational Chinese immigrants. The collaboration opened a door for the Peking Opera performance to the target audience segments who are not necessarily theatre-goers but cultural and educational event-goers.

The pitching process was not strongly supported by the company simply because they did not believe the British Library would work with a small private company. But they did agree to the attempt of trying. Coming from a higher education background, the communication between the research and the British Library highlighted the educational purpose of providing a diverse cultural perspective for the audience. Endorsed by the artistic quality of the China National Peking Opera Company and the academic and industrial leaders in performing arts from the pan-China region, the proposal was happily accepted for shared benefits. The event team from the British Library was surprised that a private company could provide connections with the national cultural institutes and the industrial leaders, and the company was overjoyed to provide a different stage for the Peking Opera events to the British audience. The obstacle to the collaboration was the little knowledge about each other, especially the offerings smaller cross-culturally oriented companies could provide to enhance the international programme for the national cultural institute in the UK.

The role the researcher played in this process is a broker to bridge different institutes based on the understanding of their own demands and resources. To work in the industry with the community makes it clear that there is a big communication gap among different types of institutes. In this scenario, the private producing company, the theatre venue, and the subsidised cultural and educational institutions do not share their understanding about their audience and lack the strategy to provide "new experiences" for them. The communication and sharing inside the community vertically and horizontally would inspire new collaborations and create new contents and cultural events for the public, and the action researcher plays a key role in this process.

Little did the researcher know that inter-institutional collaboration could extend to commercial organisations. Developed from the audience segment that the audience with experience of travelling to China would be interested in similar cultural experiences in their home country, K reached out to tourist agencies to provide a special "authentic Chinese cultural trip" in London. And thinking out of the box, different from the mindset of a theatre practitioner and a researcher, K approached the London-based companies which focused on the UK-China business exchange to promote the Peking Opera performance event as a cultural communication evening for the business purpose. Profit-oriented approaches from the company introduced the researcher to a domain of non-subsidized cultural organisations which operate and function differently from many other cultural institutes, especially the local British ones. Moreover, the idea that the community of the theatre industry could reach out beyond the cultural and educational institutes inspired many new collaboration ideas for the author and the team she was working with.

In the rest few years of the Peking Opera project in the UK, educational events became part of the programme and reached out to Oxford and other regions of the UK, and engaged with middle schools and museums in the region. Observation from the audience motivations in return contributes to the collaboration in the community to provide new experiences, high artistic quality contents, educational and social events for the audience. Until the outbreak of the global pandemic, acting with the community extended to other projects and the established collaboration within the company as well as the partners in the industries provided a solid ground for further experimental actions to confront more challenges. Before more changes could be made through working together, the cross-cultural exchange was forced to pause and the action-reflection cycle of this project came to an uninformed end, but the theoretical and methodological reflection from the practice has just started.

Author's Lessons Learned and Suggestions

The author's practical experience, coupled with her research in cross-cultural theatre events dating back to 2013, has established close connections with various stakeholders. However, this long-term engagement has given rise to certain issues during both the practical implementation and theoretical evaluation processes in this action research project.

The first lesson learned from this close collaboration and co-worker relationship is the blurring of boundaries between research and practice. The author's deep immersion in the daily operations of the company, maintained over five years as an insider, provided a unique perspective to observe and analyse the industry landscape. Nevertheless, the lack of distance hindered a clear understanding of the macro context of cross-cultural live events in the research and practice, and also limited the impact of findings from this project. This is primarily attributed to the author's role as a "full-timer" in the company, leaving little time for evaluation and reflection as a researcher. Simultaneously, this role distanced the author from the academic environment necessary for critical analysis.

A suggestion for researchers engaging in action research and deeply immersing themselves in a community, drawn from this project, is to schedule regular moments of detachment to reflect and evaluate observations from practice. Additionally, it is advisable to maintain affiliation with academic institutes, especially with research centres of shared topics. This not only sustains connections with like-minded researchers but also ensures access to up-to-date theories for the action researcher. Importantly, it facilitates the dissemination of community actions to academia for a more extensive impact.

From an institutional perspective, the suggestion from this lesson is to promote closer ties between research institutes and industry organisations, fostering the application of action research from within the community. In this scenario, research institutes take on a supportive role, aiding practitioners in initiating action research endeavours. This involves training practitioners to adopt a "researcher" mindset and facilitating regular meetings for the exchange of up-to-date information between academia and practice. This collaborative approach not only contributes to practical impact but also ensures the continuous refinement of theories based on insights derived directly from real-world experiences.

The second lesson learned is the importance of learning from co-workers. While the author's dual experience in both practice and academia in the theatre industry instilled confidence in proposing solutions to challenges, it also hindered openness to learning from colleagues. The author, in internal discussions and meetings, focused on convincing the team that her suggestions could impact the challenges. If more time had been spent inviting ideas from the team and industry partners, there might have been more inspirations, such as K's approach to international businessmen as potential audience members. Equal and open conversations among different roles and institutes in the industry can lead to more innovative ideas and a broader impact in real scenarios.

The suggestion derived from this lesson for all researchers is to remain humble and open-minded when working with the community. More importantly, it is crucial to establish and maintain open communication channels for different stakeholders in the industry. Inviting diverse voices and perspectives can lead to better solutions, more efficient implementations, and a wider industrial impact.

Conclusions

The interaction between the theatre industry and academia predominantly centres on the stage, where the spotlight shines. The audience, shrouded in darkness, often remains obscure, and the knowledge exchange between practice and research is also limited. Cross-cultural theatre, being a niche market within the industry, caters to an audience whose profile is even less clearly defined than the regular theatre audience. Action research applied in this project was led by a trained researcher with industrial experience and connections, serves as a catalyst for bridging the gap and fostering knowledge exchange between academia and the industry in this specific area.

As a methodological approach, action research establishes a platform for the professionals with diverse roles but a shared interest in a particular subject to convene and collaboratively address the community challenges. The action research project discussed in this chapter illustrates the researcher's participatory role in daily practices within the community, effectively reaching out to the audience for Peking Opera performance events in the UK. The successful transformation of knowledge between practice and academia, facilitated by the application of action research methodology, resulted in a more effective marketing strategy, improved audience engagement, and, significantly, enhanced organisational collaborations to initiate new events. Insights garnered from previous action-reflection cycles, in which the researcher actively participated, significantly informed the approach to new challenges with a new action-reflection cycle. The culmination of these experiences will undergo evaluation and reflection in subsequent action research projects, further influencing the practice in the industry. Undoubtedly, challenges and conflicts arose during collaboration with the community. The communication gap among different organisations and practitioners with varied roles has been consistently evident throughout the researcher's action-reflection cycles. However, reflections based on original, first-hand experiences not only bridged theoretical gaps in understanding cross-cultural theatre events from audience and marketing perspectives but also had a tangible impact on the community. In the aftermath of the global pandemic's catastrophic effects on the theatre industry, enhanced collaboration between academia and the industry through various action research approaches has the potential to expedite industry recovery. Moreover, it can extend cultural event experiences to broader audience segments, fostering diversity within the sector.

References

Argyris, C., Putnam, R. and Smith, D.M. (1985) *Action science* (Vol. 13). San Francisco: Jossey-Bass Publishers.

Bell, J. (2010) *Doing your research project*. Milton Keynes: Open University Press.

Bennett, S. (1990) *Theatre audience: A theory of production and reception*. London: Routledge.

Bennett, S., (2013) *Theatre audiences*. New York: Routledge.

Carlson, M. (1990) Peter Brook's The Mahabharata and Ariane Mnouchkine's L'Indiade as examples of contemporary cross-cultural theatre. *The Dramatic Touch of Difference: Theatre, Own and Foreign*, 2, p. 49.

Checkland, P. and Holwell, S. (2007) Action research: Its nature and validity. In *Information systems action research: An applied view of emerging concepts and methods*, edited by Ned Kock, pp. 3–17. New York: Springer.

Chen, W., Tajeddini, K., Ratten, V., & Tabari, S. (2019) Educational immigrants: Evidence from Chinese young entrepreneurs in the UK. *Journal of Enterprising Communities: People and Places in the Global Economy*, 13(1/2), pp. 196–215.

Colbert, F., (2003) Entrepreneurship and leadership in marketing the arts. *International Journal of Arts Management*, 6(1), pp. 30–39.

Cooper-Martin, E. (1991) Consumers and movies: Some findings on experiential products. *Advances in Consumer Research*, 19(1992), pp. 756–761.

Cunningham, J.B., (1993) *Action research and organizational development*. New York: Bloomsbury Publishing Inc.

Denscombe, M. (2014) *The good research guide: For small-scale social research projects*. Berkshire: Open University Press, McGraw-Hill Education.

Finkel, R. and Sang, K. (2016) Participatory research: Case study of a community event. *Critical event studies: Approaches to research*, pp. 195–211.

Ginters, L. (2010) On audiencing: The work of the spectator in live performance. *About Performance Issue*, 10, pp. 7–14.

Heim, C.L. (2010) *Theatre audience contribution: Facilitating a new text through the post-performance discussion*. Saarbrucken: Lambert Academic Publishing.

Heron, J. (1996) *Co-operative Inquiry: Research into the Human Condition*. London: Sage.

Ingold, T., (2008 March). Anthropology is not ethnography. In *Proceedings of the British Academy* (Vol. 154, No. 11, pp. 69–92).

Kotler, P. and Armstrong, G. (2008) *Principles of marketing* (12th ed). London: Pearson Education Limited.

Kotler, P. and Scheff, J. (1997) *Standing room only: Strategies for marketing the performing arts*. Boston: Harvard Business School Press.

Lewin, K. (1946) Action research and minority problems. *Journal of Social Issues*, 2(4), pp. 34–46.

Maguire, J.S. (2015) Cultural omnivores. In Cook and Ryan (Eds.), *The Wiley Blackwell encyclopedia of consumption and consumer studies*, pp. 1–2. New Jersey: Wiley Blackwell.

Malinowski, B. (1922) Ethnology and the study of society. *Economica*, 6, pp. 208–219.

Martorella, R. (1977) The relationship between box office and repertoire: A case study of opera. *Sociological Quarterly*, 18(3), pp. 354–366.

Nicholson, R.E. and Pearce, D.G. (2001) Why do people attend events: A comparative analysis of visitor motivations at four South Island events. *Journal of Travel Research*, 39(4), pp. 449–460.

O'Brien, R. (1998) An overview of the methodological approach of action research. In Roberto Richardson (Ed.), *Teoria e Prática da Pesquisa Ação [Theory and Practice of Action Research]*. João Pessoa, Brazil: Universidade Federal da Paraíba.

Peterson, R.A. (1992) Understanding audience segmentation: From elite and mass to omnivore and univore. *Poetics*, 21(4), pp. 243–258.

Peterson, R.A. and Kern, R.M. (1996) Changing highbrow taste: From snob to omnivore. *American Sociological Review*, 61(5), pp. 900–907.

Reason, M. (2004) Theatre audiences and perceptions of 'liveness' in performance. *Participations: Journal of Audience and Reception Studies*, 1(2), pp. 1–23.

Roose, H., Van Eijck, K. and Lievens, J., (2012) Culture of distinction or culture of openness? Using a social space approach to analyze the social structuring of lifestyles. *Poetics*, 40(6), pp. 491–513.

Sanford, N., (1981) A model for action research. *Human inquiry*, pp. 173–181.

Silvers, J.R. (2012) *Professional event coordination* (Vol. 62). New Jersey: John Wiley & Sons.

Swanson, S., Davis, J. and Zhao, Y. (2008) Art for art's sake? An examination of motives for arts performance attendance. *Nonprofit and Voluntary Sector Quarterly*, 37(2), pp. 300–323.

Tedlock, B. (1991) From participant observation to the observation of participation: The emergence of narrative ethnography. *Journal of Anthropological Research*, 47(1), pp. 69–94.

The Audience Agency. (2017) *Audience Spectrum: Segmenting the UK population by their attitudes towards culture, and by what they like to see and do*. Accessed August 2017. https://www.theaudienceagency.org/audience-spectrum

Throsby, C.D., (1990) Perception of quality in demand for the theatre. *Journal of Cultural Economics*, 14(1), pp. 65–82.

Walmsley, B. (2011) Why people go to the theatre: A qualitative study of audience motivation. *Journal of Customer Behaviour*, 10(4), pp. 335–351.

Walmsley, B. (2015) Audience engagement and the role of arts talk in the digital era. *Cultural Trends*, 24(4), pp. 322–323.

Wu, F. (2018) Attracting the "Sojourner": Insights into cross-cultural arts marketing through a case study of Chinese theatre in the UK (Doctoral dissertation, University of Leeds).

Yu, J.E. (2004) Reconsidering participatory action research for organizational transformation and social change. *Journal of Organisational Transformation & Social Change*, 1(2), pp. 111–141.

13

THE CREATIVE IS CRITICAL

Critical Creative Methods for
Post-Critical Event Studies

Rita Grácio

Universidade Lusófona, Lisbon, Portugal

Adalberto Fernandes

University of Algarve, Faro, Portugal

Introduction

Critical Event Studies emerges as a response to the imperative for a more profound and nuanced understanding of events in contemporary society. Scholars in event studies assert the need for a critical examination that transcends non-critical paradigms (Pernecky and Lück, 2013; Jackson, Morgan and Laws, 2018; Spracklen and Lamond, 2021). Situated within the intersections of cultural and creative industries, tourism, hospitality, leisure studies, and marketing, Critical Event Studies, by introducing the element of "critical", deliberately disrupts the conventional trajectory of event studies, signalling a departure from the often profit-driven orientation associated with the field. As opposed to confining itself to the examination of the formal aspects of events—such as their forms and contents—the critical lens of this sub-discipline extends its gaze towards the intricate interplay of social, cultural, environmental, and political dimensions. This reimagining prompts a fundamental questioning of the assumptions that underpin traditional event studies, urging scholars and practitioners to adopt a more reflexive stance. In sum, the critical expansion of event studies is a call to action. It challenges researchers to embrace a more comprehensive, interdisciplinary, and socially engaged approach.

However, as the burgeoning field of Critical Event Studies matures, the danger of adopting a superficial critical stance looms large, posing the risk of unintentionally replicating the accomplishments of preceding critical schools of thought and presenting them as, erroneously, novel. This challenge arises from the chronological constitution of Critical Event Studies—emerging after

DOI: 10.4324/9781032686424-13

the establishment of event studies as a non-critical discipline and considerably after the crystallisation of various critical schools of thought outside event studies. Positioned as a newcomer within the critical discourse, Critical Event Studies grapples with the complex task of shedding its conceptual baggage rooted in non-critical paradigms of event studies. This endeavour requires a meticulous understanding of its historical context, acknowledging its genesis within the context of an academic landscape that preceded the critical turn. Moreover, the potential for non-criticality is accentuated by a discernible gap in its engagement with the broader discourse surrounding the concept of critique. Effectively addressing the role of creative methods within Critical Event Studies necessitates a comprehensive response to this dual challenge— critiquing established non-critical schools of thought in Event Studies while actively engaging with well-established critical ones.

Herein lies the pivotal role of creativity as an instrument of critique and, by being a field that researches and methodically uses creativity, Critical Event Studies are at the front of this pivotal role. Creativity becomes a dynamic force that not only challenges the status quo of "non-critical" event studies but also fosters a robust and constructive dialogue with existing critical and post-critical paradigms. In the current landscape of de-financing of social sciences and the arts, we need to take very seriously the use of "creative methods" and "the arts" in the social sciences, so that creative methods can indeed "help us address societal questions that traditional methods cannot" (Kara, 2015), instead of either depoliticising social science through playful "anything goes" aestheticisation or merely "art-ificate" ornamentally the social sciences. As Critical Event Studies navigate this intellectual terrain, its deliberate fusion of creativity and critique emerges as a guiding principle, ensuring its resonance as a dynamic and transformative force within the ongoing dialogue with critical scholarship. This deliberate fusion positions Critical Event Studies as an active participant in shaping the future trajectories of critical thought.

Creative Methods in Social Sciences

Social sciences already deployed artistic, fictional, aesthetic, and creative methods since their inception, even if in the last ten years there has been a flourishing of creative methods in social sciences (Barone and Eisner, 2012; Kara, 2015; Leavy, 2017), which the COVID-19 pandemic gave more visibility to (Lupton, 2020). However, creative methods in social sciences do not show up necessarily under the name of "creative methods" as such. For instance, Helen Kara in her popular book on *Creative Methods in Social Sciences Research* (2015) proposes that creative methods can be analytically grouped into four key areas: 1) arts-based research (ABR), 2) research using technology, 3) mixed-methods research (Archibald and Gerber, 2018), and 4) transformative research frameworks (such as participatory, feminist and decolonising methodologies). These are not mutually exclusive categories. For instance, art-based and narrative research have been considered particularly suitable for projects concerned with social justice and social change, where a participatory, ethical and multivoiced ethos is in place.

ABR refers to the use of arts in the research process, including narrative inquiry, fiction-based research, poetic inquiry, music, dance and movement, theatre, drama, film, and visual art, mixed media arts, quilting and sculpture, among others (Barone and Eisner, 2012; Kara, 2015; Leavy, 2020). However, artistic inquiry as knowledge production can be traced back much before the postmodern turn in social sciences in the second half of the 20th century (Leavy and Chilton, 2020, p. 404), and it emerges closely linked to other qualitative research paradigms, such as narrative, hermeneutic and phenomenological research (Leavy and Chilton, 2020, p. 405). ABR is now claimed to be a "methodological genre" on its own or even an emergent research paradigm (Leavy, 2020). What is now clear is the burgeoning literature on the topic across different disciplines—from organisational studies (Broussine, 2008), to communication and media studies (Carpentier and Sumiala, 2021).

Art and art making have been used across all research stages in social sciences, from data gathering to data analysis and data representation, as well as combinations of these (Finley, 2008; Kara, 2015). Arts-based research is consensually employed in research projects that aim to describe and explore social, emotional, and other meta-cognitive experiences, as well as sensitive topics of so-called vulnerable people, as art affords specific ways of knowing (e.g. meta-verbal, embodied, emotional, aesthetic) (Inckle, 2010; Kara, 2015; Leavy, 2020). Hence, it is well suited to capture the multiplicity of meanings and meaning-making processes, but also to evoke empathy and a transformative understanding of the social (McNiff, 2008; Hogan and Pink, 2010).

The issue of who should conduct ABR is not consensual regarding the extent to which the researcher should be artistically skilled and the impact on the quality of the artwork produced. Those who argue in favour of the researcher-artist, claim that if the research outcome is not a proper artwork or has poor "aesthetic quality", then the arts in arts-based research is not fulfilled (Bagley and Cancienne, 2001; Piirto, 2002; Faulkner, 2009). Those who argue against, claim that the figure of the artist-researcher reinforces power imbalances between researcher and participants, and that requiring aesthetic quality—or "aesthetic powers"—reproduces pre-existing dominant criteria that are produced by elites, and does not allow redistribution of artistic resources for social transformation for those that don't usually have access to it: "If we embrace rigour, if we engage in hegemonic control of the beautiful in research, then we run the risk of missing the opportunity" of the arts to inform and transform our world (Finley *as quoted in* Leavy and Chilton, 2020, p. 416). A middle-ground solution to this dilemma has been the constitution of multidisciplinary teams, where social scientists and artists work together in the field with the research participants, under the criteria of "fit": what matters is if the methods are appropriate to the research and its context (Kara, 2015, p. 23).

However, the most controversial issue in ABR is the issue of assessing the scientific results produced. The knowledge claims produced in this kind of research practice are intended to be ambiguous enough "to allow for multiple, multidimensional, complex, dynamic, intersubjective, and contextual interpretations" (Leavy and Chilton, 2020, p. 417). If this is understood by their practitioners as these methods' strength, it is understood by their detractors as "subjective", "biased", and "non-scientific" (Adams St. Pierre and Roulston, 2006), hence reproducing the qualitative-quantitative epistemological, ontological and methodological "wars". We claim that arts-based research has to be included as part of the methodological pluralism repertoire of social sciences. What is interesting is the reconstruction of new criteria for what counts as quality in this field, as situated action, emerging from the interaction between actors that have asymmetrical power and the work itself, in specific times and places. Before exposing the critical role of creativity it is necessary to understand the difference between critical and post-critical approaches as this will help situate the critical or post-critical role of creativity.

Critical and Post-Critical Schools of Thought

By delving into the historical roots of critical thought, a certain trajectory unfolds from the seminal works of the Frankfurt School (Horkheimer and Adorno, 1982) to the contemporary proposals of post-critical sociology (Latour, 2004). The historical journey through critical scholarship unveils a rich discourse dedicated to unravelling the intricacies of critique. Following the description of the critical school made by Sloterdijk (2010), it can be identified with, at least, the following three traditional traits: 1) *Identification of Oppressors and Oppressed*: it involves an intricate examination of how individuals and groups assume roles as either oppressors or oppressed; 2) *Analysis of Hidden Social and Economic Structures*: engagement in analyses that go beyond surface-level manifestations of inequality. This entails uncovering the intricate and hidden webs of influence that contribute to systemic issues, including an exploration of historical legacies and the complex interplay of various structural elements like class, race and gender; 3) *Emancipation from Ideological Illusions*: Critical thought is not solely about exposing illusions but actively working towards emancipation. This involves not only deconstructing existing ideologies but also envisioning alternative frameworks that promote justice and equality. It acknowledges that the path to emancipation requires a continual reassessment of ingrained beliefs and a commitment to transformative practices that challenge oppressive ideologies.

An infusion of post-critical perspectives into the Critical Event Studies discourse, through the incorporation of post-critical theorists like Michel

Foucault (2008) and Jacques Rancière (2011), necessitates a more profound exploration of the critical school contentions. These contentions challenge traditional critical frameworks and introduce layers of complexity that significantly contribute to the nuanced understanding of critical inquiry in the realm of Critical Event Studies: 1) *Transversality of Power Relations*: The emphasis on the transversal nature of power relations underscores the need to move beyond simplistic binaries of oppressor and oppressed. This requires scholars to delve into the intricate ways in which power manifests across diverse contexts, where an oppressor can become oppressed and vice versa; 2) *Questioning the Notion of Hidden Ideological Structures*: The post-critical lens challenges assumptions about the researcher's idealistic capacity for self-reflectivity to escape the power structures that, apparently, only rule the individuals under study but not the researcher; 3) *Problematic Idealised Self-Reflectivity*: Delving deeper into the problematics of idealised self-reflectivity, scholars must confront the feasibility of momentarily escaping the powers that influence academic work. This introduces a critical dialogue on the researcher's positionality and the potential perpetuation of power imbalances; 4) *Presuppositions and Acknowledgement of Illusions*: Post-critical perspectives highlight the danger of presupposing an inherent incapacity among individuals to recognise illusions independently.

Creative Methods in Event Studies

A literature review of event studies shows a weak critical approach to creative methodologies. We identified two main trends: 1) The studies use creative methods to achieve solely cognitive results; 2) they reduce creativity to artistry, or gamification and playfulness. In the first case, creative methods serve aims of intelligibility, understanding, of cognition: "we would argue that there is great potential in using such digital co-creative methods in conjunction with more "traditional" methods, such as interviews and observation, to better our understanding" (Leer and Juel-Jacobsen, 2022, p. 307). Creative methods also serve to attain comprehensibility: "This will enable tourism researchers to develop in-depth understanding about the complex and strategic tourism destination planning processes" (Ivanova, Buda and Burrai, 2021, p. 6). As for the second point, event studies rely on traditional artistic or gaming practices to infuse creativity in their methods, be it through existing games (Wengel, McIntosh and Cockburn-Wootten, 2021), or with dramatic (Wright, 2021), dancing (Cisneros, Crawley and Whatley, 2020) or drawing approaches (Barry, 2017).

In the critical examination of event studies' creative methodologies, a concerted effort must be made to transcend the prevailing emphasis on cognitive outcomes and traditional conceptions of creativity, marking a paradigmatic shift. This recalibration is crucial to challenge the existing assumption that confines creativity to a mere instrument for achieving rational results, thereby neglecting its multifaceted expressions, including emotional, affective, and ethical dimensions, as well as the embodied. Delving into the domain of arts-based research, it is imperative to adopt a nuanced perspective on creativity and its agents. Rather than rigidly defining creativity within the confines of traditional artistic or gaming frameworks, researchers are encouraged to exercise caution and broaden their acceptance of diverse manifestations of creativity within research. Extending the methodology to encompass creativity beyond the boundaries of artistry or the extraordinary, necessitates a reevaluation of preconceived notions regarding who qualifies as a creative agent. Rejecting *a priori* judgements, this approach invites researchers to remain open to the political possibilities embedded in unconventional forms of creativity, which elude stringent definitions and conventional categorisations.

Three methodological considerations serve as integral guideposts for researchers navigating the landscape of creative methodologies in event studies. The first serves as a cautionary reminder, urging researchers to broaden their conceptualisation of creativity beyond cognitive realms, to embrace its effective results. The second suggestion advocates for a reexamination of ostensibly "non-creative" acts and objects within the scientific domain as creative. Lastly, the third consideration underscores the significance of acknowledging and celebrating the creativity inherent in ordinary actions and individuals, challenging established aesthetical hierarchies associated with artistry and gamification.

The Affect-Turn in Critical Event Studies

In navigating the evolving landscape of Critical Event Studies, the recognition of the affective turn within social sciences assumes a paramount role. Within the methodological landscape, the creative process's epistemic role dictates how creative tools align with knowledge acquisition objectives. This implies that creativity is confined to generating cognitive outcomes. While this rational approach resonates with critical perspectives elucidating power dynamics and fostering emancipatory reasoning, it can be understood as a "cognitive authoritarianism". This criticism emerges from the prioritisation of cognitive dimensions, often at the expense of overlooking crucial aspects such as emotional, bodily, affective, or ethical dimensions of research. A post-critical perspective challenges this traditional stance, asserting that focusing solely on the cognitive might perpetuate ignorance rather than fostering true emancipation. The "affect-turn" (Lemmings and Brooks, 2014) in social sciences, calls attention to the limitations of rationalisation and advocates for recognising the political and epistemic implications of affects and emotions. Creative methods, therefore, should not solely pursue cognitive results but also embrace affects, emotions, and sensibilities as legitimate outcomes of arts-based research. This approach not only prevents the reduction of the world to rational calculability but also acknowledges the political possibilities these non-cognitive dimensions open up, especially for those marginalised or affected by technoscientific domination. In the realm of Critical Event Studies, the aspiration extends beyond mere results to foster a new way of critically engaging with feelings and understanding their transformative potential. This change signifies a scholarly pursuit focused on understanding how events can be felt and experienced, embracing the *emotional* nature inherent in the very definition of an event as something dynamic in time and space.

Creativity in Knowledge Production

The recognition of creativity within the realm of knowledge production underscores the notion that the demarcation between creative and non-creative endeavours in social science is inherently porous. The creative dimensions inherent in scientific research manifest across various facets of the research process, weaving a complexity that transcends conventional boundaries between art and research. While a critical approach meticulously demarcates the boundaries between science, fiction, creativity, and emotion to construct an objective critique of the existing state of affairs, a post-critical perspective challenges the absoluteness of these distinctions. It delves into the symbiotic nature of scientific practice and the creative act, acknowledging their interwoven existence. In this light, a post-critical approach to creative methods advocates for expanding the array of agents and tools considered creative, unlocking new possibilities for research. This expanded conception seeks to interrogate the political dimensions of creativity, scrutinising its power effects and questioning who is deemed creative or not. Essentially, it aims to challenge and reshape the politics of creativity by inviting diverse voices and forms of creativity into the discourse, thus fostering a more inclusive, dynamic, and equitable research landscape that acknowledges and celebrates the myriad expressions of creativity and scholarly endeavour.

Scientific inquiry involves the strategic selection and adaptation of methodologies, which can be viewed as a creative endeavour in its own right. Researchers navigate the nuanced landscape of methodological choices, strategically aligning them with the unique contours of their investigative pursuits. This creative orchestration encompasses the thoughtful design of experiments, surveys, and observational approaches, each a deliberate aesthetical stroke contributing to the broader canvas of scientific exploration by privileging, for instance, aesthetical simplicity in scientific explanations and models (McAllister, 2002). For instance, the utilisation of language, a seemingly utilitarian tool, is an inherently aesthetic practice (Ortony, 1993). Letters possess designs, oral communication carries tonal nuances, and language simultaneously persuades through both reason and emotion. Scientists creatively adapt established linguistic codes to pragmatically address the unpredictability of academic life, demonstrating that creativity permeates even the most routine academic activities. Moreover, the analysis and interpretation of data—central tenets of the scientific endeavour—bear the imprints of creativity. Researchers engage in the creative act of deciphering patterns, discerning trends, and deriving meaningful insights from seemingly disparate data points. This interpretative dance with data demands a creative approach, allowing scientists to discern the subtle nuances that may elude a purely analytical gaze. The very formulation of research questions and hypotheses is an exercise in imaginative inquiry. Scientists embark on a creative journey of conceptualisation, framing questions that propel investigations into uncharted territories. This process mirrors the artistic endeavour of posing novel queries that challenge existing paradigms, opening avenues for intellectual exploration.

Furthermore, the presentation of research findings transcends the mere dissemination of information; it assumes the guise of a creative performance. Whether through written publications, conference presentations, or visual representations, researchers engage in the art of communication, strategically crafting narratives that resonate with diverse audiences. This creative dimension extends to the use of multimedia, innovative visualisations, and compelling storytelling techniques to amplify the impact of research dissemination.

While the utilisation of arts in research methodologies is undoubtedly valuable for yielding fresh insights, it is essential to avoid reducing creativity within academia solely to artistic inputs. The risk lies in perpetuating a false dichotomy between "creative methods" and purportedly non-creative scientific approaches. This separation fosters a misleading image that science lacks creativity, potentially hindering the appreciation of the creative techniques employed by scientists in non-artistic contexts. The conventional labelling of "arts-based research" may thus emerge as a potential misnomer, as it implies an original separation between arts and research that obscures the inherent artistry and creativity embedded in all facets of research. We challenge the restrictive conceptualisation of creativity, urging to transcend reductive notions that confine artistic expression solely to traditional forms (such as painting, gaming, creative writing, storytelling, photography, etc.).

Also, the inadvertent consequence of this separation is the imposition of a competitive relationship between arts-based research and more traditional scientific methods. By challenging this dichotomy, we open avenues for arts and science to engage in a reciprocal exchange of creative methodologies. Embracing a more inclusive understanding of creativity within academia encourages the recognition of creative moments in various forms, whether they stem from the arts or from the intricacies of scientific practice. The objective is not to diminish the importance of arts-based research but to expand the conceptual boundaries of creativity within academic pursuits. By dismantling the perceived divide between science and creativity, we foster an environment where both can mutually benefit from the diverse array of creative techniques employed in scholarly and non-scholarly endeavours. This paradigm shift emphasises that creativity is not confined to specific methods or disciplines but is an intrinsic aspect of the dynamic and multifaceted landscape of any knowledge creation.

Creativity in Everyday Life

Expanding upon this perspective, it is crucial to recognise that the traditional designation of creative and non-creative acts carries inherent political implications. This designation influences the distribution of social power by shaping notions of legitimacy in creative endeavours. A critical approach to creative methods shoulders the responsibility of identifying and defining the multifaceted dimensions of creativity and its various actors. There are perils associated with adopting an excessively rigid definition of creativity, such as construing it solely as the generation of art and pigeonholing the creator into predefined archetypes like the genius or the artist. Such rigidity risks the establishment of what can be termed an "aesthetics police" (Rancière, 2004)—an entity that vigilantly monitors instances of creativity and categorises certain acts and individuals as non-creative. This risk not only curtails the expansive potential of creativity by imposing predefined boundaries but also undermines the critical power by excluding unconventional forms of creativity.

A critical task for creative methods, therefore, extends beyond the mere utilisation of arts or games as instruments for empowering marginalised groups. Instead, it aims to embrace and elevate the diverse creative repertoires intrinsic to everyday life. From a critical standpoint, the examination of the aesthetics of everyday life exposes how certain individuals are deemed capable of leading extraordinary lives while others are confined to a realm of perceived ordinariness reduced to the consumption of mass culture (Adorno, 2001). The post-critical perspective, however, challenges this dichotomy, recognising it as a political construct that diminishes the value of seemingly mundane forms of creation. Through repeated acts of creativity within the fabric of daily life, individuals assert resilience and resistance against prevailing norms (DeNora, 2014). To delve further into the critical exploration of everyday creativity, it becomes imperative to understand the socio-political implications of designating certain acts and individuals as creative or non-creative.

Adopting a post-critical approach, we seek to redefine the very concept of creativity, liberating it from predetermined categories and recognising its presence within the ordinary. This redefinition disrupts hierarchical distinctions, challenging established narratives that prioritise specific forms of creativity over others. Everyday creativity emerges as a site of resistance, where individuals reclaim agency and challenge societal norms. Moreover, the post-critical perspective prompts a reevaluation of the researchers' role, acknowledging their intrinsic involvement in the politics of creativity. Researchers participate in the complex relationships between creativity, power, and societal norms.

By questioning and redefining traditional dichotomies, scholars pave the way for more inclusive and politically aware approaches to studying creativity in everyday life. This expanded perspective not only opens new avenues for inquiry but also provides a foundation for fostering a more equitable and insightful engagement with the multifaceted dimensions of creativity within diverse social contexts. Furthermore, this reevaluation prompts a methodologically critical exploration of the criteria governing who qualifies as a creative individual. A critical approach works by scrutinising the social and economic factors influencing creative agency, both of researched subjects and researchers. This involves examining the disparities in resource access that either empower or constrain certain individuals from engaging in creative acts or having their creative acts recognised as such.

A post-critical methodological approach needs to unravel the creative potential inherent in acts and agents traditionally deemed non-creative. This means that subjects are not passively waiting for the scholar to bring creativity through methods that use games and arts as means of producing knowledge but have their own non-artistic and non-gamified forms of producing creativity that can change research methods. By transcending conventional definitions and acknowledging the creative capacities embedded in everyday practices, post-Critical Event Studies can tap into a broader spectrum of experiences. This expanded scope not only challenges preconceived notions but also interrogates the political consequences of selectively ascribing creativity to specific acts or individuals. Moreover, adopting an inclusive stance towards everyday creativity contributes to the democratisation of creative contributions, offering a platform for the voices and expressions that might be marginalised in traditional artistic paradigms. It opens avenues for exploring the political implications of recognising, or neglecting, the creative agency embedded in ordinary experiences. This methodological approach cultivates a holistic understanding of creativity within Critical Event Studies, recognising its multifaceted manifestations and the intricate interplay of social, economic, and political dynamics. By delving deeper into these dimensions, Critical Event Studies can better navigate the complex landscape of creative practices, fostering a more comprehensive and equitable discourse within the field.

Conclusions

The critical examination of event studies' creative methodologies calls for a post-critical paradigm shift. This shift challenges the assumption that confines creativity to a tool for achieving rational results, emphasising the need to recognize its diverse expressions in emotional, affective, and ethical dimensions, as well as in embodied struggles against injustices. Instead of rigidly defining creativity within non-academic, artistic or gaming frameworks, researchers are also urged to broaden their acceptance of diverse manifestations of creativity within the scientific domain. The extension of methodology to encompass creativity beyond artistry or the extraordinary calls for a reevaluation of preconceived notions about who qualifies as a creative agent. This approach encourages researchers to remain open to the political possibilities inherent in ordinary and unconventional forms of creativity that elude stringent definitions and traditional categorisations.

Acknowledgements

Funding Note for the First Author: The first author acknowledges the writing of this chapter as part of her research work at CICANT (DOI 10.54499/UIDB/05260/2020), and as part of her research work for European projects at Lusófona University, namely filmEU+ (HORIZON-WIDERA-2023-ACCESS-03/101136627), WIRE (Project: 101136627 — WIRE FilmEU — HORIZON-WIDERA-2023-ACCESS-03), filmEU_RIT (H2020: 101035820).

Funding Note for the Second Author: This chapter is financed by National Funds provided by FCT – Foundation for Science and Technology through project UIDB/04020/2020 with DOI 10.54499/UIDB/04020/2020 (https://doi.org/10.54499/UIDB/04020/2020).

References

Adams St. Pierre, E. and Roulston, K. (2006) 'The state of qualitative inquiry: A contested science', *International Journal of Qualitative Studies in Education*, 19(6), pp. 673–684. https://doi.org/10.1080/09518390600975644

Adorno, T.W. (2001) *The culture industry: Selected essays on mass culture*. Edited by J.M. Bernstein. London: Routledge (Routledge Classics).

Archibald, M.M. and Gerber, N. (2018) 'Arts and mixed methods research: An innovative methodological merger', *American Behavioral Scientist*, 62(7), pp. 956–977. https://doi.org/10.1177/0002764218772672

Bagley, C. and Cancienne, M.B. (2001) 'Educational research and intertextual forms of (re)presentation: The case for dancing the data', *Qualitative Inquiry*, 7(2), pp. 221–237. https://doi.org/10.1177/107780040100700205

Barone, T. and Eisner, E.W. (2012) *Arts based research*. Los Angeles: SAGE.

Barry, K. (2017) 'Diagramming: A creative methodology for tourist studies', *Tourist Studies*, 17(3), pp. 328–346. https://doi.org/10.1177/1468797616680852

Broussine, M. (2008) *Creative methods in organizational research*. SAGE Publications Ltd. https://doi.org/10.4135/9781849208772

Carpentier, N. and Sumiala, J. (2021) 'Arts-based research in communication and media studies', *Comunicazioni sociali*, (1), pp. 3–10. https://doi.org/10.26350/001200_000125

Cisneros, R., Crawley, M.-L. and Whatley, S. (2020) 'Towards hybridity', *Performance Research*, 25(4), pp. 125–132. https://doi.org/10.1080/13528165.2020.1842606

DeNora, T. (2014) *Making sense of reality: Culture and perception in everyday life*. Los Angeles: SAGE.

Faulkner, S.L. (2009) *Poetry as method: Reporting research through verse*. Walnut Creek CA: West Coast Press.

Finley, S. (2008) 'Arts-based research', in J.G. Knowles and A.L. Cole (eds.), *Handbook of the arts in qualitative research: Perspectives, methodologies, examples, and issues*. Los Angeles: Sage Publications, pp. 71–81.

Foucault, M. (2008) *The history of sexuality: 1: The will to knowledge*. Camberwell: Penguin.

Hogan, S. and Pink, S. (2010) 'Routes to interiorities: Art therapy and knowing in anthropology', *Visual Anthropology*, 23(2), pp. 158–174. https://doi.org/10.1080/08949460903475625

Horkheimer, M. and Adorno, T.W. (1982) *Dialectic of enlightenment*. Translated by J. Cumming. New York: Continuum.

Inckle, K. (2010) 'Telling tales? Using ethnographic fictions to speak embodied "truth"', *Qualitative Research*, 10(1), pp. 27–47. https://doi.org/10.1177/1468794109348681

Ivanova, M., Buda, D.-M. and Burrai, E. (2021) 'Creative and disruptive methodologies in tourism studies', *Tourism Geographies*, 23(1–2), pp. 1–10. https://doi.org/10.1080/14616688.2020.1784992

Jackson, C., Morgan, J. and Laws, C. (2018) 'Creativity in events: The untold story', *International Journal of Event and Festival Management*, 9(1), pp. 2–19. https://doi.org/10.1108/IJEFM-10-2017-0062

Kara, H. (2015) *Creative research methods in the social sciences: A Practical Guide*. 1st edn. Bristol: Policy Press.

Latour, B. (2004) 'Why has critique run out of steam? From matters of fact to matters of concern', *Critical Inquiry*, 30(2), pp. 225–248.

Leavy, P. (2017) *Handbook of arts-based research*. New York: The Guilford Press.

Leavy, P. (2020) *Method meets art: Arts-based research practice*. 3rd edn. New York: The Guilford Press.

Leavy, P. and Chilton, G. (2020) 'Arts-based research practice merging social research and the creative arts', in P. Leavy (ed.), *The Oxford handbook of qualitative research*. 2nd edn. Oxford, New York: Oxford University Press (Oxford Handbooks).

Leer, J. and Juel-Jacobsen, L.G. (2022) 'Food festival experiences from visitors' perspectives: Intellectual, sensory, and social dimensions', *Food and Foodways*, 30(4), pp. 287–309. https://doi.org/10.1080/07409710.2022.2124729

Lemmings, D. and Brooks, A. (2014) 'The emotional turn in the humanities and social sciences', in D. Lemmings and A. Brooks (eds) *Emotions and social change* (pp. 3–18). Routledge.

Lupton, D. (2020) *Doing fieldwork in a pandemic (crowd-sourced document)*. Available at: https://docs.google.com/document/d/1clGjGABB2h2qbduTgfqribHmog9B6P0NvMgVuiHZCl8/edit?ts=5e88ae0a#

McAllister, J.W. (2002) 'Recent work on aesthetics of science', *International Studies in the Philosophy of Science*, 16(1), pp. 7–11. https://doi.org/10.1080/02698590120118783

McNiff, S. (2008) 'Art-based research', in J.G. Knowles and A.L. Cole (eds.), *Handbook of the arts in qualitative research: Perspectives, methodologies, examples, and issues*. Los Angeles: Sage Publications, pp. 29–40.

Ortony, A. (ed.) (1993) *Metaphor and Thought*. 2nd edition. Cambridge England; New York, NY, USA: Cambridge University Press.

Pernecky, T. and Lück, M. (2013) *Events, society and sustainability: Critical and contemporary approaches*. London: Routledge.

Piirto, J. (2002) 'The question of quality and qualifications: Writing inferior poems as qualitative research', *International Journal of Qualitative Studies in Education*, 15(4), pp. 431–445. https://doi.org/10.1080/09518390210145507

Rancière, J. (2004). *The politics of aesthetics: The distribution of the sensible*. London: Continuum.

Rancière, J. (2011) *Althusser's lesson*. London: Continuum.

Sloterdijk, P. (2010) *Critique of cynical reason*. Translated by M. Eldred. Minneapolis: University of Minnesota Press (Theory and history of literature).

Spracklen, K. and Lamond, I.R. (2021) *Critical event studies*. London: Routledge.

Wengel, Y., McIntosh, A. and Cockburn-Wootten, C. (2021) 'A critical consideration of LEGO® SERIOUS PLAY® methodology for tourism studies', *Tourism Geographies*, 23(1–2), pp. 162–184. https://doi.org/10.1080/14616688.2019.1611910

Wright, R.K. (2021) '"Que será, será!": Creative analytical practice within the critical sports event tourism discourse', *Tourism Geographies*, 23(1–2), pp. 296–317. https://doi.org/10.1080/14616688.2019.1648542

INDEX

Pages in *italics* refer to figures and pages in **bold** refer to tables.

Printed in the United States
by Baker & Taylor Publisher Services